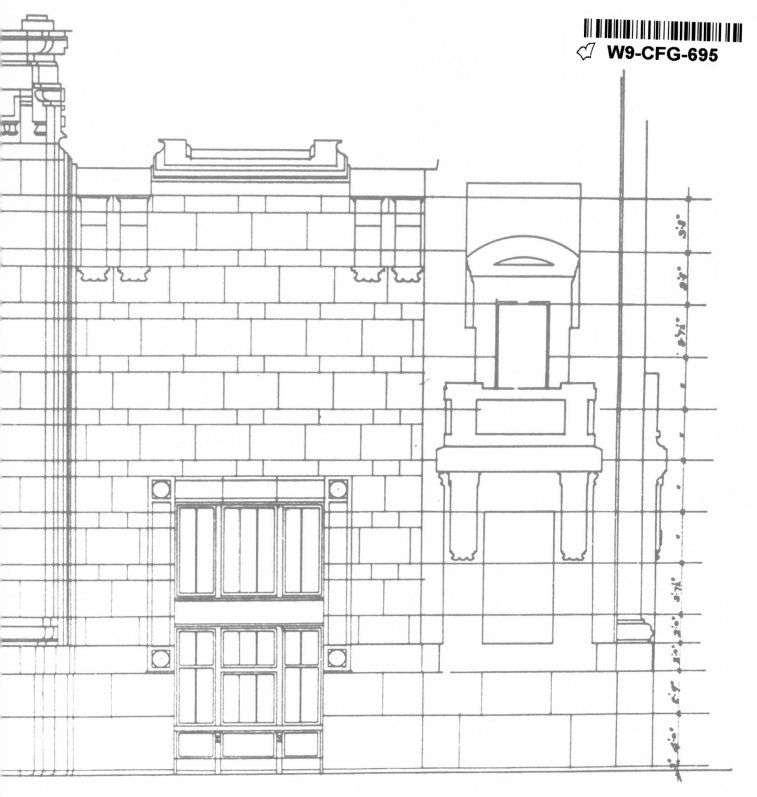

PASSAGE WAY

JOINTING IN WAITING ROOM

y. 19. 1912

UNION STATION
KANSAS CITY

Jeffrey Spivak

KANSAS CITY STAR BOOKS
KANSAS CITY, MISSOURI

UNION STATION

KANSAS CITY

Author
Jeffrey Spivak

Editor
Monroe Dodd

Book Design
Jean Donaldson Dodd

Associate Editor
Les Weatherford

Graphics
Dave Eames

Dust jacket photo:
Illustrator's rendering of Grand Hall and entrance
into the waiting room

Endsheet:
Elevation from Jarvis Hunt's architectural plans
for terra cotta jointing in waiting room,
Union Station, 1912

Title page photo:
Aerial photo of Union Station and its train sheds,
circa 1930

Published by KANSAS CITY STAR BOOKS
1729 Grand Boulevard, Kansas City, Missouri 64108

First Edition, Second Printing

Library of Congress Catalog Card Number: 99-66593

Cataloging-in-Publication Data

Spivak, Jeffrey, 1963-
    Union Station : Kansas City / Jeffrey Spivak.
- 1st ed.
        p.   cm.
        Includes bibliographical references and index.
        1. Union Station (Kansas City, Mo.)-History. 2. Railroad stations-
Missouri-Kansas City-History. 3. Kansas City (Mo.)-Buildings, structures,
etc. I. Title.
TF302.K3S64 1999
99-66593

CIP

ISBN 0-9604884-1-3

Printed in the United States of America by
Walsworth Publishing Co. Inc.

To order copies, call StarInfo, (816) 234-4636.
www.kcstar.com

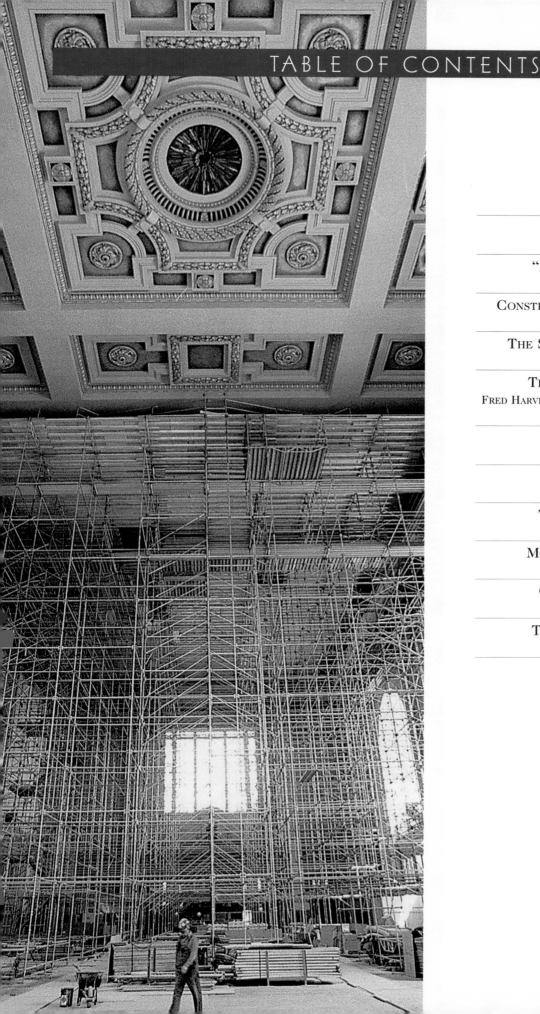

INTRODUCTION

hile compiling this book, I searched for people with the oldest memories of Kansas City's Union Station.

Because the station opened 85 years before this writing, they had to be at least 90 years old to have even the slightest recollections of its celebrated beginning and its early days. One way I tracked them down was to take a computer database of Kansas City voters and break up that list of more than 200,000 names into a sublist of those born from 1900 to 1908.

Then I wrote those people, asking what they recalled of the station's first years, the times when presidents passed through and steam engines still ruled the rails, when romances blossomed under the clock and Union Station was the gateway to the biggest city in America's heartland and the city's gateway to the world.

One of the handwritten replies I received was from Gladys Watkins, 93. Apologizing for her wobbly handwriting, she filled six pages. She first saw the station, she wrote, on Aug. 24, 1924....

...I lived in Salisbury, Mo., then and had just graduated from high school in May. I was 19 years of age. Everybody that was somebody was coming to Kansas City to visit. It was a sign of prestige. My father had two sisters living here, so I decided that I too would come here for a visit. It was on a Sunday afternoon that I left Salisbury for the long train ride on the Wabash to Kansas City. It was

wonderful! I had never been out of Chariton County before.

As we entered the railroad yard here I began to get excited. The train finally stopped and my heart almost did too. I was in Kansas City — about to enter that great building, the Union Station. All I had to do was get my suitcase and climb the long stairway to the main lobby. When I had done just that, I could hardly believe what I saw and heard. It was truly a place to behold — a place where dreams could be made. The beautiful high ceilings. The large and powerful clock. People rushing from one place to another.

I fell in love then and it never left me — the hollow sound of the men calling the trains. It was a fascinating sound, and no matter how many times I heard it, I liked it. I passed through the station many times over the years and the feeling was always the same....I'm sorry I do not have many more facts — like getting married under the clock, etc. My romance was with the station. I am 93 now, and I pray I may live to see the great Union Station come back to life again. I still have a real soft part in my heart for it.

Indeed, the station was only a building, a place where Kansas Citians and cross-country travelers spent an hour or so at a time, where many rushed through or hurried out on their way someplace else, and where America played out the demise of its first great industry.

Yet, the building has come to mean so much more to its

patrons, its city and its epoch. At its heart, Union Station was and remains a monumental embodiment of liberation, as much about linking places as about leaving them, as much about capping a confident age then as symbolizing an age of renewal today, and as much about celebrating changing times as about fostering a changed community. As such, Union Station represents not one, not two but four separate sagas about Kansas City.

The first involves a town bursting at the seams and full of big ideas, clamoring for a bigger station and, by a stroke of luck, getting it. The second saga highlights how the citizenry embraced their monument, made it their town square and experienced magical moments there. The third entails powers out of the city's control abandoning the station and letting it decay, while the city watched and fumed. The final saga is one of redemption, the historic pairing of a grand vi-

sion and the region's disparate parts, the likes of which had never been done before — here or anywhere else in the country.

During each of these sagas, the station reflected the city around it. Now, near the end of the century, it's a grand symbol of revival. As Walter Cronkite, who worked for a while in Kansas City, said in one of his pitches to save Union Station: "It is integral to the entire history of Kansas City."

Jeffrey Spivak
Summer 1999

PROLOGUE

Kansas City: 1993

In the twilight of a summer day, Andy Scott was working late. He was the only one left in the downtown suite of the city's economic development recruiting agency. There was something bugging him, something that had been in his head for weeks. He had to get it written down.

So Scott turned on a computer, tapped a few keys and produced a blank document. On the one side of the screen he typed "advantages." On the other side he typed "disadvantages." Then he began weighing the future of Kansas City's most cherished landmark, Union Station, which sat on the edge of downtown, boarded up and falling apart.

Scott was an unlikely participant in the station's crisis. He hadn't grown up in Kansas City, he had never taken a train out of the building, and he had no particular railroad station interest or expertise. But this summer Scott had landed an important post in his adopted city, one that would immerse him in the saving of the station. He had become Mayor Emanuel Cleaver's part-time chief of staff.

In Scott's first meeting in that position, he heard some lawyers brief the mayor on the status of a court case involving Union Station. The city had sued some companies for failing to restore it. The city had essentially lost in court. So the two sides were trying to reach a settlement while the city considered an appeal. But those talks were going nowhere. The attorneys told the mayor that their phone calls to the companies weren't being returned anymore. After that meeting, Cleaver told Scott to work on this issue, to follow its progress.

Now it was weeks later. Scott sat at the computer terminal in the economic development agency, where he still kept an office. He felt that the crisis had to end and that it was up to the city to end it. To him the city was quibbling, holding out for a few million dollars when actually it would cost tens of millions to restore the station and tens of millions more to create a new use for it.

So under "advantages" Scott began typing some of the reasons the city should just gulp, take whatever settlement terms it could get and move on: 1, 2, 3.... On and on the list went: 10, 11, 12.... Things such as: It would end a public relations nightmare, and Union Station immediately would get a new start. Then Scott directed the cursor to the other side of the screen, for the "disadvantages" — things such as: The city would not get as much money as it sought. He paused, typed a little, pondered, typed a little more. The list on this side didn't reach 5. Scott wasn't finished yet, but the lists were lopsided enough already.

He picked up the phone and called the mayor in his car. "Maybe we ought to re-evaluate our position and lower the dollar demand," Scott told him.

"That sounds good to me," the mayor replied. "Let's go."

Within four months a settlement was reached and plans were unveiled to put a new museum inside Union Station, giving the landmark new life.

Andy Scott, Emanuel Cleaver and others responsible for this milestone were unaware that Union Station's history was actually repeating itself. That this was only the latest turning point in the station's fabled yet arduous history, which stretched for most of this century. That long ago, before any of them were born, before Union Station's blocks of stone were set in place, the building was embroiled in local politics, trapped by years of frustration and at the mercy of powerful out-of-towners....

Facing page: Union Station, closed and deteriorating in the mid-90s

CHAPTER 1

A ROCKY START

Chicago: February 1905

It was one of those gray, blustery, wintry days in the Windy City when some of the leaders of American railroads met to finally decide the fate of Kansas City's next train station. Or so they hoped.

These six men formed an executive committee of the Union Depot board of directors. This board represented the 10 passenger lines using Kansas City's dingy, overcrowded and rat-infested depot in the West Bottoms, at the confluence of the Kansas and the Missouri rivers. Several of those lines were headquartered in Chicago, so they typically handled Kansas City's business at an oval, wood table on the 10th floor of the LaSalle Street Station, the offices of the Chicago, Rock Island & Pacific railroad. Out the office window, a commuter train rattled and screeched past every few minutes on the elevated rail below.

By this day, several of the men in this room had finished studying Kansas City's long-festering depot problem. For a decade, Union Depot leaders had come close to choosing new station locations — a south site at 23rd Street and Grand Avenue before the turn of the century, but one railroad vetoed it; then another West Bottoms site near the existing depot, but the 1903 flood showed the folly of that locale.

Now they had another site in mind. It was along the banks of the Missouri River east of Grand Avenue and north of the city's governmental center at the City Market. This site offered 165 acres and was owned by a partnership of the Armour-Swift meatpacking interests and the Chicago, Burlington & Quincy railroad, one of the Union Depot lines. Sketches for the new station showed a Victorian facade, gables on the roof and a central clock tower rising about 100 feet.

The Burlington, of course, was adamant about picking this north site, and the Union Depot charter required that all decisions be unanimous. If other railroads didn't exactly prefer this site — like the Atchison, Topeka & Santa Fe — they had to go along with the Burlington if they wanted something better than the existing depot.

So at this February meeting, Union Depot's executive committee, which included the Burlington's Daniel Willard, welcomed Armour-Swift officials.

LaSalle Street Station, Chicago

COMING OF THE RAILS

Kansas City owed its existence as a boom town to the coming of the railroad, and city fathers had worked hard to get it. The story was one of perseverance and desperation, hope as well as greed.

Before the Civil War, Kansas City was in a railroad frenzy. Rallies, parades and speeches stirred up enthusiasm for a train line, considered the key to big-city status. The prize would be a bridge across the Missouri River. After the Civil War, its economy ravaged, Kansas City was considered the underdog for a bridge.

But in 1866, Kansas City beat out Leavenworth, a town about three times its size, with better economic inducements. It got what would come to be known as the Hannibal Bridge, linking Kansas City to Chicago. This was a triumph won with strokes of luck and greed, such as a railroad official's buying up land where tracks would go in the West Bottoms. The city became a major cattle and grain shipping point and meatpacking center beginning in the 1870s.

Kansas Citians, though, soon came to curse the railroads, just as the rest of the country did.

This form of industry came to dominate transportation, and before the days of government regulation the railroad barons abused their power. They set such high shipping rates that it cost more for farmers to transport grain to New York than to transport it overseas. The railroads, in fact, set arbitrary rates that infuriated most everyone. And the railroads showed favoritism toward the privileged and the powerful, whether it was lower rates for Standard Oil or free passes for politicians who could generate favorable laws. This meant everybody who bought food, clothes or shelter was taxed to compensate for the rebates.

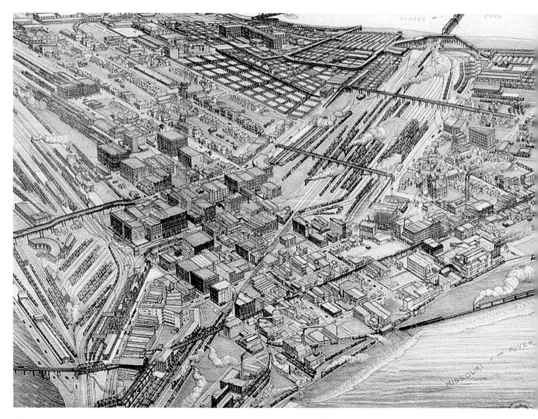

This panoramic view of the West Bottoms from 1895 shows the area between the Kansas River at top and the Missouri River at bottom jammed with rail yards, stockyards, packinghouses, grain elevators, bakeries, farm implement distributors and wholesale warehouses. In the midst of all this, hemmed in on all sides, was narrow Union Depot, barely visible on the diagonal street at lower left above the streetcar line.

They all expected to wrap up negotiations.

The railroads considered the land to be worth about $10,000 an acre. They were hoping for that price to keep this site cost-effective. Willard knew this, but he also was aware that Armour-Swift had a surprise in store. He had to wonder whether the other lines would cave in again to the Burlington. Throughout the decade-long site-selection process, the Burlington had been difficult to deal with, always pushing for a decision that best fit its track alignment and routes. This time would be no different.

Armour-Swift officials sat down and presented their offer. It was $30,000 an acre.

The executive committee members hardly spoke. Except for Willard, they were stunned. They politely told the meatpacking officials that the offer would be submitted to the depot's full board, and then they ushered the negotiators out the door. But the committee members had no intention of taking that offer to their board. They felt deceived and betrayed.

The meeting had "resulted disastrously," a Santa Fe official recounted years later for the Interstate Commerce Commission. It looked as if the railroads were never going to find a site they all could accept. Samuel Felton, a railroad industry takeover artist who headed the Chicago & Alton line for railroad baron Edward Harriman, was particularly incensed. Or as the Santa Fe

Cable cars from Union Depot brought passengers up the harrowing Ninth Street Incline to the top of the bluffs, and then east to the busy heart of downtown, the Junction at Ninth, Main and Delaware streets.

official put it, in genteel terms, "very much chagrined."

Yet this disastrous meeting marked the key turning point in the long, arduous saga of locating a new depot.

A civic clamor

Of course, the entire crisis never would have arisen had Kansas City not emerged as a boom town on the prairie.

When Union Depot was built in 1878 by a group of railroads, it was the pride of the burgeoning river town. By far the city's architectural showpiece, its fancy French-styled turrets and tall clock tower made it a landmark. It was situated, though, amid some of the city's busiest industries and most nefarious activities, below a tall bluff separating the West Bottoms from the City Market and the rest of the business district on top.

Across the street from the depot was a roaring row of saloons, cheap hotels, gambling joints and novelty bazaars. These kept the sidewalks jammed with a mixture of travelers, booted cattlemen, silk-hatted gamblers, sheepskin-clad Mennonite settlers from Russia and blanketed American Indians. They were drawn to the storefronts by a cacophony of barkers from each doorway, yelling things such as, "Right here — biggest beer in Kansas City for a nickel." William M. Reddig wrote of the city's early days: "Union Avenue society took a swashbuckling pride in a reputation for picturesque sordidness which was believed to compare favorably with the iniquity of New York's Bowery."

Kansas City was still very much a Wild West town then, with low-slung, wood-boarded buildings and horse manure on the ground. In dry times, dirt and dust swirled in the air, and most everyone stepping inside a building took a few seconds to brush off their coats and pants. When it rained, muck in the streets was an incessant hazard; none of the main commercial thoroughfares was paved. Women had to hike up their dresses to cross muddy streets.

At the Missouri River front, the city was growing by cutting back the bluff

At its opening in 1878, headlines called Union Depot the "handsomest and Largest Depot West of New York." It symbolized the remarkable growth of the young Kansas City, which within a year would install its first telephones and, a few years later, its first electric lights and streetcars.

Saloons, rooming houses, hotels and restaurants lined Union Avenue, the first things incoming passengers saw upon leaving Union Depot.

Narrow, umbrella sheds at the depot gave little protection from the elements, left. Like most activities at the depot, the news agency occupied tight quarters, above.

The Star's editorial of complaint, Sept. 8, 1897: "The Union Depot company is a close and profitable corporation. The lines in the organization know that their depot is not the depot Kansas City deserves, but they will not build a new one because, they argue, they don't have to."

Above: Accompanying drawing was captioned, "Slivers in the planks keep travelers alert."

and clearing trees and brush, which left ravines of bare, red earth. When it rained, the water rushed down in gullies, leaving so much muck that a carriage could be swamped on Main Street.

Ten years after Union Depot opened, it suffered from filth, just as the rest of the city did. Black smoke from steam engines settled on everything — the roof, the walls, clothes. Complaints about the depot's size, soot and crowded conditions had started in the mid-1880s. The train platforms were so narrow that travelers were often hit by fast-moving baggage wagons. The wood planks in those platforms were so uneven that travelers tripped over them. Once, a late-arriving passenger ran after a Union Pacific train pulling out of the station, stepped on a splintered plank and fell, tearing his clothes and cutting his face so badly that he had to go into surgery. Then there was the waiting room, where there never seemed to be enough seats.

The depot had been built to accommodate a Kansas City population of 60,000, but the city was outgrowing it fast, doubling to 132,000 by 1890.

On February 22, 1888, the city's outspoken afternoon newspaper, *The Kansas City Star*, called for a larger train station: "In this dilemma the natural question is, why does not the Union depot company go somewhere else and build another grand union depot which will accommodate all the roads?" But the railroads were not hard-pressed to spend much money. As the 1880s ended, rail passengers and traffic were declining from a severe economic depression, which would consume much of the 1890s.

Not until 1897 did *The Star* again pick up the charge for a better station. One front-page editorial was headlined: "The Union Depot won't do for the Kansas City of to-day." Civic leaders pursued the issue, too. William Barton, president of the Commercial Club, the predecessor to the chamber of commerce, asked in a speech: "When will Kansas City have a depot at least commensurate with its importance as a commercial and railroad center?"

The out-of-town railroads, civic leaders knew, were a stingy bunch who at first weren't even giving pledges toward a convention hall the city wanted built. As far as Kansas Citians were concerned, the railroads were relegating the town to second-class status.

Later in 1897, as the country was coming out of the depression, Union Depot's own manager joined in the carping about the crowding. Finally, the railroads moved into action. The 10 Union Depot lines privately started negotiating land options around 23rd Street and Grand Avenue, along the Kansas City Belt Railway freight line. That line skirted the city to the south, along O.K. Creek, rather than following the Missouri River bottoms like the other main lines into town.

This land had been bought and held for railroad development by Charles Adams, a descendant of U.S. Presidents John Adams and John Quincy Adams. Born and bred in Boston like the rest of his prominent family, Charles Francis Adams Jr. had looked west to make money in railroad speculation. His Kansas City investments were managed by Charles F. Morse, a Boston-born railroad agent who had helped develop the exclusive Hyde Park subdivision. One Kansas City historian, Daniel Serda, believes Morse lobbied the directors of the Chicago railroads to build a new passenger station along the Belt line on the Adams land, parts of which were owned by Morse and the Santa Fe.

As the years took their toll, Union Depot was stripped of the lacy ironwork that had marked its roofline. In the late 1890s, the railroads expanded and remodeled the station, below (from a hand-colored postcard of the era), giving it a plainer look. Gone were the clock tower and many of the dormers.

But under the Union Depot railroad partnership, all decisions had to be unanimous. In this case one railroad, the Chicago & Alton, vetoed it. The Alton, in the period before Samuel Felton was brought on to run it, was one of the few conservatively run lines and didn't want the expense of a new station, having suffered declining earnings in the 1890s depression. The Alton was known for being, in the words of one railroad historian, a "constant thorn" in the side of larger systems seeking harmonious relations.

This became Kansas City's first site-selection decision to go sour.

So instead of building new, the railroads decided to expand Union Depot, and the depot board issued a statement in November 1897 declaring: "It is difficult to see how any change can be made in location." After this expansion, the depot had no more room on its crowded block. The depot's superintendent kept telling the board about "the great need for additional track capacity." And complaints about its dirty condition — and rat sightings — continued. *The Star* called the depot "the old shack" and wrote about "rats that act as scavengers. Experts who have seen these massive rodents say they can eat anything."

Then in 1902 the Union Depot board's executive committee recommended a new site in the West Bottoms. One line, the Santa Fe, opposed this proposal, believing "a satisfactory union station in the present location is impossible" because of all the freight traffic crossing the passenger tracks and creating a bottleneck. The Santa Fe, of course, had a built-in self-interest. It still wanted something at 23rd and Grand, where it already participated in a small passenger station adjoining the Belt line.

Meanwhile *The Star* campaigned for non-West Bottoms locales, the south site and a newly announced north site along the Missouri River. The paper ran renderings and interviews with anonymous experts touting the virtues of each alternative. Both sites, for instance, adjoined existing railroad tracks used by several Union Depot lines. *Star* Publisher William Rockhill Nelson served on a Commercial Club committee lobbying for a new site.

To civic leaders it was clear what was at stake. The city was growing atop the bluffs. To keep the train station and the city's largest daily crowds down in the bottoms would stunt the city's expansion. Besides, it was dirty and dingy down there, and pedestrians kept getting hit by trains where rails crossed the streets.

The civic clamor grew while train ticket sales increased more than 10 percent every year of the new century. So in May 1903 the depot board created a committee of five engineers to study two sites in earnest — one in the West Bottoms, which appeased a majority of railroads, and the other north of down-

UNION DEPOT

Tickets sold

Year	Tickets sold
1879	139,350
1881	216,577
1883	264,079
1885	295,780
1887	452,018
1889	404,184
1891	336,980
1893	310,931
1895	298,641
1897	294,347

Trains handled

Year	Trains handled
1879	14,380
1881	20,181
1883	27,007
1885	27,670
1887	36,175
1889	41,303
1891	46,001
1893	44,838
1895	42,853
1897	41,044

Source: Union Depot's Co. treasurer reports

town, which appeased the locals. The south site was dropped from consideration because it had only one supporter.

At this moment peace reigned among the titans who controlled most of the main lines and whose sign-off was necessary on any big decisions. Two of the legendary turn-of-the-century railroad barons, Edward Harriman and James Hill, had vied for control of the Burlington by buying up its stock on Wall Street. Each ended up with half, and financier J.P. Morgan negotiated a truce in which Harriman and Hill created a shell corporation, the Northern Securities Co., to hold all the stock and jointly run the line. Besides this, Harriman had established a business relationship with another baron, George Gould, son of railroad titan Jay Gould. Harriman and George Gould each served on the boards of the other's main lines.

As all this related to Kansas City, the mighty Burlington controlled the Hannibal Bridge across the Missouri River and the only tracks rounding the bluff by the river, called the gooseneck. The Burlington wasn't interested in a new station somewhere that diminished either of those advantages. After all, the Burlington charged other railroads for their use of those tracks. By this time, too, Harriman had gobbled up the previous site-decision holdout, the Chicago & Alton, to go along with his Union Pacific. George Gould, meanwhile, headed the Missouri Pacific and the Wabash in Kansas City.

Together they went along with the Burlington, forming a cooperative partnership among competing lines that Harriman liked to call a "community of interest." *The Star*, meanwhile, likened the partnership to something else: extortion. "With these (trackage rental) contracts for a club, the Burlington line has whipped these lines into a position where they dare not oppose the Burlington in its selection of the West bottoms site," the paper opined in April 1903.

Nature intervenes

In June 1903 everything changed. Floodwaters swamped the West Bottoms and Union Depot. First the torrents swept through the depot's downstairs, tearing down doors and ripping out window sashes. At the flood's peak the waiting room was filled to a depth of 6 feet 7 inches, while outside only the black humps on top of locomotives were visible. The depot was closed for a week.

That was Kansas City's lucky break.

Reed

No one argued for a site in the bottoms anymore. That left only the north site in serious consideration.

Kansas City leaders remained antsy. A delegation led by Mayor James A. Reed addressed the Union Depot board in January 1904 "requesting action." The board kept appointing study committees. This served two purposes: It gave the railroads a chance to draw up estimates and confirm that buying land and track right of way for the north site would cost less than any alternative, and it bought time for the railroads to persuade some of their partner lines, especially the Santa Fe, to go along by promising adequate connections to their main tracks.

Water engulfed the West Bottoms in 1903, severing Kansas City's water supply and knocking out electricity, natural gas and streetcar service. On June 2, these spectators looked on from the shantytown along the bluff. Inside Union Depot, the flood rose to the tops of doors. The catastrophe ended talk of placing a new railroad station in the bottoms.

Then came that blustery day in Chicago in February 1905. The Union Depot board's executive committee convened on the 10th floor of the LaSalle
Street Station. All the issues for a new Kansas City station had been ironed
out except one seemingly small matter — the price for the land. After eight
years of bouncing around among a south site, the West Bottoms and the north
site, the railroads were finally all in agreement on a location to pursue. The
Burlington, led by Daniel Willard, Hill's hand-picked man, cemented its stake
by buying into the new north-site ownership group, the Armour-Swift meatpackers.

And that's when the Burlington and the meatpackers jacked up the land
price. Committee members all left the LaSalle Street Station knowing a golden
opportunity had been lost.

At that point the Chicago & Alton's Samuel Felton took command of the
situation. Soon after the meeting, he contacted the Santa Fe's committee
member. Felton, according to a later account by another Santa Fe official, resolved "that we go to the (south-side) site whether the balance (of railroads)
would go there or not; that he was tired of fooling with the north end site."

Samuel Felton

Felton, a respected railroad executive who would later be put in charge of
all U.S. railroads in World War I, was the chief Harriman representative on the
depot board. He also had been the swing vote who had kept the fragile Harri-
man-Hill-Gould railroad coalition intact. Now he was switching sides, plotting
with the Santa Fe, which had usually been the outcast on the depot board.

The reason for this switch was simple, but it wasn't recognized then by
Kansas Citians, including the newspapers: Harriman's "community of interests" among railroad barons was falling apart.

The Harriman-Hill truce consisting of a dual-owned railroad holding company over the Burlington was ruled unconstitutional by the U.S. Supreme
Court, forcing the two to negotiate some sort of settlement. Harriman and Hill
couldn't decide how to divest their holdings, so they went to court, and in
March 1905 the U.S. Supreme Court sided with Hill, giving him the Burlington. This turned them back into bitter adversaries, as they had been toward
the end of the 19th century. Harriman also had a falling out with Gould over
railroad construction in the West. Gould resigned from Harriman's boards,
and the two also became adversaries. Meanwhile, Harriman had patched up a
short-running squabble with the Santa Fe over western expansion, and two of
his associates were elected to Santa Fe's board.

James Hill

George Gould

For a Harriman man such as Felton, then, his allegiances had to shift. So
at the next Union Depot meeting in May, a motion was made for a vote on the
south site. It fell far short of the unanimous requirement but received support
from more than half the railroads — the Alton, the Santa Fe, the Rock Island,
the Union Pacific and two others.

Then these maverick lines resolved to do something that changed the
course of Kansas City history. They decided to go ahead on their own, breaking away from the other railroads and buying options themselves for the land
that would be needed around 23rd and Grand.

Behind this bold move was the era's foremost railroad financier, Harriman, who was the invisible hand behind Kansas City's station selection. Together, Harriman and his trusted agent, Felton, played the key roles in the

A REPUTATION FOR RUTHLESSNESS

Edward Harriman grew up on the East Coast, the son of a low-paid minister. In school he was better-known for mischief-making than for study, and at age 14 he dropped out. He found a job as an office boy at a brokerage firm on Wall Street, soon became a broker and quickly developed a reputation for ruthlessness. He brazenly pocketed commissions on stock orders he took from his fellow brokers' customers while they were at lunch. C.J. Osborne, one of the boldest speculators in New York, called him "the best broker on Wall Street." When Harriman married in 1879, his new father-in-law was president of a small railroad and immediately put

Harriman on its board. Harriman immersed himself in the railroad business and soon bought into another small line. He spent a year as vice president, giving the roadbed, locomotives and cars a general face-lift, and then set about selling it for a tidy profit. This became his formula: spend money to make money. From this beginning he quit Wall Street, operated the Illinois Central in the 1880s and then took over the Union Pacific and the Chicago & Alton in the late 1890s. He would become one of the renowned names of American railroading around the turn of the century before his death in 1909.

---

jockeying and the eventual breakthrough.

Any way you look at the site decision, Harriman's fingerprints were all over it. His chief engineer, John Berry, had been preparing reports in 1904-05 touting a south-side site, even as Harriman was prepared to go along with the other railroads on the north-side site. Berry had been with Harriman from the beginning of the baron's takeover of the Union Pacific in the 1890s. He was one of a handful of officials who went with Harriman on a tour of Union Pacific properties in 1898, a trip that started in Kansas City, Union Pacific's easternmost outpost. This trip undoubtedly gave Harriman a sense of the West Bottoms' crowded conditions.

The mythology about Harriman was that he got into the railroad business as a profit-sucking speculator. In reality, he increased profitability by improving railroad equipment so his trains ran more efficiently.

Harriman rebuilt track and facilities, a departure from the industry's typical penny-pinching policies. During Harriman's 10 years guiding the Union Pacific, the railroad put up 58 new stockyards, 45 section houses and 36 depots. And Harriman put Felton in charge of the Alton to do the same thing.

All of Harriman's correspondence in the first years after the turn of the century was destroyed by fire, so his thoughts about Kansas City are not entirely known. Yet, surely he considered a new Union Station a major project for his railroads. After all, it would be the largest depot ever built by his lines in his lifetime. With Berry's work, he was keeping his options open, and with Felton part of the decision-making process, he was kept apprised. As Felton himself related at the end of his career in a 1925 magazine article titled "The Genius of Edward H. Harriman," the baron "kept in his head the exact conditions everywhere.... In all his plans, he took the initiative.... He was always

The mythology about Harriman was that he got into the railroad business as a profit-sucking speculator. In reality, he increased profitability by improving railroad equipment so his trains ran more efficiently.

the sole director." Felton also indicated: "I was always in close touch with him."

With Harriman's instant recall and understanding of conditions everywhere, the baron undoubtedly knew Kansas City had to resolve its depot crowding, and after the land-price debacle of 1905, that meant going with the south site.

For decades it would be repeated that Union Station's location was chosen after some sort of rational review. "The site was a logical one," a mayor's Union Station Task Force reported in 1986. Yet, what happened was a combination of luck, greed and intrigue among some of the most powerful men in America.

Finally, a decision

In 1906 everything came together.

As the year began, the split on the Union Depot board was unequivocal. Hill's Burlington and Gould's Missouri Pacific and Wabash lines kept pushing for the north site. Harriman's interests sided with some of the independent lines, such as the Santa Fe, the Rock Island and the Chicago, Milwaukee & St. Paul railroad, to form a new coalition to get the badly needed, modernized station done.

Stealthily, the Harriman lines and the independents acquired land for a new station. The acreage wasn't exactly ideal: swampy, on the outskirts of town and bisected by O.K. Creek, by then little more than a sewer. The site contained the Our Lady of Sorrows church, which had 145 members, and a few rows of bungalow homes on a steep, hilly slope between the creek and Penn Valley Park. The church, for instance, was bought for $51,000.

In the spring the Harriman lines and the independents announced the new station site publicly. Amid much hoopla made about the decision in the pages of *The Star*, the Alton's Felton was deemed "chairman of the Committee of Six" and started making arrangements for an architect.

To formalize their relationship, the six lines formed a new company, the Kansas City Terminal Railway Co., which was separate from the Union Depot Co. It comprised the Union Pacific, the Alton, the Rock Island, the Santa Fe, the Milwaukee and the Frisco.

The Terminal Railway then hired a president to handle all the planning for the new station. Observers had to read between the lines of newspaper accounts to realize that not all the railroads were included.

Before long the other railroads realized the truth of the adage: If you can't beat 'em, join 'em. By the middle of 1906 the Hill and Gould recalcitrants joined the Terminal Railway and the long-raging dispute had come to an end. Those, along with two new railroads, made a total of 12 lines — a "union" of railroads, hence the name of the station.

As the Kansas City Terminal Railway, the new board met to consider who should design its new station. Felton already had an architect in mind. Another man seeking the job was Daniel Burnham of Chicago, probably the nation's pre-eminent architect around the turn of the century. He had overseen the wildly successful 1893 World's Fair in Chicago, whose architecture would influence city planning for years afterward. He also had already designed the na-

In the late 19th century, O.K. Creek ran through undeveloped parts of Kansas City. By the time Union Station was proposed, a scattering of factories, lumberyards, warehouses and other businesses stood along the creek.

tion's next great train station, Washington, D.C.'s, Union Station.

Yet, the railroad leaders expecting to build what would be Kansas City's largest building to date instead chose another architect from Chicago, a man with little experience designing railroad stations and a man whose eccentric nature was at odds with the very prim-and-proper Victorian era. Simply put, Felton's choice was a man who, based on his background, had no business winning this commission.

CHAPTER 2

"MAKE A MONUMENT"

Jarvis Hunt
Architect

U nion Station owes its quiet dignity to a man who was anything but quiet. He was equal parts unpredictable and bombastic. He was Jarvis Hunt.

Hunt was a medium-sized man with a dapper, mustached appearance. He laced his language with profanity and often ranted and raved with a booming voice. His chief architectural aide, Charles Bohasseck, years later recalled Hunt as "an individual as distinctive and unpredictable as any I ever knew" and one who had "the ability to soften his blunt and harsh comments with the neatest kind of profanity artistically rendered."

In Hunt's country home outside Chicago, there was a stuffed crocodile on the floor. Once, in a tale that became family legend, Hunt rode a horse inside that house. Across the road was a golf course, and Hunt was so hooked on golf, he played straight through Chicago's snowy, windy winters with a red ball. He was, in a nutshell, flamboyant.

Fortunately for Kansas City, though, Hunt also was a man with vision, plus enough stubbornness and arrogance to see that vision through. In spring 1906 he spent weeks preparing his conception for Kansas City's station. He drew and redrew his plans and erected a three-dimensional model of them, complete with stained glass in the windows. Then in June, when Hunt was scheduled to make a presentation to the Terminal Railway building committee, he didn't show up.

Finally, one of the committee members telephoned him. "Get your plans together and come over at once; we are waiting," Hunt was told.

"At once?" Hunt reportedly questioned. "Why, damn it. It will take days to move my depot plans. I must have time."

He not only got a week's extension, he got the job.

A man with connections

One big factor in Jarvis Hunt's favor was his family name.

In the blooming architectural profession before the turn of the century,

Facing page: Jarvis Hunt.

few figures loomed larger than Richard Morris Hunt. He designed many mansions and estates in Newport, R.I., and in New York City, based on connections he made in New York society. Jarvis Hunt was a nephew, and he developed the same penchant for using his social relationships to advance his career.

Jarvis Hunt's friendship with the founder of the Chicago Golf Club, the first 18-hole course in the U.S., led to jobs designing the clubhouse and several homes along the course. His practice eventually evolved from clubs and country estates to office buildings and warehouses. Several of these were noted in national architectural journals for their classical designs, their attention to detail and, in the case of the homes, how well they fit with wooded settings. Typical of the critiques of Hunt's early work was one in *The House Beautiful* in 1897 for the Saddle and Cycle Club in Chicago: "The architect, Mr. Jarvis Hunt, has indulged in no particular aggressiveness of style, but has produced a building which, while thoroughly original, is still simple enough in character."

In his golf outings, in his downtown Chicago club memberships, in his home designs for other wealthy businessmen, it's likely that Hunt became friendly with executives from the era's largest industry, the railroads.

And so, with no railroad stations on his resume at the time, Hunt was enlisted to do some drawings for Kansas City's Union Depot board as early as 1901 or 1902, when the board got serious about a new station and procured drawings from several architects. Four years later, when the Chicago & Alton-led faction for the south station site began making arrangements for an architect, Hunt was already working on a new Alton station in Mexico, Mo. This cemented his link to Alton President Samuel Felton, a fellow Chicagoan. By then, Felton headed the new Kansas City Terminal Railway's committee on station and plans. In his rush to pick an architect, it's probable Felton turned to one he already knew and trusted.

At the "official" Union Station architectural selection in June 1906, Hunt was obviously the hand-picked choice all along, a man in the right place at the right time.

Daniel Burnham and a Kansas City architectural firm were asked to submit proposals only after a couple of railroads requested competition. In the first vote on the architect, seven of the newly united railroads were present. Hunt received five votes, Burnham two. Minutes of the meeting indicate that the votes of the remaining railroads would be sought, but no record exists of the final tally for Hunt. Having Felton on his side meant Hunt had Edward Harriman on his side, too. Harriman, perhaps the most powerful of all railroad barons, was over Felton's shoulder on the Alton board and lobbied for Hunt.

Jarvis Hunt's station for the Chicago & Alton railroad in Mexico, Mo.

Harriman had just one piece of advice, the architect remembered, one that would become part of Union Station lore:

"Make a monument."

A PROSPEROUS BEGINNING

Jarvis Hunt was born into privilege. A grandfather, William Jarvis, was a consul to Portugal. The consul lived one of those remarkable, early American adventures in which he made a fortune as a merchant capitalist on the high seas and then seized an opportunity with European instability to buy Spanish merino sheep.

Hunt as a young man

He imported those sheep into this country, which spawned a boom in woolen manufacturing. The consul settled in Vermont and built a sprawling farm named Elmsholme. He died in 1859, and the property eventually was turned over to the consul's daughter, Katherine Jarvis Hunt.

By this time Katherine had married Leavitt Hunt, who himself came from a distinguished family. His oldest brother was William Morris Hunt, who became an acclaimed painter. Leavitt's third brother was Richard Morris Hunt, who became a renowned architect. Leavitt and Richard were close growing up, going to school together in Europe and sightseeing in Rome and across America with their mother. Leavitt apparently distinguished himself early. He was said to have been the first American to photograph the ruins of Egypt, and he later earned the rank of colonel in the Civil War. He settled down as a lawyer in New York, though the law was a struggle for him because of an eye injury from the war.

So Leavitt and Katherine would raise their five children on the consul's estate. Jarvis Hunt was their second child. So little is known about Jarvis' early life that the Withey & Withey architectural reference guide listed his birth year wrong and didn't even give a birth day. He wasn't born in 1859, as passed along by many publications, but on Aug. 6, 1863. Jarvis also is described in architectural refer-

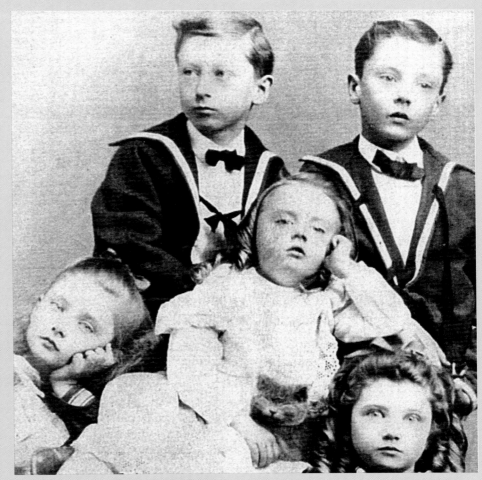

Hunt, upper right, and his siblings. Bottom row from left: Maud, Leavitt and Katherine. Top left: Clyde.

ences as having attended Harvard, but the school has no record he went there. He actually attended the Massachusetts Institute of Technology. MIT was the only architectural school in the country at the time. It was patterned after the celebrated Ecole des Beaux-Arts in Paris, which stressed classical designs, such as arches, columns and symmetry. Hunt stayed at MIT just one year, long enough to receive a smattering of architectural training before proceeding to flunk chemistry and a class called "projections."

Hunt didn't accomplish much early in his career, partly because of bad luck. A poem his father wrote about his son in this period was titled "I Am Looking for Something To Do." One verse went:

I've dotted New England peak and shore,

With plans, elevations, o'er and o'er,
A big job in Boston was decided
When patron mine — he up and died.

Going to booming Chicago for the World's Fair in 1893 catapulted Hunt's career and his social life. He married Louise Coleman, the granddaughter of one of Chicago's pioneers, and their wedding was a society event worthy of newspaper coverage. She was a prize-winning equestrian, and the country home Hunt built along the Chicago Golf Club in far suburban Wheaton included large stables in back. The marriage ended in divorce in 1909, and Hunt got custody of his two young children. After designing more stations, though none as big as Kansas City's, he retired in 1927. Hunt died in 1941.

That mandate certainly fit Hunt's personality and work. His own country house was oversized, with a 20-foot ceiling in the family room. "His signature was big, and he liked things big," his granddaughter, Diana Hunt Edgerton, recalled decades later. Indeed, Jarvis Hunt's personality might have been extraordinary by Victorian standards, but his work reflected his times. And those times influenced him in many ways. Beaux-arts monumentality, his friendship with Daniel Burnham, Kansas City's beautification crusade and the national shift in railroad architecture toward classical structures — all these shaped Hunt's planning for Kansas City's station.

The Court of Honor at the Chicago World's Fair, formally the World's Columbian Exposition, was dominated by Daniel Chester French's 65-foot Statue of the Republic. The 1893 fair marked the 400th anniversary of Christopher Columbus' first voyage to the Western Hemisphere — one year late. The event lasted from May to October. The grand buildings had walls of a temporary material, and all but one were demolished afterward.

The City Beautiful

It's appropriate that Jarvis Hunt's first big break, the one that really launched his career and profoundly influenced his architectural outlook, was the result of his connections. It came at the Chicago World's Fair in 1893.

Fairs were wildly popular in the 19th century, a combination of Disney World, the Smithsonian Institution and Fourth of July picnic all in one place. As Hunt entered his teens, he had visited the last great U.S. fair, the Centennial Exhibition in Philadelphia in 1876. Now, as a man approaching 30 years old, unlucky with early commissions and hungry to establish himself, he would contribute to the fair.

The Chicago fair stretched over a square mile of Jackson Park along Lake Michigan. Most visitors arrived by train at the fair's beaux-arts Terminal Station, paid a 50-cent admission and walked out into the Court of Honor, where the fair's major buildings stood, all covered in white stucco. Orchestra music drifted up from the lakefront. Men strolled around tapping walking sticks. Women twirled umbrellas in the sun.

To their left, past Richard Morris Hunt's domed headquarters for the fair's organizers, was the Electricity building, with Thomas Edison's 82-foot Tower of Light displaying a phenomenon still relatively new for most Americans. Next to that was the Manufactures and Liberal Arts building, more than a quarter-mile long, where such consumer products as Cream of Wheat and Aunt Jemima syrup were making their debut. From there, across a lagoon, was the 14-block-long Midway Plaisance with an Eiffel Tower model, an ostrich farm and the first Ferris wheel, which rose higher than any building on the grounds. Then at the fair's far north end, past the floor-to-ceiling aquarium, near the elevated railroad tracks and partly hidden by the state of Massachusetts' reproduction of John Hancock's barnlike house, was Jarvis Hunt's contribution.

It was the official state building of his native Vermont, a reproduction of an ancient Roman villa, containing a display of Vermont marble. Hunt got this commission through his uncle Richard Morris Hunt, a supervisory architect for the fair. Jarvis sketched it and Richard approved it before Vermont even set aside enough money for it late in the fair's planning. The distinction of being a World's Fair architect, though, was only part of the plum for Jarvis Hunt. For the fair is also where he first encountered Daniel Burnham and the changing face of architecture.

Burnham was the fair's mastermind. His status as America's foremost architect had been cemented with his selection, over Richard Morris Hunt, as the building director. Burnham organized the Court of Honor, the series of monumental buildings around a vast rectangular reflecting pool. Because 10 firms were involved in designing these major buildings, Burnham and his chief architects decided to adopt a uniform style to avoid creating a hodgepodge.

They could have adopted the popular Victorian Gothic or even the developing modernism. Yet, they chose classical beaux-arts. It was simple and clean, with an emphasis on horizontal monumental structures. This repre-

Hunt's building for the state of Vermont.

sented a step backward in architectural innovations. Classicism drew inspiration from ancient Roman temples rather than modern American phenomena, such as the budding skyscraper, that the World's Fair was celebrating. Burnham's World's Fair guidelines specified "symmetrical and rectangular plan.... The architecture should be dignified in style, formal rather than picturesque." So all the buildings around the Court of Honor shared a standard flat cornice or roof line, arches and rhythmic repetition of architectural elements like columns. The buildings became known collectively as "White City."

By all accounts it was a hit. With more than 27 million visitors, this fair outdrew all previous ones, so the neoclassic theme of long, block buildings embellished with arches and columns became etched in America's mind. Children's writer L. Frank Baum was so enthralled by White City that it served years later as inspiration for Emerald City in *The Wizard of Oz*. While the fair's architecture flaunted the old, it looked new. Certainly no major city had many, if any, buildings resembling it. Thomas Tallmadge summed up these feelings in *The Story of Architecture in America*: "The spectacle of the exhibition had been so overwhelmingly beautiful that laymen and professional alike returned home convinced of the superiority of the art of Greece and Rome."

Daniel Burnham

By this time Kansas City was trying to transform itself from muddy boom town to dressed-up metropolis through a crusade for parks and boulevards. *The Star* led this charge, through the bullying personality and vision of its publisher, William Rockhill Nelson, who had been a road builder in his native Indiana.

His theme was civic shame: Kansas City must beautify itself or lose the race for municipal importance, an argument for major-league status that would be conjured time and again in the city's history. In the latter days of the Chicago World's Fair in October 1893, the new parks board presented its first report on the city's needs. It read like a regurgitation of Nelson's theme. At one point the report stated that "by beautifying our city...we shall create among our people warm attachments to the city, and promote civic pride, thereby supplementing and emphasizing our business advantages and increasing their power to draw business and population."

The fair, mapped out as an urban setting with tree-lined promenades and ample open spaces, gave Kansas Citians a glimpse of this new aesthetic. "For its visitors," Thomas S. Hines wrote in a biography of Daniel Burnham, "the fair provided a model, against which they might compare their own urban centers." In the two decades after the fair, Kansas City developed nearly 2,000 acres of parks, such as Penn Valley and Swope, plus 61 miles of divided thoroughfares, such as the Paseo. It achieved "one of the most remarkable instances of continuity of purpose in city planning," in the words of one parks report. As such, Kansas City became one of the nation's leading examples of the so-called City Beautiful movement.

This Progressive-era movement was more than a crusade against ugliness and dirt. It was an attempt to tame the cluttered, squalid and unseemly urban scene with order, harmony and planning. For many cities, this meant not just parks and boulevards but also street sweeping, nighttime streetlights and storm sewers. And at the movement's ideological apex was an ensemble of monumental public buildings around a plaza — introduced at the Chicago World's Fair as the Court of Honor.

After the fair, Daniel Burnham elaborated on his concept, spawning what's known as the civic center. His plan for Washington in 1902 enlarged Pierre L'Enfant's 1791 blueprint, adding a Lincoln Memorial and a new train station, plus filling in the Capitol mall with grass as a central plaza. A year later he proposed grouping government and cultural buildings along the shore of Lake Erie in Cleveland, and then moved on to San Francisco and Chicago.

That last plan borrowed an idea to turn Michigan Avenue into a grand lakeshore drive from fellow Chicago architect Jarvis Hunt. Once in Kansas City, Hunt would make his own contribution to the City Beautiful — and try his own hand at civic-center planning as a climax to the parks and boulevards movement.

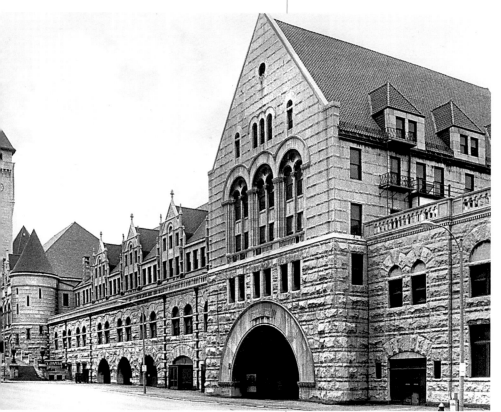

St. Louis Union Station, built in 1894 in the Romanesque style.

As the world awoke to the beaux-arts ideal, railroad station design was in the midst of a revolution.

Terminal architecture was shifting from decidedly Victorian Gothic and its vertical towers to beaux-arts and its horizontal monumentality. The most grandiose and well-known stations before the turn of the century were rich in red stones or bricks, asymmetrical roof lines with turrets, gables and the like, plus pointed-top clock towers rising a couple of hundred feet. Typical of this look were Kansas City's own Union Depot and the medieval-like fortresses in St. Louis and Indianapolis patterned after European cathedrals. Towers were in vogue during this period, rising from nearly every building of importance. But this style was going out of style.

Again, the Chicago fair played a decisive role. One of the monumental buildings around the Court of Honor was the Terminal Station. It had three soaring arched windows above portals, wings on each end — and no tower. This was, in the public's eyes, how futuristic depots should look. And that's what they became.

The economic depression after the fair slowed opportunities to build new things, but beginning with Burnham's design for Washington's Union Station after the turn of the century, the beaux-arts trend took off. That station featured a rectangular front dominated by three large, arched windows and a

Forebear of a trend: Terminal Station at the Chicago world's fair, outside and in.

straight cornice line, just like at the World's Fair. Inside, the lobby/waiting room was an expansive, cavernous, open-air space, like an atrium. The room was flanked by Roman columns and an arched ceiling decorated with gold-leaf paint.

The classical form instantly influenced plans for New York's Grand Central and Pennsylvania stations. These also featured high, arched windows letting in sunlight, columns along the facade, and gigantically tall and long halls inside. This building spurt ripened into the golden age of railroad station construction. Railroad station historian Janet Greenstein Potter wrote in her 1996 book, *Great American Railroad Stations*: "In railroad's gilded age, before World War I, opulence earned respect rather than being regarded as undemocratic. The railroads lavished money on a game of architectural one-upmanship by competing to build the most spectacular monuments to their arrogant success."

Another architectural historian derogatorily called this design shift "elephantiasis." In this view, bigger was not better, just less convenient for travelers. Either way, all these architectural and engineering trends would find expression in Kansas City's Union Station.

The plan emerges

So here was Jarvis Hunt near the end of the century's first decade, facing the biggest commission of his life. He had begun the decade designing homes and then had progressed to commercial buildings. Now he was sketching a big-city railroad station, among the biggest buildings then being conceived. Hunt knew this could be his masterpiece. But he had never done anything so immense or extensive before. Instinctively he turned to the forms he admired and respected most — the works of Daniel Burnham.

As a result, Hunt's initial drawings in Kansas City were strikingly similar to what Burnham was doing.

Before his plans were reduced, Jarvis Hunt in 1907 envisioned this grand design for Kansas City's Union Station.

After the Chicago World's Fair the two had become friends. Hunt's business records no longer exist, but letters written by Burnham show they knew each other well and worked together on architectural issues in Chicago. Even the office Hunt occupied in downtown Chicago, the space where he sketched Kansas City's new station, was inside one of the Burnham firm's first creations, the 16-story Monadnock Building, a pioneering skyscraper. It was as if Hunt were following in Burnham's footsteps, feeding off the master's energy.

In 1907, Hunt made public his creation. The main building occupied the equivalent of three city blocks. Jutting out from the main building was a portico-covered entry with three 70-foot-tall masonry arches. The triple-arched motif was then repeated in the three giant windows in the lobby's front wall. The lobby itself was lined with columns and trimmed with marble 70 feet high along the walls. The ceiling curved in a wide arch that reached 115 feet high at its peak. Flanking the lobby on each side were four-story wings. The lobby and wing together formed the top of a "T" shape. A long waiting room formed the stem of the "T," and the triple-arch motif continued in the passageways be-

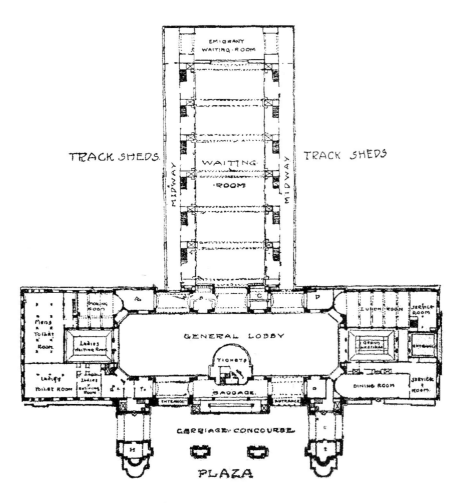

tween the two colossal halls. The waiting room, also topped by an arching roof, contained 12 train gates. Each was equipped with "moving staircases," or escalators, to shuttle travelers to and from the trains parked underneath the waiting room. *The Star* declared that the design added up to "a magnificent building, elaborate in proportions and monumental in appearance."

Hunt's edifice was a virtual clone of Burnham's Washington station. That terminal also featured a triple-arched entrance concourse jutting out from the front, triple arches repeated inside, columns around an enormous lobby, arched ceilings, plus adjoining wings. About the only touches Jarvis Hunt did not copy were Burnham's stone statues above the entrance outside and circling the lobby's balcony inside. In a sense, Hunt's design harked back to before Washington's station — to the Chicago World's Fair terminal, with its triple archways in front. Yale architecture professor Carroll L.V. Meeks observed later in his study of railroad depots that the fair's terminal "engendered a whole family of permanent stations....After it, the completely romantic stations...seemed old-fashioned."

In this new period of railroad architecture, was Hunt plagiarizing or simply following the latest trend? Whichever, he would continue doing it.

Once Hunt completed his station layout, his attention turned to its surroundings. George Kessler, the designer of Kansas City's parks and boulevards

The Star declared that the design added up to "a magnificent building, elaborate in proportions and monumental in appearance."

system, broached the subject with Hunt. Kessler hoped to include some of the Terminal Railway's lands south of the station into the parks system. In a letter to Hunt, he also advised: "Possibly some of this land might have to be used for public buildings, perhaps around the border, if a general grouping scheme can be accomplished there using your building as a key." That sparked Hunt's next proposal for Kansas City.

At that time all the main government buildings were scattered around the City Market, away from the commercial downtown growing to the south. What Hunt had in mind for his grandiose station was an equally grandiose setting: a civic center, something that wouldn't just add parkland but would also crown the City Beautiful aesthetic. He devised a semicircular plaza surrounded by city and county buildings, a federal post office and an art museum spanning the six blocks between Broadway and Grand Avenue. He situated a domed City Hall — resembling his uncle Richard's Chicago fair headquarters — directly across from Union Station's entrance. It would be a mammoth town square befitting a flourishing city with major-league ambitions, a city with seemingly unbridled potential. And, again, it followed exactly in the footsteps of Burnham.

The master's plan for Cleveland, for instance, included a new railroad station to act as the "city gate" and provide a "favorable" first impression, according to Burnham's proposal. This was Hunt's thinking, too, and it caught the imagination of Kansas City's leading businessmen. Jesse Clyde Nichols, a real estate developer who himself would later change the city's landscape, argued: "Don't you believe that the creation of a beautiful setting would do much to bring fresh capital here?" Soon the idea received a boost when Mary Atkins bequeathed a six-figure gift for an art museum.

Years later, however, after the fate of all these buildings around Union Station became clear, a Missouri state historian would look back at the station's place, by itself, in city history. She would designate the station "the most prominent architectural contribution to the City Beautiful movement in

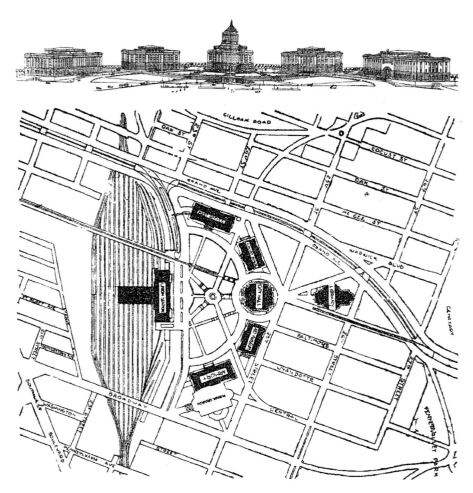

What might have been: In August 1910, Hunt made public in *The Star* this plan for a Civic Center opposite the entrance to Union Station. City Hall would have stood in the middle, flanked by buildings for the post office, a library, an art museum and Jackson County offices.

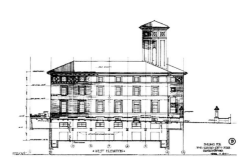

In 1911, *The Kansas City Star* moved into its new, Jarvis-Hunt-designed building at 18th Street and Grand Avenue, only a few blocks northeast of the site of Union Station.

Kansas City."

Cost, cost, cost

In November 1907, just weeks after unveiling his drawings, Jarvis Hunt appeared at a Terminal Railway board meeting in Chicago. The railroads were worried. They loved his plans. What was not to love in that temple of railroad affluence? But a financial panic had started a few months back. Bank credit — needed to pay for construction — was drying up. So the railroads summoned Hunt. They wanted to know how much their temple was going to cost. The railroads had first set a budget of $2 million, but everyone knew Hunt's design surpassed that. As the railroad chieftains sat in leather chairs on the 10th floor of the LaSalle Street Station, Hunt hemmed and hawed. A true cost couldn't be determined, he told them. Various features were still undecided. Detailed specifications hadn't been done. But the railroads pressed him. Hunt finally provided an estimate: $3.5 million, almost double the budgeted amount.

That was just what the railroads feared. The board members told him to scale it back. They "agreed that the plans might be modified and portions omitted," according to the meeting minutes. They further instructed a separate building committee to become a watchdog and proceed "with the idea of further reducing cost of Station in any possible way without seriously affecting its efficiency, which is considered by the Board to be the paramount issue at (this) point."

To Jarvis Hunt, the railroads might as well have thrown a brick at his head. He hated rejection of his creations. While the station was being planned, William Rockhill Nelson of *The Star* hired Hunt to design a new newspaper building at 18th Street and Grand Avenue. Nelson had wanted it Italian Renaissance, done in brick. Hunt presented a watercolor showing a classical structure, dressed up with marble. Nelson looked it over. "Oh, it's a beautiful building, of course," he said, "but it wouldn't do for a print shop." Hunt recoiled. "Kick a hole through it," he bellowed. "Back to Chicago for me." Nevertheless, Nelson got what he wanted.

As for what the railroads wanted for their building, it was back to the drawing board for Hunt. He eliminated the portico-covered entryway. Replaced the arched roofs. Pruned the wings from four stories to three. Abandoned an east entrance. Cut all the columns around the grand lobby. Trimmed the interior marble from 70 feet high to the balcony level. Reduced the ceiling's height from 115 feet to 95 feet. Pared the waiting room's size. Traded stone for terra cotta on the waiting-room walls. Removed the escalators at train gates. Substituted one big central clock for several throughout the two main halls. On and on he went, though the monumental stature and triple-arch motif remained, along with the best decorative materials he could find, various kinds of limestones, marbles and cast iron.

Yet, as 1907 turned into 1908 and 1908 became 1909, the recession softened, and the railroads soon replaced one worry with another. Passenger business in Kansas City was jumping. The number of tickets sold, which had remained quite steady during the middle of the decade, suddenly doubled from 650,000 to 1.3 million by decade's end. Union Depot's on-site managers asked for more tracks at the new station. Certainly the railroads didn't want to make the same mistake twice — build a lavish Kansas City station and then see it become obsolete after several years. They knew what respected New York railroad superintendent John Droege was writing at the time: "The average passenger station…has rarely retained its adequacy more than 25 or 30 years. It has been practically impossible to anticipate the exact degree of growth of business, and the cases are few where the railroads with all their foresight have been able to anticipate the future sufficiently." So Hunt was directed to add four tracks and four gates.

And in November 1909, Hunt appeared in front of the Terminal Railway board's building committee with his revamped design. Even with all the reductions, he now announced an even higher cost, $5.7 million. This time Hunt came prepared to argue his case. Alluding to the growing passenger traffic at Union Depot, the architect explained how he had calculated Union Station's space needs. As the Terminal Railway's chief engineer later related: "Counting all of the space to be used by passengers, including general waiting room, lobby, ladies waiting room, smoking room and second-class waiting rooms, Mr. Hunt's allowance was about two square feet per passenger per day." Of course,

UNION DEPOT

Tickets sold

1900	1901	1902	1903	1904	1905	1906	1907	1908
444,308	503,148	539,288	602,238	657,754	649,893	721,948	975,541	1,308,892

Trains handled

1900	1901	1902	1903	1904	1905	1906	1907	1908
47,577	53,348	57,412	57,679	64,529	69,158	73,322	74,207	71,175

Source: Union Depot's Co. treasurer reports

Instead of a single large span over the tracks, Hunt used a new, lower design for the train shed. It allowed smoke and fumes from locomotives to be quickly vented away.

> **"...I believe every one identified with the Terminal Company realizes that the Station is none too big, that there is no wasted space and that the general arrangement serves satisfactorily every public convenience in an orderly and economical way. The design is monumental, as it should be, but is plain and without useless ornament and certainly shows no extravagance."**
>
> *— Jarvis Hunt, in a letter to Samuel Felton, defending himself against accusations of extravagance. It was written five years after the station opened, indicating the controversy had not died.*

not all those passengers would be in the station at the same time, but apparently no one quibbled with his computations. Building committee members, according to the meeting minutes, lamented that "they saw no way to wisely reduce the plans."

The architect-client battles were far from over, however. Hunt proceeded to spar with the railroads for the next few years. This was going to be his masterpiece. He wasn't going to let his client mess it up for him.

On several occasions railroad officials suggested small changes, even during construction, and Hunt had the audacity to turn them down. As correspondence from the period shows, Hunt didn't countenance meddling and he bullied his clients into giving him almost total control. For instance, the railroads' chief engineer kept making suggestions, such as enlarging a room or proposing how a counter should be situated. At one point Hunt wrote back defiantly: "...you keep returning to us drawings altered to meet with your ideas, which we have turned down before, and you seem to persist in making these changes according to your ideas. I therefore see no further sense in our making drawings in connection with same, as I certainly will not incorporate them in the plans, as they will not at all carry out the design of the building."

Another time, the chief engineer demanded that the waiting-room support columns not be placed on the passenger platforms, where they would obstruct the traveler and redcap traffic. "In looking over the plans I have seen no reason why the columns could not be placed between the tracks (within) each pair of station tracks," he wrote Hunt. Yet Hunt was devising a novel kind of train shed over all the tracks. It wasn't a traditional, semicircular span of several hundred feet but a virtual duplicate of a new shed at the Hoboken, N.J., station. This shed was lower, closer to the top of trains, and it allowed their smoke to filter outside, instead of leaving a foggy, sooty environment for passengers to walk through. In Hunt's view, each pair of tracks had to remain close together. There couldn't be columns between them. He won.

Meanwhile, the architect repeatedly objected whenever the Terminal Railway attempted — however justifiably — to control costs. The company asked about omitting marble lining the rest rooms in the off-site powerhouse, which would supply the station's heat and electricity. The architect balked. The company asked about swapping concrete for brick on the powerhouse facade, because the construction company had thousands of leftover bricks. The architect balked. The company asked about simplifying the lobby floor pattern so the marble pieces could be cut easier and faster. The architect balked. The company president asked about saving $750 by not having the big central clock, situated between the lobby and the waiting room, light up inside. Again, the architect balked. Sometimes Hunt lost, as with the powerhouse bricks and the marble floor, and sometimes he won, as with the clock.

Even scaled back, Union Station would be one of the largest in the country, larger even than Burnham's Washington station. In square feet, Kansas City's main building would be the third-biggest in the country. Only those in New York City would be larger. Kansas City's basement baggage-handling area would be the largest of any U.S. railroad station. The men's and ladies' rest rooms each would be the nation's second-largest, as would be the train sheds.

The building's massive scale reflected the city's monumental aspirations. After all, this was a city about which local and visiting dignitaries had been promising great things for decades, a city whose population was on its way toward breaking into the nation's top 20 in the 1920 census. The new station would accommodate a city of 2 million people — or five times the size of the entire metro area then.

But the terminal wasn't big solely for bigness' sake. Kansas City's unique status as a railroad stop demanded something out of all proportion to the city's size. It was a transfer town, after all. It served both as an outpost to the West, much as it had been in the days of the Santa Fe Trail, as well as the hub of a region stretching from the Dakotas to Texas. Because Kansas City served such a vast area, travelers changed trains here. The amount of baggage handled in Kansas City equaled Boston's South Station and exceeded New York's gigantic stations, which handled thousands of daily commuters. The volume of mail matched that of stations in those larger cities, too. "The problem of providing for the passenger traffic at Kansas City," declared the magazine of the Santa Fe railroad, "is radically different from that at any of the other large stations recently built."

The building's sheer size, though, added to the challenge of arranging all its varied functions. The ideal arrangement, according to architectural histori-

Before construction began, photographs were made at the site of the station and along the route that would be cut through the city by the Terminal Railway tracks. To document the study, an employee held a chalkboard containing the number of each site. This photo was made along the course of O.K. Creek.

an Carl Condit, was placing the entrance, the ticket offices, the baggage check and the passenger concourse "in as close to a linear series as possible." But there were nearly as many solutions as there were stations. The vaunted Pennsylvania Station was "needlessly complex," while Washington's Union Station was "astonishingly close" to Condit's ideal. For Kansas City, ticketing and baggage-check services were placed near the west front doors, while traveler waiting and arriving areas were toward the back.

This layout was partly dictated by a terrain sloping upward to the south.

THE NEW UNION STATION AND SURROUNDINGS.

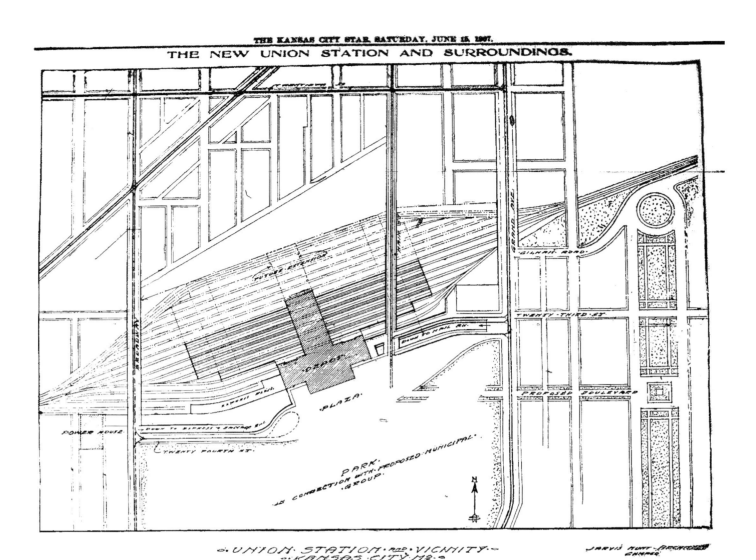

UNION STATION AND VICINITY
KANSAS CITY, MO.
SCALE

JARVIS HUNT, ARCHITECT
CHICAGO

This slope, as well as the existing Kansas City Belt Railway line of freight tracks at the site's north end, necessitated the station facing south. This also allowed for "through" tracks at the station so trains didn't have to back up. The building's layout, then, became innovative for big-city stations of the day. For one thing, only a couple of other stations in the country had waiting rooms over a set of "through" tracks. For another thing, the layout accommodated different uses. Outgoing passengers would wait in one room, while incoming passengers flowed through side corridors, called midways. Operational work such as mail and baggage hauling would take place below the passenger level in the several basements.

This separation made full use of the lobby's grand scale. Travelers would arrive through the front doors or from trains below, pass through vestibules with low ceilings, and then go into the lobby, heightening the effect of the tall ceiling. What Hunt had in mind was the same effect shown decades later in the movie "The Wizard of Oz": When Dorothy's house landed after being swept up in a tornado, she opened the door and stepped out into a vast, lush

Plans for new Terminal Railway tracks into and out of the station stirred disputes between the railroads and the city over what to do about cross streets, among them Broadway and Grand Avenue.

garden, with the movie changing from black-and-white to color.

The city approves

Finally, a political hurdle needed to be cleared: an agreement with the city over how the new tracks in and out of Union Station would cross streets. City officials were obstinate. They demanded that the railroads build bridges at main thoroughfares, such as Broadway, Grand and the Paseo. The railroads balked, and it took three years for the two sides to negotiate a 140-page agreement.

The final deal set the total number of required bridges and underpasses at 40 and made the railroads pay for relocating O.K. Creek on the station grounds, blowing the railroads' budget even more than Hunt's architecture. Still, the City Council decided only by a slim majority to put the deal up for a public vote. An election was required, because the city had to give away small slices of boulevard rights of way for the Terminal Railway to build some of its bridges.

At this time, in 1909, the city's most powerful politician was Jim Pendergast, the boss of the 1st Ward and big brother of later citywide boss Tom Pendergast. Jim's ward encompassed the West Bottoms area that would be economically savaged if Union Depot moved. That was reason enough for boss Jim to instruct his minions to vote against the new station. But he didn't. The mayor then, Thomas Crittenden, later wrote in a family memoir that Pendergast did this for the good of the city. That seems to be true. He was quoted in the 1906 announcement as supporting a new station if it benefited the entire city. He consistently supported civic improvements, because his blue-collar constituents usually stood to gain lots of work from those improvements. But also, Pendergast was fed up with politics and about to retire to his farm.

Voters approved the land deal in a landslide, 24,522 to 708. The day after the election, *The Star* opined on its front page: "The solution to the station and terminal problem marks the beginning of a new epoch for Kansas City. The best terminal system in the country is now in sight. The finest, most convenient and up-to-date station building will mark Kansas City for all travelers and give pride to every Kansas Citian."

Yet once construction work finally got under way, Hunt pondered whether Kansas Citians would take a liking to his station the same way they had first appreciated the old depot a generation before. With his typical flair — and hyperbole — the architect ranted on one visit:

"You don't show enough enthusiasm....You've got $50 million worth of parks and boulevards and $50 million worth of terminals. You ought to be howling."

In time, they would be.

CHAPTER 3

CONSTRUCTION AND CELEBRATION

Preceding page: Construction workers at Union Station, bundled against the cold in January 1912.

Left: Excavation begins Aug. 27, 1910.

On a sweltering, sunny Saturday in 1910, a photographer captured a group of men wearing overalls and hats and carrying shovels, all working around a steam shovel. The great machine hovered over them like a dinosaur. It rested on railroad tracks, taking its first scoop from the rocky hillside and officially kicking off the construction of Union Station. A smattering of official-looking men watched. It was August 27, and already the project was behind schedule.

Several months had passed since construction was supposed to start. Almost a year had passed since voters gave a green light to the undertaking. And four years had passed since railroad executives announced the site. To the public, the delay eroded some of the good will the railroads had renewed with their original proposal. Going back decades, Kansas Citians had voted to subsidize railroads proposing to build tracks into town. Some had panned out; many hadn't. Now this station. No one knew for sure whether it would come to be.

Certainly there had been signs of work. Dozens of tiny clapboard bungalows along with the Our Lady of Sorrows church had been torn down on the hillside south of the Kansas City Belt freight tracks, leaving sidewalks and carriage driveways to nowhere. That was something, but not much. So by the time the first construction workers gathered by the steam shovel that Saturday in August, Kansas Citians probably held the age-old Missouri attitude toward the new station: Show me. Union Station, then, began with little fanfare. None of the local newspapers showed up to take a photograph or sketch the scene. It was only as the citizenry slowly saw more that it dawned on them what they were getting.

Dangerous work

In the early mornings downtown, garment workers scurrying to work or businessmen sitting at desks with their office windows open could faintly hear

END OF WEST HEADING.   5-1-12
FILE 11-15-29. O.K. CREEK SEWER TUNNEL.

Rerouting O.K. Creek — converting the polluted, open stream into an underground sewer — was one of the less-glorious tasks of the Union Station project.

Foundation piers arose for the station even before the creek was permanently moved.

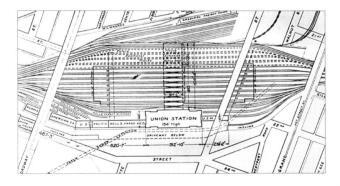

For the creek's new path, sewer casing was installed. *Left*, eventually the stream flowed underground just south of the station entrance.

The cost of the approaches to Union Station exceeded that of the station itself. This work took place to the east, near Woodland Avenue.

blasting a mile away. Dynamite explosions were a constant occurrence on the station site. Part of the hillside was being leveled. It contained mostly solid rock — the kind of shale or limestone still visible poking out of the hill south of the station. A contraption resembling an oil-well drill sank holes in the ground. Into them dynamite was packed and then detonated. Once the daily blasts loosened the rock, two steam shovels, each on temporary tracks and belching black smoke, scooped up debris and dropped it into railroad cars. Scoop and drop. Scoop and drop. On and on this went, day after day, month after month.

Every so often, the temporary tracks were moved farther into the hill, edging closer to the point where the slope would be cut 74 feet deep. Meanwhile, just to the west, another steam shovel dug a wide trench. This was for the underground diversion and enclosure of O.K. Creek, which now crossed the area where the waiting room would go. Here, wooden carts drawn by horses were parked by the steam shovel, filled and hauled away to a railcar and unloaded. The slow process stretched over a year, as the steam shovels excavated about 670,000 cubic yards of dirt and rock — the equivalent of digging 50 feet deep over eight football fields. And this covered only the preparatory work, not the station foundation. In August 1911, at a ceremony in which the station's brick-and-mortar construction contract was signed, the contractor was asked: "When will you begin building the station?" That might have drawn a chuckle.

The morning of Oct. 10, 1911, began like any other. With the foundation work a month old, about 100 men reported to the job. Some worked with the two steam shovels, digging a row of 30-foot deep pits for waiting-room piers. Some pushed wheelbarrows of concrete from four on-site mixers to the

The progress, slowly at first: The view looking west on Sept. 10, 1911.

Two and one-half months later, on Nov. 23, a few temporary excavation tracks had been altered and some cuts were deeper.

By July 3 of the next year, the waiting room and lobby had begun to rise. The scaffolding, called falseworks, was used to build the walls and later to decorate the interior.

The week of June 16, 1913, more than 500 men were on the job at Union Station. It was a typical week in the seemingly endless life of Union Station's creation. There were dozens of tasks being done all over. Among Union Station laborers, specialization was the norm.

Inside the building scaffolding filled the lobby. The "falseworks" contained four floors, each with platforms that allowed access to the walls. Thick stone pieces made up the facade, and behind the stone, brick was laid 3 feet thick. Now 2-inch thick slabs of Kasota limestone were being placed on the walls. Stone setters and plasterers occupied all four floors of the falseworks. Some lifted slabs of mustard-colored Kasota stone with a clanking chain hoist. Others silently scraped a flat trowel across the cornice of scagliola plaster — a faux stone — being formed high on the wall.

Atop the scaffolding were the decorative ceiling plasterers, theirs one of the only crafts that hadn't changed much in previous decades and wouldn't change much the rest of the century. Already they had hung metal framing bars from ceiling beams and then covered the frame with metal mesh lath. For ornate plaster pieces, such as the center rosettes and the egg and oak-leaf patterns, casts had been produced and put in place. Now the men were in the midst of applying three coats of plaster to the mostly flat background surfaces and to the beamlike plaster strips between and surrounding the ornate areas. This was a painstaking job, requiring an artist's touch and quick hands as the plaster mix dried. On the beamlike strips, groups of men worked in tandem. Some slapped on thick clumps of plaster, and others followed by pushing a wood cutout through the mudlike glob to produce the desired shape. Later, a few men with surgical-like scalpels applied extra plaster in

The lobby, still containing scaffolding, in March 1914.

the shape of a criss-crossing ribbon at the ends of the beamlike strips.

Elsewhere in the building, other plasterers finished walls in the upper stories of the headhouse wings, while plumbers followed and roughed in spots in the walls and floors for pipes. Electricians pulled conduit through as the walls were put up, and steamfitters installed radiator pipes and ductwork before ceilings were plastered.

The project took on the look of a scrap heap. Piles of marble slabs or ductwork or conduit tubing lay on the floors throughout the building, gobs of plaster or pieces of wood or just trash were scattered everywhere, and a constant blanket of dust hung in the air. But the building was remarkably quiet. The big lobby muffled the sounds of voices or clinking chains. It was as if the workers were in a cathedral and keeping down the noise out of respect.

Pouring concrete was the most pervasive work the week of June 16, 1913. The building's bottommost basement floor was being poured, as were some of the floors in the headhouse office wings and the mezzanine-level floors between the lobby and the waiting room. Outside, the passenger platforms were being filled with concrete. So was the plaza deck in front of the station, and the walls for the west-side baggage tunnel that passed under all 16 tracks.

At this time, concrete and steel had become the favored structural support materials of the day, replacing iron, which itself had replaced wood. A booklet published by the leading concrete manufacturing company in 1909 stated: "In the past few years concrete has had a marvelous growth, and in railroad construction perhaps more than in any other branch of engineering it has been universally adopted as a building material." Concrete — a mixture of sand, water, small stones and a gray powder called cement — was considered solid and strong, especially in compression, when weight was applied on top. And because concrete was cheaper than steel, it was applied liberally throughout Union Station. Men pushing

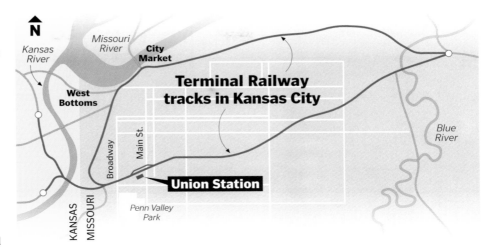

Terminal Railway lines to the station extended for miles east and west.

wheelbarrows or tubs on makeshift tracks from on-site mixers had poured concrete into the waiting room's 15-foot-thick underground piers, then around the room's steel support columns and into the foundation and basement walls before even starting inside.

In fact, Jarvis Hunt had designed the building with separate appearances for public and industrial uses. For the public, the exterior above street level was finished in elegant stone. For railroad services under the street level — including the parcel-express building adjoining the station on the west and a food-storage commissary building adjoining the station on the east — the facade was simply done in concrete.

For a complex so big, the concrete work was time-consuming. Before anything could be poured, the men spent weeks joining 2-by-8 boards. These made forms to hold the mixture in its desired shape and thickness. When the concrete dried and the wood forms were removed, the outline of the boards could still be seen. Concrete production, though, proved to be spotty at times. On some occasions, workmen complained about concrete mixes' being shortchanged of Portland cement, making the batches weaker. And a fall 1911 Terminal Railway memo asked Hunt's office for more concrete in-

spectors. Inadequate concrete would come back to haunt the building in later years, adding to its deterioration and its cost.

As for the rest of the job, outside windows were still being set, the first steel beams for the train shed over the eventual tracks were being erected, and, as always, dirt was being dug or moved. Steam shovels burrowed lanes for the tracks, and to the east and west of the site, excavation continued for the various bridges the Terminal Railway had agreed to build. More than half the Terminal Railway's spending was on widening track lanes, building bridges and adding freight stations. This work, extending from the state line to the Blue River valley, formed the approaches to the station. The digging to do all this encompassed 1.14 million cubic yards of soil and rock, almost twice the amount removed for the station site.

Not every man outside was on the concrete or steam shovel crews. A city alderman sent a man out to the site who had been dismissed recently in a Police Department shake-up. A memo from the Terminal Railway's engineering office to a subcontractor asked whether a watchman was needed and simply suggested that "it might be a good thing to have an alderman's friend on the job."

Positioning limestone for the station walls.

Walkouts

Not everyone who was supposed to be on the job was there. During this week in the summer of 1913, the marble setters and the bricklayers were on strike. The marble setters, in the midst of putting up the dark, red Tennessee marble wainscoting around the lobby, had been out since the beginning of May, the bricklayers since the end of April. The bricklayers, part of the stone-setters union, felt that any marble more than 1-inch thick was stone and should be done by their men. The marble setters, meanwhile, felt that the type of material should determine which craft handled it. Marble couldn't go up until a wall was erected, so when the bricklayers walked off the job, it was just a matter of time before the marble setters followed.

Union Station's construction had been tormented by these interunion squabbles almost since the first crafts joined the steam shovels on the site. Kansas City was a hotbed of organized-labor militancy at this time, as was much of the country in the Progressive era. Workers in such diverse industries as mining, garment manufacturing and railroad construction fought employers for the right to organize, demanding better treatment and shorter

STATION MEN STRIKE

All Work on the New Depot Site Stopped by a Walkout This Morning.

hours. When their demands weren't met, they went on strike and took sympathetic trades with them — or worse.

There had been an outbreak of dynamitings against projects whose owners had met labor's resolve with equal determination. In Kansas City, girders were blown up on a railroad bridge under construction the same month that Union Station's excavation started. Soon after, steelworkers shut down construction projects all over town.

By the time work began on the station building itself, the station's main contractor tried to signal its interest in working with organized labor. The company bought a front-page ad for the special Labor Day 1911 edition of *The Labor Herald*. For a while there was peace.

It didn't last long.

In spring 1912, a few months after two local labor leaders were arrested in a national dynamite-conspiracy case, Kansas City's Building Trades Council called a general strike on the site. At 8 a.m. May 4 nearly 700 men put down their tools. They didn't want higher wages. They didn't want better working conditions. They didn't want shorter hours. Their complaint was that workers in Indiana cutting the Bedford limestone for the station's facade were not affiliated with the American Federation of Labor, to which the stone setters in Kansas City belonged. This typified labor's grievances on the station job.

All the station workers returned four days later, except for the local stone setters. Still, every six months or so something interrupted the work. Later in the year the marble helpers wanted more money, followed by the common laborers, then the bricklayers and the marble setters in the spring of 1913. This strike would drag on through the summer, and there would be several more in 1914, stopping parts of the work for weeks. But there was no sabotage.

The station's south facade quickly took shape from mid-September 1912, top, to Nov. 27, bottom.

At the dig, 1912: Black and white laborers worked together, despite the fact that society was largely segregated.

craters and dumped the concrete into wooden column forms. Some manned the 12 locomotives that hauled the 300 railcars on the site. And some made up the dynamite crews, working with 15 steam drilling machines. As usual, a few onlookers lined the banks of the carved-up hill, and on this morning one of those watching was a Terminal Railway train brakeman, F.A. Kirk. About 7:35, Edward Donahue and Joseph Berg, both middle-aged and quite experienced in what they were doing, were packing 60 sticks of dynamite in a hole. Other two-man crews were doing the same thing nearby. None of the explosives had been connected. Yet, suddenly, Donahue and Berg's dynamite prematurely ignited.

With a louder-than-usual boom from the uncovered discharge, Berg was thrown over a steam shovel 250 feet to the west, Donahue was hurled 150 feet to the southwest, and rock rained down like hail around them. Both died, so mangled and blackened that they were hardly recognizable. Two other workers were injured, and one small stone blown into the air came down on Kirk's head 50 feet away, knocking him unconscious.

It turned out that after Donahue and Berg had drilled their hole, they enlarged it by detonating a little gunpowder. Too soon afterward, they packed their dynamite in what was called a "hot hole" with enough heat to set off the explosives. They were the first, but not the last, fatalities on the construction site — and among the few ever reported to the public. Months later a construction superintendent was sitting in his shanty office when a rock fragment from a dynamite blast crashed through the tin roof and split open his leg, causing so much blood loss that he soon died. In all, the project claimed five lives, and several more persons suffered serious injuries as things fell on them or they fell between floors. Some of these accidents, for which the typical

Laborers taking a rest: Not a hard hat in sight.

worker had no insurance and received no pay while recovering, were cited in a city Board of Public Welfare report pushing for a state workers' compensation law. This was, after all, the Progressive era, during which new laws were being proposed to improve work and health conditions.

By today's standards, however, hardly anything was progressive about the way Union Station was constructed.

As a preteen boy, Leo Ernstein lived along 18th Street next to Troost Avenue. He went to school right by Hospital Hill, part of the hillside that sloped upward from the Union Station construction site. It was a 10-minute walk from the school to the site, so sometimes on his way home in spring and fall afternoons, Ernstein detoured by the work. Grand Avenue and Main Street did not cross the rail yard yet, so he and sometimes a friend walked along the bare, dirt slopes and got pretty close to the action. "You're curious when something new is happening," Ernstein remembered decades later. This wasn't just something new; it was Kansas City's counterpart to the Pyramids. It was the largest single piece of construction in this part of the prairie to this point, an undertaking demanding so much manual labor that extras were brought in from outside the region.

From a late-20th century perspective, construction techniques then were crude. There were no mixing trucks delivering concrete, or pressure hose pumps through which to pour it. There was no welding to fuse steel beams together. There were no power sprayers for painting or fireproofing. There were no Bobcats buzzing around the site delivering materials and cleaning up scraps. Ernstein and those who brought lunches out on the stub of the Main Street bridge witnessed a tedious and labor-intensive process of men assembling the building shell.

First, towers of criss-crossing wood beams, like scaffolding, were erected where the two giant halls would rise. These were called "falseworks," and derricks were bolted on the top of them to lift the roof beams and the exterior

Union Station construction wages
- Carpenters: 60¢ an hour
- Unskilled laborers: 27.5¢ to 30¢ per hour (with a Sept. 1912 raise)

What would become train sheds and tracks was a cluttered staging area on the east side, above, and the west, below left.

The Grand Avenue Station was used for passenger service by the Santa Fe, the Milwaukee Road and the Rock Island. It sat east of the Union Station site and was scheduled to be retained as a freight office. But to make way for the new tracks, the brick structure had to be moved a short distance.

Roofing was under way on the waiting room by August 1913.

stone blocks. The work progressed north to south, starting with the waiting room. There the derricks lifted a knee-high, 82-foot-long, steel I-beam girder, swung it up and over the room, and then slowly, slowly, like the docking of two spaceships, set it down. Men at both ends of the girder directed it into place, pointing and shouting above the constant din of hydraulics and hammers.

Every piece of steel for the frame, the floors and the roof trusses was fastened into place by rivets. A rivet was a solid iron bolt with a round head at one end only. Riveting took smooth-flowing cooperation among the four men who made up riveting gangs. One, the heater, used three-foot tongs to pick out a red-hot rivet from a forge of flaming coke. He tossed the rivet with an easy motion to the second man, who caught it with a battered metal can. This second man fished out the rivet with tongs, tapped it on the beam to remove cinders and then stuck it into one of the holes in a steel plate overlapping the beams. The third man forced the rivet head against the plate, while the fourth

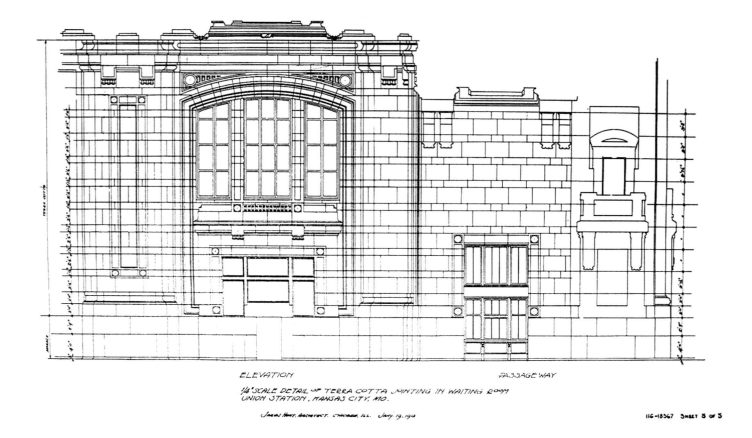

ELEVATION   PASSAGEWAY

¼" SCALE DETAIL OF TERRA COTTA JOINTING IN WAITING ROOM
UNION STATION, KANSAS CITY, MO.

Jarvis Hunt, Architect, Chicago, Ill.   Jany. 19, 1912

116-18367 SHEET 5 OF 5

Jarvis Hunt's office continued to alter plans well into the project.

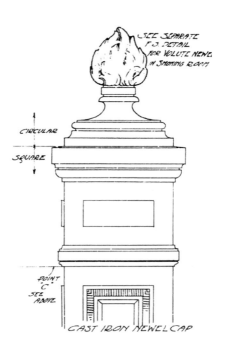

SEE SEPARATE
F.S. DETAIL
FOR VOLUTE NEWEL
IN SMOKING ROOM

CIRCULAR

SQUARE

POINT C
SEE ABOVE

CAST IRON NEWEL CAP

man took a yard-long riveting hammer and pounded the other end of the hot rivet into a cap. Each blow resounded with a loud clang, and sparks spat out from the red-hot metal as the heat fused the metal parts. As the completed rivet cooled, the metal contracted and shrank, holding the two pieces of steel together in a viselike grip.

Meanwhile, the derricks above the headhouse hauled up pieces of Bedford limestone — some wider than a man's extended arms. These pieces were stacked on top of each other, forming the exterior walls like a Lego tower of Roman proportions. This buff-colored limestone already was the most distinguished building material in the country, used on most state capitols, banks, courthouses and beaux-arts federal buildings in Washington. Each piece for Union Station had a ring embedded in the top, where a hook was fastened to hoist it. Workers stood on platforms extending from the falseworks and carefully and slowly maneuvered one stone on top of another. Doing one piece, from hoisting to setting, took roughly an hour. Forty to 50 were placed in a week's time, and little by little from spring 1912 into the next winter, the facade of Union Station took shape.

Throughout this time, there were innumerable additions and changes in the work, mostly things the architect's office did not foresee or do on time.

Initial surveys of the land, for instance, wrongly estimated where the bedrock was. This required lengthening foundation piers and cost tens of thousands of dollars. The same thing happened with a retaining wall in front of the station. Also, architect Jarvis Hunt's office, without the convenience of today's computer-aided design programs, was constantly late delivering blueprints or letting contracts. The project went without an electrical contractor for months in 1912, delaying the pouring of concrete floors through which conduit had to be placed. And Hunt decided to add miniature wings at the south ends of the waiting room for extra concessionaire space — but not until the main contractor had begun cutting stone, which then was wasted. Sometimes when drawings were finally produced, they didn't sufficiently instruct laborers what to do, such as where ductwork should go in the station's restaurant kitchen.

A post-construction report from the Terminal Railroad's engineering office noted: "A comparison of the completed building with the contract plans will reveal the fact that they differ in almost every important detail except the outside design of the building, and even many features were changed there."

'Do something big'

As construction progressed in 1913 and the huge structure took shape on the former marshy bed of O.K. Creek, Kansas Citians began to see results. At a meeting of a subcommittee of the Commercial Club in February, one E. T. Orear broached the subject of a mammoth party befitting a mammoth structure. "We should have thousands of visitors, and we should provide ample entertainment," Orear said. "We should invite the big railroad men and the noted newspaper men to come to Kansas City to see what we have done and are doing. We should give them a big dinner, the biggest ever undertaken in the West."

The next day the Commercial Club itself decided to start planning such a fete, and immediately the entire city jumped on the bandwagon. Representatives from nearly every major organization joined planning committees. Adding one of the nation's largest buildings in the nation's largest industry was a sign of supreme confidence in the city's prospects. This would be an opportunity to show off Kansas City's big-league status.

"It's time for Kansas City to do something big, something that will turn the eyes of the country this way," said the club's secretary, E.M. Clendening. Railroad officials, too, felt the need to celebrate. George Charlton, general passenger agent for the Chicago & Alton railroad, called the new building "the best station in the country. It deserves a large noise, and Kansas City will be falling down on its reputation if the noise isn't larger."

Consequently, the planning settled on not one parade, but two. Not just one day of revelry, but two. Not just one concert, but two. And after much cajoling from city leaders, the railroads promised to lower their fares throughout the Midwest for those coming from hundreds of miles around for the celebration.

While the city was getting excited, Jarvis Hunt was getting downright giddy. As 1914 dawned, the architect paid one of his occasional inspection visits.

The waiting room, ready to accept passengers.

Foremen stood at attention. Painters paused in midstroke. Others dropped their tools and turned to listen. It was hard to miss him. Hunt's blustery persona included a booming, baritone voice. As he peered up at the dark, red Tennessee marble wainscoting surrounding the lobby up to the balconies, he bellowed: "Magnificent! Looks like it had been carved out of a solid block of marble. Those arches — and balconies!"

Another time, before giving a speech to a Commercial Club committee, Hunt made a quick tour — prodding his walking stick into corners and closets, peering into the vast baggage area to get a sense of the lighting — and met with some of the lobby ceiling plasterers. One-quarter of the giant falseworks scaffold had been removed. Hunt gazed up at the chestnut-colored swirling rosettes and oak-leaf patterns set against maroon and silvery blue backgrounds. "We've hit it," he exclaimed, the plasterers nodding in agreement. "By the Lord Harry, it's the finest thing in the United States. Not a station in the United States with such decorations. The Penn in New York is the best, but it can't compare with this."

By this time Hunt had parlayed his Union Station job into a career niche. Soon after getting this contract, Hunt won station commissions in Joliet, Ill., (again for the powerful Edward Harriman) and Oakland, Calif., both of which were completed before Kansas City's. He would soon move on to his next-largest station in Dallas. All of these were designed with the beaux-arts and Chicago World's Fair hallmarks of three high-arched windows spread across

the front facades. Several American architects designed more railroad stations, but Hunt could be classified, in terms of big-city commissions, as one of the top five railroad terminal architects ever, according to railroad station historians Hans and April Halberstadt.

Still, Hunt wasn't entirely happy with Union Station's progress, particularly its outside setting. His civic center idea from years past had gone nowhere. The only thing the city government had done was create a no-booze zone for a few blocks around the station. It was a way to ensure that another Union Avenue row of saloons did not spring up across the street. The Terminal Railway had donated to the city a patch of land south of the station, but the city hadn't built on it, landscaped it or even graded it in all the years of the station's construction. And it hadn't paved some of the surrounding roads. All of this led to a Jarvis Hunt rant.

The railroads, Hunt said at one point, "are preparing to bring the big men from all over the country to see that new station. There will be national figures there from New York to San Francisco. There will be men from Montreal. And what will they see? They'll see...Kansas City's front yard, eh? Yes, they'll see those clay banks.... But that's Kansas City, those clay banks. They'll see Kansas City, all right!...Oh, say, it's a crime. It's an outrage."

Eventually those visiting dignitaries grumbled, too, but for Hunt there was a maddening feeling of lost opportunity. The City Beautiful movement had lost its luster and it leaders. William Rockhill Nelson of *The Star*, for instance, was sick and close to death. In the welfare-oriented Progressive era, the longtime criticism of parks being only for the rich finally held sway. The city didn't have the money or the will for such an ambitious undertaking, so Hunt's civic center plan sat on a shelf, his station destined to be an oasis for more than a decade.

On one of Hunt's visits a question was asked that clearly perturbed him.

To the architect and many Kansas Citians, the unimproved hill opposite the station was ``an outrage."

Opening-day parade participants missed no chance to advertise. This vehicle was decked out to boom a perfume.

"When will you be ready to open the station, Mr. Hunt?" a *Star* reporter inquired. "I can't tell you that," Hunt thundered. "My Lord, how would I know?" The railroads originally thought construction would take only a couple of years. Then, with Hunt's changes and delays and labor troubles, a grand opening was set for August 1913. That was moved to October, then the next January, then March, then May, then July, and then the Terminal Railway stopped predicting when the station would open, even to its member railroads. A final company report tallied a year's worth of delays in the construction timetable.

So as the seasons came and went in 1914, construction crews and the Terminal Railway scurried to finish things. During a labor strike that summer, the Terminal Railway employed its own workers for such duties as erecting steel in the powerhouse. The company's president, Herbert Adams, wrote a memo to the chief engineer in June stating: "I do not feel that we can afford to let the completion of the Power Station meet with further delay."

As summer turned to fall, small scaffolds were put up around the waiting room to wire electricity to the soda fountain pumps or to get lights into some of the shopping booths. And even when the day finally came at the end of October for the station to open, the midway stairs weren't enclosed, the steam heat wasn't ready and the basement was littered with debris left behind, like cement bags, piles of plastering metal lath and unused lumber.

A celebration . . .

The morning of Friday, Oct. 30, 1914, Julia Elledge woke up around sunrise as she usually did, but this day she didn't get dressed for school. At the end of school the day before, the 8-year-old had received a miniature American flag and been told that school was closing for the week so everyone could participate in the city's train-station opening. So Elledge put on her Sunday dress and walked with her father and her younger sister one block to the streetcar line, which they rode downtown.

The city was in the midst of an awful epidemic of diphtheria, a sore throat that impeded breathing. It was going around the schools and already had claimed 11 lives. Meanwhile, in the budding European war, the Germans were plowing through Belgium. But in the streets of Kansas City, it was one of those glorious Indian summer days, not a cloud to be seen, the temperature rising to the low 70s.

The streetcar was packed with riders, some holding that morning's *Kansas City Journal*, which had these words to say about the events they were to witness: "Nothing in all the history of Kansas City has so appropriately fitted into the essential character of its development as this station and terminal system. It marks the closing of one era and the opening of another. Kansas City has emerged into full fellowship with the few really great cities of the land." When everyone got off downtown, the crowds weren't much thinner on the sidewalks. The Elledges squeezed into a spot along the route of the celebration's first event, the Manufacturers Parade.

American flags hung from every window of most every building. Bands

marched by first, followed by automobiles carrying officers of the Commercial Club's manufacturing division. Then came the floats, all 140 of them. Most of them were dressed-up trucks, others were wagons pulled by teams of horses. One float had model trains. Another showed a printing plant in full operation. Another resembled a battleship with gun turrets. And one car carried an over-sized key inscribed, "The Key to the New Union Station." The procession was more than two miles long and took two hours to pass, but the Elledges didn't wait out the entire thing. They wandered away from the cheers and horn-blowing and flag-waving children, and walked south out of downtown to the new station.

Julia's father was a carpenter and wanted to see the building. Already a crowd for the official afternoon ceremony was forming, and the Elledges walked right up to the front sidewalk. There, some of the new Harvey Girl waitresses from the famed railroad restaurant were exhibiting their outfits and showing off some of the restaurant's giant cooking pans. Near noon, the Elledges walked back downtown, where the two girls enjoyed their first restaurant meal, and then went home. But the station's day was just beginning.

Around 2 p.m. that afternoon another parade started downtown, this one made up of a dozen bands and some 4,000 marchers, all headed to the station down Main Street, which was decorated with streamers. There were hundreds

Done! Crowds gather outside the brand-new landmark Oct. 30, 1914, leaving room for the parade of dignitaries to enter the east doors.

Idealized in this hand-tinted postcard view, the new station was nevertheless an architectural spectacle.

of Boy Scouts in their khaki uniforms, hundreds more Commercial Club members, plus groups from the Kansas City Cooperative Club, the Traffic Club, the Mercantile Club and just about every large civic group. Spectators spilled onto the roadway, hung out windows and even climbed onto the station roof. Some women stood out with their Victorian flower-wrapped hats, while others donned the latest turban-styled headpiece. Skirt fashions were just starting to rise from the knob of the anklebone to the shoe top. Men were eschewing black, so some stood in gray or light-brown suits, with ever-present shoulder padding, new-style cuffs in the trousers and lace-up boots.

Those beholding Union Station for the first time saw a massive, elongated facade, the length of two city blocks in front and almost 11 city blocks with train sheds and express buildings included. The headhouse facade was a light-tan, "Indiana Blue" Bedford limestone, with gray Vermont granite at the base, punctuated by three arched windows extending roughly 40 feet high and flanked by giant columns. The public entryways, with projecting cast-iron and glass marquees, were directly under the easternmost and westernmost arches. The entire composition was symmetrical, with columns and windows and pavilions, and decorative pilasters and entablature moldings under the roof line added stylistic touches in repeated patterns.

At 2:47 p.m. a battery of cannons boomed a salute from atop the hill opposite the station, and a throng estimated at 100,000 — roughly half the city's population — answered with shouts and horns. Mounted police cleared a lane amid the packed masses in front of the building, and the afternoon parade, with bands playing, men waving their canes and drums pounding, continued right on inside. After all the marchers got in, the station doors were opened to the public.

It was popularly reported — and repeated for decades afterward — that President Woodrow Wilson pressed a gold-plated button on his desk in the

White House to electrically open the doors. This tradition had started just a year before when the president ceremoniously unlocked the doors of New York's newest skyscraper. But Wilson for some reason never pushed the Kansas City button. A daily log kept by one of his secretaries showed that he had picked up a friend at Washington's train station at the time and then gone out on an automobile ride.

Still, the crowd poured into Union Station, jostling and pushing, filling every corner and crevice of the lobby and main waiting room, crunching folks against the walls. In the mad rush more than a dozen women fainted, and a 75-year-old man suffered two broken ribs when he was pinned against the marble wainscoting. The newspapers would call it Kansas City's largest crowd under one roof. It was estimated at 25,000, the building's capacity.

At 3:35 p.m., Charles Keith, president of the Commercial Club, held up his right hand from a makeshift platform in the middle of the Grand Hall lobby, signaling the start of the official ceremony. The Grand Hall carried that name because it was more than 200 feet long and 95 feet high. The walls were the rich, mustard-colored Kasota stone, and the floor was embellished in a geometric pattern of polychromatic marble, with borders echoing the design of the ornate ceiling above. The sun's afternoon rays beamed through the three giant arched windows, bathing parts of the crowd and stage in bright light. Folks closest to the stage began uttering "sh!" and the surrounding horde quieted somewhat. Then a band in the balcony struck up "America the Beautiful," and thousands of voices took up the song, their volume echoing off the great walls from end to end, nearly one-tenth of a mile in all, a city rejoicing in its new industrial temple.

It wasn't until more than 32 hours later that the first trains rolled in. Late Halloween night, the Missouri-Kansas-Texas (better known as the M-K-T or Katy) Flyer bolted through Paola, Kan., instead of stopping. Conductor J.W. Burnes wanted his to be the first train arriving at the new station. It was, just after midnight on the morning of Nov. 1, 35 minutes ahead of the Flyer's regular schedule. As the train pulled in, thousands lined the track, cheering. The locomotive slowed to a halt. Some rushed to touch the train and others climbed aboard, even into the engine cab. "There was a huge celebration for the passengers and members of the train and engine crew," mail clerk Rolla Lyon recalled later in the Missouri-Kansas-Texas company magazine. One woman ran up to Burnes and handed him a pretzel for a souvenir.

Travelers and curiosity seekers seeing the station for the first time would pass — starting on the west side of the Grand Hall and proceeding clockwise — the baggage-check area near the west door, a parcel checkroom, the men's smoking room with benches and white marble wainscoting, then a barber shop with 12 chairs and a fruit and candy store. Heading farther east, the visitor reached a coffered arch in the middle of the room — the middle of three arches on the north wall aligned with the arched windows in the south wall. Attached to that wall was a semicircular ticket office with bronze grillwork. Hanging from the top of the arched entrance to the waiting room was a 6-foot-

The striking lobby, or Grand Hall, in the colorful dress of the station's youth.

wide clock. The waiting room beyond was more than 300 feet long with its own, smaller arched windows admitting rays of sunlight on pewlike mahogany benches aligned in parallel rows. Farther eastward in the Grand Hall, the visitor passed the women's waiting room — guarded by a matron — a drugstore and, finally, through bronze doors into the east wing, the Fred Harvey Restaurant. It featured a long, U-shaped lunch counter in one room and an elegant dining room next door.

One local minister, D. Arthur Brown, wrote his in-laws after taking it all in on opening day: "I have never been in such a building. It is actually the most handsome thing that I ever saw in my life." There was so much more inside, too: six floors above with administrative and railroad offices; several basement levels below for train and building operations; adjoining express and commissary buildings. Marble ended up covering 105,000 square feet of flooring and 80,000 square feet of wainscoting. In all, the headhouse itself cost $6.36 million. Adding the costs of land, grading and adjoining buildings brought the figure to $10.6 million, still just a fraction of the $48 million total — more than $600 million in end-of-the-century dollars — that also went for building bridges and train yards and extending Terminal Railway tracks for miles from the new station.

In the midst of the opening ceremonies, former Mayor Henry Beardsley epitomized what many city leaders felt about the occasion: "There are epochs in…the life of every city. Kansas City has had several of them. The opening of the Hannibal Bridge was one, the building of Convention Hall was another, and the start of our great park and boulevard system…was a third. Today we are entering a fourth great epoch — an epoch of advancement that will be unlike any the city has known.

"Another structure might have been built here by the railroads — less beautiful, less fine architecturally — and it would have served our needs."

Mayor Henry Jost didn't quite see it that way. He didn't let the railroads' benevolence overshadow the city's decades-long frustration with them. Instead of the expected show of appreciation, Jost stood at the speakers' platform in the Grand Hall and, in a speech hardly anyone could hear because of the crowd's loud buzz, declared: "It is not a gift. The railroads built the station for profit the same as the builders of the Muehlebach Hotel."

Still, he raved about the building, as did everyone else, including architecture critics. The *Architectural Record* in August 1914 gave the nearly completed station a favorable review, commending the design as one of the most interesting station buildings in the West. Harold D. Eberlein wrote:

It is consistent, dignified, sufficiently monumental and massive to be worthy of a great city and absolutely free from meaningless and finicky adornment of any sort.…All the detail is so well adjusted to the scale of the building that there is an aspect of perfect repose, and the ornament is so judiciously managed as to convey the most desirable impression of elaborate simplicity.

At the same time, it was heralded as the last of the mammoth stations. B.F. Bush, president of the Missouri Pacific railway, told *The Star*: "It is well known that the reason the railroads build big terminals is the matter of pride and regard for the city into which their lines run, and I don't believe the railroads will ever spend so much money on a similar enterprise again in the West." He was only partly right. Subsequently, two bigger cities, Chicago and Los Angeles, would open union stations, and some of Chicago's rooms would be bigger than Kansas City's.

Jarvis Hunt was so proud of his creation that a few years later he lashed out at criticism that Union Station was too showy.

"The design is monumental, as it should be," he wrote in a letter, "but is

Railroads announced the switchover to the new station in these ads in *The Star*.

Onlookers jammed the lobby and lined balconies for opening-day ceremonies.

plain and without useless ornament and certainly shows no extravagance."

. . . and a funeral

To the denizens of Union Avenue, it was bad enough that Union Depot was closing. A 50-foot outline of the depot was burned in effigy on the hill south of Union Station to close the first day's celebration of the new building. But this wasn't the depot's real finale. That came around midnight on Halloween, the second day.

A makeshift band of musicians went up the avenue and led a rhythmic march. Their leader wore a blue uniform with gold braid. They circled the depot's waiting room and headed out the doors, quickly joined by folks flocking out of Union Avenue's saloons. It was an impromptu funeral parade, which turned into a tango line, ending in a final toast. A local character named "Kentucky Ed" Turner, a street barker by trade, climbed on a box, waved his black sombrero at the old depot and delivered an impassioned eulogy about its glory days. "Years ago, my friends, that was a howling wilderness and the beasts of

Railroad stations compared

	New Union Station Kansas City	Old Union Depot Kansas City	Union Station St. Louis	Union Station Washington, D.C.	Union Station Chicago	Penn Station New York City
Acres covered by buildings	5.6	.98	3.0	4.3	5.5	7.8
Main building (sq. ft.)	140,131	16,250	48,480	132,526	119,000	339,270
Main waiting room (sq. ft.)	26,100	8,763	10,068	26,280	26,920	33,000
Baggage room (sq. ft.)	74,678	13,484	42,100	41,683	73,550	50,000
Number of tracks	16	8	32	28	14	21

Source: Kansas City Terminal Railway Co.

Union Avenue in 1911, left, and *The Star's* eulogy for the old depot that supported business on the street.

the forest ranged there. Then the daddies of the West built that old station, my friends, that old station there. It was magnificent — magnificent, in its day."

Soon, the band continued on, marching down "the row," in and out of all the garishly lighted saloons, playing mostly "A Hot Time in the Old Town Tonight." After the stroke of midnight, after the last tickets were sold, two employees began nailing windows and doors closed. They were nailing Union Avenue's coffin. The two finally left the dark, turreted building in silence, and the West Bottoms never recovered. It retained its stockyards workers for a half-century or so, but its honky-tonk and burlesque culture moved up over the bluff, forever.

Here's Goodbye to An Old, Old Friend

The Old Union Depot, ancient and worn at 36 years, has encountered the whole category of human endeavor and emotions in her day = Glimpses into her past.

Facing page: An illustrator's version of the Grand Hall and waiting room.

THE STATION AS CITY CENTER

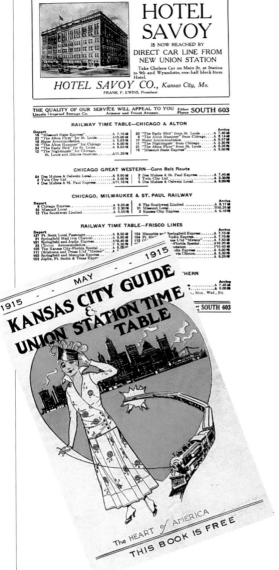

Even after Union Station's grand opening, the building continued drawing crowds. Overflowing crowds. Boisterous crowds. Curious crowds. They weren't all there to catch trains. There usually was something else going on. Hardly a year went by without some event drawing thousands of people.

In 1915 a train carrying the Liberty Bell passed through on a cross-country tour. A noontime throng, swelling with packinghouse men on their lunch break, lined the terminal tracks and formed a cheering escort, even climbing on the sides of the train cars and the engine. Early the next year, President Woodrow Wilson arrived in town for a speech, and, of course, his train went through Union Station. Masses gathered on the Grand Hall balconies and along a roped-off lane across the hall. They cheered the president as he emerged from the midway doors, and they craned their necks to catch a glimpse of his new, younger wife, whom he had married only two months before.

The next fall, former President Theodore Roosevelt visited to begin a stint writing a newspaper column for *The Star* and distributed to other papers. As he walked through the midway, Roosevelt paused to shake the hands of a station employee and pat little Gladys Steeves on the head — something she would remember the rest of her life. Out on the plaza in front of the station, Roosevelt raised his hat to the multitudes held back by military guards. Then four trumpets sounded, and a 200-man band began "The Star Spangled Banner," with Roosevelt standing at attention, his hat pressed against his chest. "The picture was perfect," the newspaper declared that afternoon.

Why all this at Union Station? Why such crowds there? Because it quickly became more than a place to pass through, more than another public building. It became the city center, the town square, the barometer of Kansas City's spirit, its trends, its happenings. It was a mirror that reflected the city.

Before there were shopping malls, there was Union Station. Before there were two-deck sports arenas, there was Union Station. And before there was a transportation hub for airliners, there was Union Station.

All the trains of the 12 railroads were listed in this 1915 publication, which also promoted Kansas City.

Facing page: Night enhanced the cathedral-like character of Union Station in this scene, produced for a postcard.

Preceding page: As a choral director atop the ticket booth led the singing, travelers and residents paused to join in carols at Christmastime.

The new terminal in its first decades served Kansas Citians in myriad ways. They took trains in and out, of course. They also celebrated there. Mourned there. Encountered crooks there. Cheered presidents there. Got their hair done there. Drank ice-cream sodas there. And bought toys there. Union Station handled multiple uses before the term "multiuse" entered the real estate lexicon. Nowhere else could Kansas Citians do all this under one roof. Not around the square in the City Market. Not at the convention hall. Certainly not on 12th Street's burlesque strip or in J.C. Nichols' new housing-shopping communities.

By the end of the 20th century, cities would have entertainment-retail districts and sports-and-hotel complexes — and sometimes both — wrapped together in so-called festival marketplaces or downtown revitalizations. At the beginning of the century, however, those didn't exist. So in Kansas City, there was nothing quite like Union Station.

First impressions

Typically the first thing anyone noticed at the station, the first thing anyone talked about, was its size. Its immense spaces provided an unusual sensory experience. Coming through the front entryways, you stepped into a tight, cramped vestibule between two sets of doors and then proceeded into the vast, hazy openness of the Grand Hall. It was the same when you arrived by train. You walked along a concrete platform as the locomotive hissed and steam poured from the underside of its cars. Up the stairs, you came to a low-ceiling brick midway, where your footsteps and those of other travelers fused into a cacophony of continuous, random taps. Then you moved into a vestibule at the end of the midway. And just as your eyes and ears were adjusted to enclosed spaces, you advanced into the Grand Hall, where life seemed to proceed in slow motion.

Vast and resonant, one low hum seemed to be evenly distributed throughout the great room, pleasant in parts, regular in its rhythms, all inside a "silent bubble of space," as *New Yorker* writer Tony Hiss once described Grand Central Terminal's grand lobby. You could see two things clearly: first, an unmoving framework of marble floor, stone walls and arched windows; second, the swirling, crossing motion of hundreds of people milling and walking in all directions, two or three abreast. The vastness of the room subconsciously cast a restraint on your behavior, akin to walking into church. And it made you feel good.

Kansas Citians understood this only intuitively in Union Station's first decades. Scientists today know it for a fact. In a groundbreaking study on the effect of surroundings on a person's mental condition, Abraham Maslow and Norbell Mintz of Brandeis University rigged up three rooms, a "beautiful" one, an "average" one and an "ugly" one. The ugly room resembled a janitor's storage closet, while the beautiful room had large windows, paintings and comfortable chairs. Volunteers were told to study photos of people's expressions. Invariably the volunteers found energy and well-being in faces when they looked

In the hall, life seemed to proceed in slow motion. The vastness of the room subconsciously cast a restraint on your behavior.

Facing page: The lobby, or Grand Hall, in an illustration produced for a postcard.

at them in the beautiful room and saw fatigue and sickness in the same faces when they looked at them in the ugly room. According to the researchers, "setting had a real impact on judgment." That was the case at Union Station, too.

In its prime years the terminal was a busy, bustling, buzzing kind of place, with crowds chattering and scurrying about. The same scene observed on a city street at lunch hour would seem chaotic and uninteresting. But inside Union Station it appeared animated, jovial, coordinated, almost choreographed to a rhythm of the human heartbeat. Thomas Wolfe, in his novel *You Can't Go Home Again*, saw ethereal timelessness in big-city railroad stations: "For here, as nowhere on earth, men were brought together for a moment at the beginning or end of their innumerable journeys, here one saw their greetings and farewells, here, in a single instant, one got the entire picture of the human destiny."

In Kansas City, Katherine Edelman was so inspired by the station's whirl of activity that she crafted a poem, which was published in *The Star* in 1932:

Life, at its swiftest tide,
Flows through your gates:

"Life, at its swiftest tide, Flows through your gates...."

— *Katherine Edelman*

GLITCHES

Union Station got off to an ignominious start for something that was so grand and such an icon. Nothing seemed to work inside. Water leaked in all over the place, from the skylights in the Harvey lunchroom, from small openings in the foundation and from the train sheds onto passengers below. Somehow, water even dripped in the stairways between the midways and the tracks, prompting a 1915 Terminal Railway memo to note: "This causes a great deal of unfavorable comment from passengers using the station."

The ventilation system didn't work in the beginning, either. Some parts of the station were too hot, some were too cold, and black soot from the trains got blown through the ducts into the Harvey restaurant and the waiting room. Attendants had to dust off the benches every hour. Most of these problems were soon solved, except one — water leaks caused by faulty roofing. The architect had replaced his original arched roof with a traditional triangular one topped with a thin layer of waterproofing and heavy concrete tiles. This construction, with 9,000 tiles on sloped sections and tarpaper on flat areas, would haunt the station its entire life. It proved so leaky — the result of concrete cracks, inadequate caulking and deteriorating waterproofing — that several repair companies through the years couldn't plug it. And it proved so expensive that the Terminal Railway could never replace it.

The most maddening and embarrassing foul-up in the first years, however, occurred with the giant clock between the Grand Hall and the waiting room. Every morning some station official came to work, checked his watch against the 6-foot-wide central timepiece and invariably found it was minutes off. On April 2, 1915, for instance, the clock's south face was three minutes slow. The next day the

south face was four minutes fast. The next day it was three minutes slow again. The next day it was off 30 minutes. This created a time-consuming maintenance task.

To set the correct time, workers took several hours constructing a temporary scaffolding to reach the hanging clock and open a door to its mechanisms. Sometimes the problem was a loose screw. Other times it was a bad spring. This went on constantly for months. It didn't help that the clockmaker filed for bankruptcy soon after installing it, so its repairmen weren't immediately available to help. In June 1915 the Terminal Railway's chief engineer wrote the clockmaker's bank trustee: "The clock being in a conspicuous place

has caused a great deal of criticism on the part of the public and the press on account of its frequent failures."

Later that summer the Terminal Railway shipped the clock mechanism back to the bankrupt manufacturer in Chicago. When the clock returned, it still didn't work properly. Finally the Terminal bought a new mechanism from another company in 1916. One newspaper opined, almost forlornly: "Travelers waiting for trains at the Union Station are to be deprived of their chief diversion — watching workmen repair the station clock." Thereafter, the clock's troubles were over, and it soon turned into one of the building's endearing symbols.

The women's waiting room.

Surging, swaying,
Coming, going,
With feverish and unending motion,
A youthful bride and groom
Come smiling from a rice-strewn cab;
A shy farm lad looks up toward the big clock;
A lonely and bewildered emigrant
Sits huddled in a corner.
The departing traveler
Is stirred by the thought
Of turning wheels,
Of changing panoramas,
Of adventures in far places.
The homeward bound
By visions of lamplit rooms,
Of restful hours,
Of waiting smiles and handclasps.
Hour after hour
The tide surges.
A heterogeneous mass of humanity,
Meeting, parting,
Parting, meeting,
Pouring like an endless flood
Through your clanging gates.

Amid this constant swirl, the building drew attention to itself, and travel-

As a promotion for the Travelers Aid agency, 4-year-old Betty Neely was posed on the counter. Her father, Roy E. Neely, served as a redcap for more than four decades at the station.

So much went on at the station that newspapers treated it as a minicity. *The Star* assigned a reporter there just as it did at the police stations and City Hall. Among the first reporters to cover the station beat was Ernest Hemingway, a round-faced young man fresh out of high school in Oak Park, Ill. He stayed at the paper only 6 1/2 months, from October 1917 to April 1918, but decades later, after he became a renowned novelist, Hemingway credited *The Star* style manual's embrace of succinct writing for inspiring his own technique.

The only known surviving assignment sheet from one of Hemingway's days at the newspaper shows him dispatched to cover seven stories or places, including a hospital, a police substation and Union Station. Charles Fenton's book, *The Apprenticeship of Ernest Hemingway*, quotes Hemingway as recalling: "Union Station was everybody going in and out, various tips on stories by railroad cops, some shady characters I got to know, and interviews with celebrities going through."

Scholars have identified only two articles about the station written by Hemingway (articles in those days did not carry reporters' bylines). In one, Hemingway interviewed star baseball pitcher Grover Cleveland Alexander as the Chicago Cubs passed through Kansas City on the way south for spring training.

The other article provided an early glimpse into what became the Hemingway mystique.

On a morning in February 1918, while the city was on a smallpox vaccination crusade, Hemingway walked into Union Station and found a man lying inside the lobby's west entrance. Passers-by were stopping and gawking, and a police officer was still waiting for an ambulance an hour after calling for it. In Matthew Bruccoli's book *Ernest Hemingway, Cub Reporter*, another rookie reporter and Hemingway pal, Ted Brumback, related how Hemingway scolded the crowd around the fallen man: "Why, I wouldn't treat a dog like that. What's the matter with you people? Why didn't some of you carry him out on the stretcher and put him in a taxi and send him to the General

ERNEST M. HEMINGWAY

THEO. B. BRUMBACK

These two friends, one who has seen service in a French ambulance corps and the other who has made eleven vain attempts to get into different branches of the service, sail this week from an Atlantic port for Italy to join a Red Cross ambulance unit.

Theodore B. Brumback, son of Judge and Mrs. Hermann Brumback, and Ernest Hemingway, son of Doctor and Mrs. Clarence E. Hemingway, Oak Park, Ill., were members of the editorial staff of The Star. Brumback served the French from May to November, 1917, and was rejected from service for a physical defect which in no way interfered with his usual work when the United States took over the unit.

Hemingway, who is 19 years old, tried eleven times to get into service since the war started, but the physical tests ruled him out each time. He was a member of the 7th Regiment.

The Star noted the participation in World War I of two of its recent alumni, Ernest Hemingway and Theodore Brumback.

THRONG AT SMALLPOX CASE

PATIENT IN UNION STATION HAS LONG WAIT FOR AMBULANCE.

After Three Calls and an Hour, a Car Arrived to Take the Traveler to the City Hospital.

While the chauffeur and male nurse on the city ambulance devoted to the carrying of smallpox cases drove from the General Hospital to the municipal garage on the North Side today to

Hospital? The man's got smallpox and will die if not given care immediately….Who'll help me get him out of here?"

At the word of smallpox, the crowd apparently retreated. Hemingway then picked up the man himself and took him

in a taxi to the hospital. The article described these events under the headline, "Throng at Smallpox Case," without Hemingway mentioning his involvement. The story recounted how the ambulance dispatched to the station had encountered engine trouble, so the driver and nurse decided to get it fixed rather than go on to the station emergency. But it was written with no great flourish. In fact, it started with an exceptionally long, 56-word sentence: "While the chauffeur and male nurse on the city ambulance devoted to the carrying of smallpox cases drove from the General Hospital to the municipal garage on the North Side today to have engine trouble 'fixed,' a man, his face and hands covered with smallpox pustules, lay in one of the entrances to the Union Station."

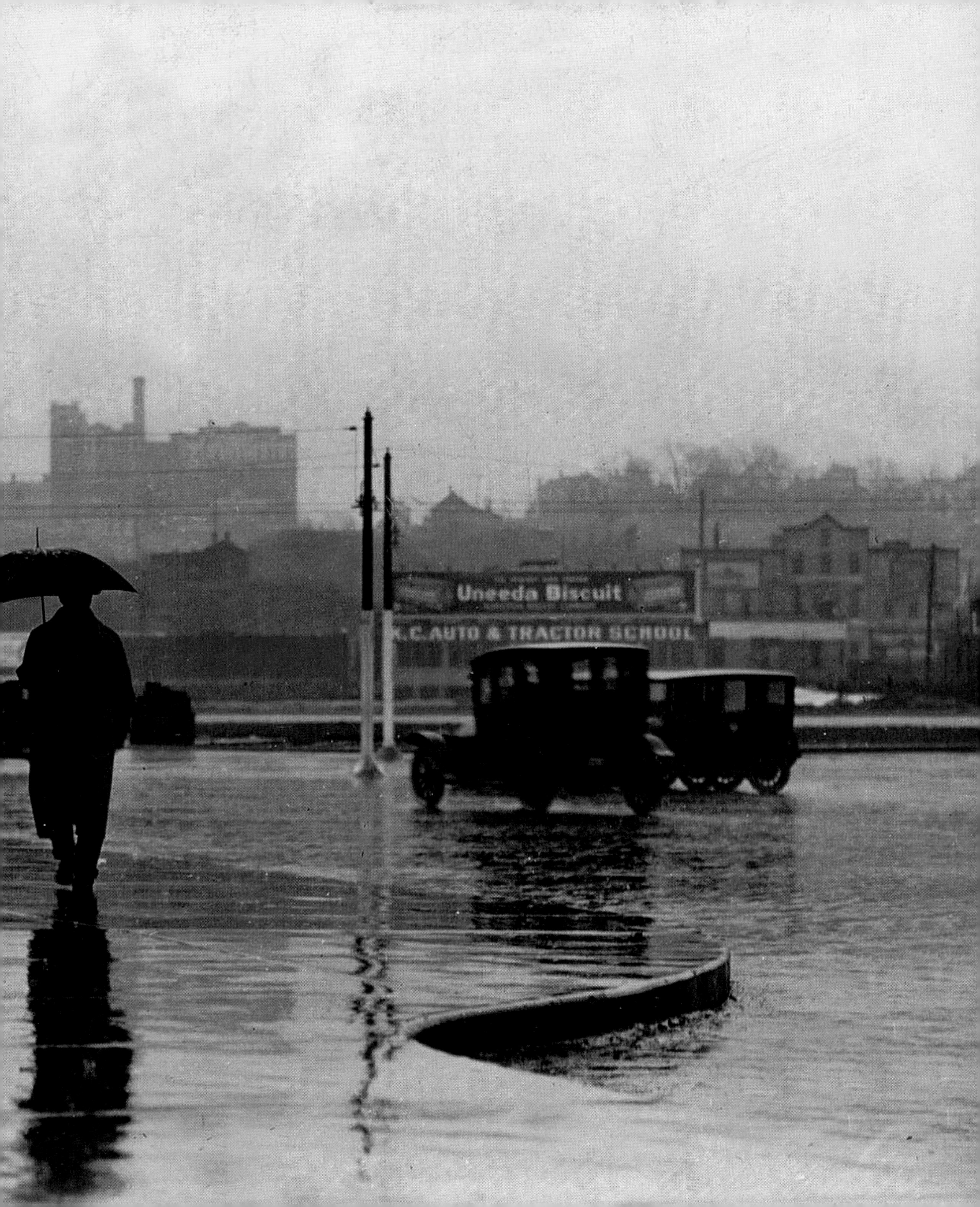
Uneeda Biscuit
K.C. AUTO & TRACTOR SCHOOL

NEWS AND BOOKS

ers stopped, turned their heads and took notice. Often they found beauty. Little, obscure things evoked delight and amusement. The minute hand of the big central clock between the two halls clicking slightly backward before springing forward to the next minute. Gleaming polished brass on all the doors. A janitor making sweeping figure-eights with a 4-foot-wide push broom across the Grand Hall floor. Helium balloons set free from small hands and scattered high across the ceiling.

Union Station wasn't some club for the privileged few, or some hall that could be rented for a private affair. It was a building for everyone, and it was big enough to belong to everyone, big enough for everyone to carve some piece of it for their memories. To its patrons the place was "gorgeous," "fascinating," "majestic" and "awesome," as expressed in letters written about it.

Consider Corval Lile from rural Kansas, who first saw the station in 1920: "All my life I had lived in very small farming communities. Coming into Union Station was entering a shocking, different world….the great big doors, the very, tall, tall ceilings and lots of people. I had never seen so many people, enormous numbers of people….The whole thing was so big, I could hardly believe it." And Ian Drake, who grew up in Kansas City: "The impact on entry into the station…was tremendous — the booming, echoing sounds in the Grand Lobby and the shafts of sunlight that beamed down through the east Waiting Room windows. They seemed to point the way along a magic carpet….It was a

A consolidated news and books shop, flanked by heavily flocked Christmas trees, marked the holiday season in 1915.

Preceding pages: Pedestrians in the rain outside the station.

By Christmas 1931, the book shop's displays spilled even farther into the lobby.

Early attractions: Fruit and candy were on sale, above, at the station's opening in 1914.

Right: At Christmas 1915, the toy store was a child's dream. A model train circled the shop on a track mounted above patrons' heads.

The drugstore, as depicted in a color illustration for a postcard.

place bigger than life in a time when life was yet rather simple. In Union Station you could have the finest meal, buy the best imported candy, smoke the best Cuban cigar and have your watch adjusted and your hair trimmed in one easy, convenient visit." It was, after all, a little city within the city.

Like a little city, Union Station offered a shopping district. In terms of variety, it might have resembled a block along Delaware Street near the City Market, except the station's offerings were more upscale and totally enclosed. As such, they preceded the climate-controlled, specialty shops in suburban malls by a half-century, albeit on a diminutive scale. It's unclear who first suggested adding stores unrelated to railroad activities at Union Station, but it's clear why — the railroads wanted to recoup some of their staggering investment. Rents tied to sales helped Terminal Railway revenue almost triple in the station's first five years, according to annual Interstate Commerce Commission filings.

Union Station's retail district extended along the Grand Hall's north wall in a straight line from the west wing to the east wing. At the far west, logically placed adjacent to the men's smoking room with its high-backed mahogany settees, was a cigar shop. A few dozen boxes rested with open lids under glass cases, while dozens more were stacked on shelves. Near this was the barber shop, and tucked around the corner from that was a shoeshine stand with raised chairs. The bootblacks, as they were called then, smacked and slapped their cloths over shoes like a flurry of boxing jabs. Whippety-whip. Whippety-whip. Whippety-whip. Sometimes when two or more of the men were going at once, they synchronized the smacks into song, humming and snapping cotton against leather in a song-and-dance routine.

Farther east, across the midway doors, was the Fruit and Candy booth, whose neatly arranged, open-air mounds of apples, oranges and seasonal fruits were more extensive than most food markets. Behind this booth, with an entrance off the waiting room, was the soda fountain topped with black Belgium marble. These food shops were operated by the Fred Harvey restaurant company, as were the other retail spaces across the corridor under the clock. Over there, at the far east end, was the drugstore. This was the Harvey company's first foray into actual merchandise. A company executive explained in a 1921 magazine article that the drugstore was stocked with perfumes in "as comprehensive an assortment as you can find on State Street or Fifth Avenue or anywhere." Such a selection didn't earn a profit, but the company didn't expect it to. It lured people into the store, and sometimes they wound up buying something else — an early case of a retail "loss leader."

Near this shop was the News and Books area, with tall display tables extending into the Grand Hall and wrapping around the marble wainscoting. A toy store filled the back and opened into the waiting room as the symmetrical counterpart to the soda fountain. Assorted dolls and wind-up figures lined the wood shelves. A model train chugged around overhead. And during the Christmas season, a spot was cleared for Santa Claus' chair.

Nearly every day at Christmastime, children waited in line for Santa to arrive. One year Jack Parkins from rural Kansas was one of those kids. Christmas trees with silvery tinsel ringed the lobby, garland graced various booth displays, and high school or college choirs stood in the balconies. Jack had surveyed the toy store first. A red-and-green metal farm tractor was his wish from Santa. Then there were cheers and shrieks. Santa came strolling along the midway from his arrival "train" and out into the lobby before making his way to his chair. The line stretched out the toy store, around the front of News and Books and back toward the east wing. Jack inched forward. It seemed like hours standing there. Finally his turn came. He climbed on Santa's lap and offered his wish. And on Christmas morning a new metal tractor sat under his family's Christmas tree.

Yet, as the big city changed, so did the little city of Union Station. In the 1920s automobile registrations quadrupled throughout the country. This fueled Kansas City's continuing southern expansion, as did development of J.C. Nichols' Country Club Plaza shopping center, which represented retail competition. From the late '20s through the Depression years, the Terminal Railway tried to adapt to these trends, with an eye toward boosting its tenants' retail revenue.

The plaza in front of the station, long a dirt-topped eyesore where drivers parked cars wherever they wanted, finally was paved. Parking spaces were laid out in front of the station's two wings and, in between, landscaped islands formed a pie-shaped entrance drive off Pershing Road instead of Main Street.

The First World War evoked a peculiar scene at Union Station. Early on in 1918, every day seemed to be Mother's Day. Moms came at all hours, some staying at the station overnight — along with sisters, sweethearts and wives. They finagled their way past the gates and down to the tracks. "If he's going across no man's land for me, I guess I can climb over a few railroad tracks for him," a gray-haired mom was heard telling an usher.

Troop-train movements weren't printed. They weren't posted. They weren't given out. So these women relied on intuition, luck and patience. They took lunches and dinners out to the railroad yards under the train sheds and even out past the Broadway viaduct, making picnics on the steel rails. "Many of them would arrive in town too late to meet their sons' trains and would pay no attention to us when we sympathized with them for the misfortune," stationmaster Vinton Bell recalled later. "Instead, they would sit at the station day after day, patiently waiting for the trains to come and turning deaf ears to our explanations."

When a train did pull in, the line of women extended as far as the cars themselves. If their boy happened to hear his name called, the mother or the wife or the sister or all of them got maybe 10 minutes to hug or kiss or tell a lieutenant to "take care of my son." Then they hoisted themselves up to the train car windows for one last hug, one final touch. And the trains moved on.

A year later, when the 110th Engineers of Kansas City's own 35th Infantry Division became the first local troops to return from overseas, men and women, fathers and mothers, brothers and sweethearts climbed over embankments, scaled walls and crawled under fences to get to the tracks. They were on the platforms 20 deep, jumping up and down, looking for their loved one, as the train engineer frantically blew the train whistle to get people off the tracks. A welcoming committee provided mess kits with rolls and hot coffee as the soldiers got off, Red Cross workers pinned a flower on each uniformed man, and women dabbed their eyes with handkerchiefs. After all three sec-

Arthur W. Duston of Washington, Kan., in his doughboy's uniform, and Kittie Smith of Burlington, Kan., couldn't find anyone to take pictures of them together, so they took these separate photos outside Union Station in 1917. Duston was on his way with the armed forces to Europe and had asked Smith to marry him; she refused, saying she did not want to become a war widow. When he returned in 1919, she said yes.

tions of the 110th were gathered from separate trains, the men joined ranks.

They marched up the stairways into the east midway and then out into the lobby, still dominated by larger-than-life banners of Uncle Sam pointing his finger, wanting you and demanding that you buy war bonds. The marchers were mobbed by another crowd that swept aside the blue-coated police and placed more flowers in rifle muzzles, in

breast buttonholes, in the folds of caps. A lane was cleared, and the marching continued out the main doors, over the beds of lilacs and tulips on the station plaza, up Grand Avenue, through a mock Arc de Triomphe and to the Convention Hall, as masses of onlookers lined the route and blocked out some of the signs on Signboard Hill. That's how the Great War passed through Union Station.

The Red Cross canteen and workers inside the station, left. *Below*: "No port but victory," a war bond display stated.

Months after the war ended, servicemen returned home to great, flag-waving crowds.

Also, Harvey's drug, fruit and toy stores and soda fountain were remodeled and expanded. A pastry shop, a beauty parlor, a liquor shop and newsstands in the two halls were added. An internal Terminal Railway memo at this time noted: "Main Street has a heavy flow of traffic and it seems to me that this artery holds potential for additional customers....New attractive facilities on the South front...would seem in the right direction." All this was completed by 1936 and cost roughly $200,000 — more than $2 million today.

As the city goes, so goes the station

Union Station's accommodations to an increasingly car-oriented society weren't the only ways the building reflected the city around it. Many incidents and events at the station in its first decades also served as a mirror image of Kansas City at the time. Out-of-control banditry on city streets? It showed up at Union Station. Livestock activity in the West Bottoms? It found its way into Union Station. Boss politics at City Hall? It was celebrated at Union Station. Whatever went on in Kansas City, Union Station usually experienced some part of it.

Consider crime. In the city, it thrived in the raw, rough streets of downtown. The station, with all its captive patrons, quickly became good pickings for swindlers. From an upstairs office lined with photos of known railroad station criminals, stationmaster Vinton Bell was constantly on the lookout for pickpockets. There were grip thieves who stole hand luggage to pawn, plus con men who duped the unsuspecting out of their cash. Or worse.

On one occasion in 1915, a Nebraska farm boy named Paul Yake went through the station after growing 2 acres of onions and selling them. He had a roll of money and made the mistake of letting it be seen. While waiting for a train to Oklahoma to visit his uncle, Yake took a walk outside. A man approached him and asked for a chaw of tobacco. Yake produced a block of tobacco. The man asked for a knife to cut off a corner of the block. Yake produced a knife. The man took it, stabbed Yake and ran off with the money roll. Yake was in the hospital for three months.

Tours of the city were led in touring cars, right. All this traffic altered the city and society in ways that foreshadowed big problems for the station and the railroads it served.

On another occasion, a 19-year-old boy from rural Kansas, fresh off the train to join the Navy in World War I, happened to ask two men where the recruiting station was. The men bet each other the boy wasn't heavy enough to get accepted. They then took turns lifting him and guessing how much he weighed. By the time the boy got on his way, he noticed his watch and his wallet were missing.

A few years later in the 1920s' rash of headline-grabbing bank robberies, two bandits climbed the stairs near the west front doors and, as hundreds of travelers mingled below, held up the Pullman company offices on the mezzanine level. The bandits walked back out the front doors with $900 cash. A witness claimed the bandits used a taxi as a getaway car, and authorities finally nabbed a similar vehicle in Lee's Summit. It turned out to contain two innocent Iowa contractors. The real bandits were captured later downtown drinking up their booty.

When Kansas City made international headlines by bringing together all the commanders of the victorious armies in World War I, Union Station was in the middle of it. The event was the dedication of the Liberty Memorial site in 1921. After World War I, local leaders briefly renewed the civic momentum for beautification with a campaign for a war memorial. The hillside south of the station still sat unused, and being next to one public monument, it was deemed a fitting locale for another. This finally settled the long-nettlesome issue of what to do with the station's front door, although urban commercialism had already elbowed its way in that door with the rise of Signboard Hill and its dozens of colorful billboards diagonally across Main Street.

On Halloween night 1921, Gen. John Pershing and Marshal Ferdinand Foch, two of the five commanders of the victorious American and Allied armies in World War I, arrived by train to a throng that spilled out of the station building and onto the railroad tracks and platforms. The gathering, *The Kansas City Times* reported the next day, "was counted not in thousands but in blocks." The two leaders could not get off the train. A billowing mass on the

The once-ugly hill opposite the station entrance had been graded and landscaped by 1921, top, when Gen. John J. Pershing and several other military leaders of World War I came to town for the dedication of the hillside as site of the future Liberty Memorial. Spectators filled every space to watch the generals arrive. Above, General Armando Diaz, commander of the Italian armies, made his way through the crowd.

In the Roaring '20s, the summer homecoming of vacationing Kansas Citians was captured by an artist for *The Star*'s Sunday magazine.

platform cheered while pushing and pressing toward the train car. The back of the mass pushed the center upward and lifted some onlookers above the heads of others. Finally, police and Marines formed a circle around the leaders and slowly wedged a lane through the jam.

The next day, a crowd as far as the eye could see formed a makeshift amphitheater in the hills around Union Station for the dedication ceremony. People were even perched on the roof. The stage stood at the edge of the station plaza. School was canceled for the day, so sixth-grade history buff Marie Heintz, later Rehkop, went on her own. Her teachers had been talking about this day, even informing the children that Foch "rhymes with mush." Standing in the crowd about 100 feet from the stage, straining on her tiptoes to see, Marie made sure she got a look at the French commander. She thought his cylindrical cap was rather daffy.

After each speech by the five commanders, polite and solemn applause rippled outward from those nearest the platform like waves, taking dramatic seconds to flow the estimated quarter-mile east and west through the vast assemblage. While the military commanders memorialized their soldiers, it took a local rabbi, H.H. Mayer, to capture the symbolism of the day's featured event, the lighting of a memorial flame. "Dear God," the rabbi prayed in the benediction, "let this flame burn in our hearts forever and go before us like a torch to light the way of peace."

During the next two decades, Union Station shared in what Kansas City was known for most — cows, jazz and Boss Pendergast.

One night in 1928, a train carrying cattle bound for the West Bottoms stockyards overturned on the Terminal Railway tracks. Close to 150 head of cattle escaped and scampered all over the city. They hoofed it through streets, charged into downtown doorways and went as far south as the County Club Plaza. One steer even apparently crossed railroad tracks and climbed a midway staircase inside the station.

In the early morning of July 24, assistant stationmaster Charles Clancy spied it lumbering through the east midway doors. The steer then paused a moment in bewilderment before turning left and heading into the women's waiting room. A woman saw the animal and shrieked, "Bull! Bull!" Clancy ran into the waiting room and got the animal turned around. Then he and a bunch of redcaps surrounded the large-horned steer in a wide circle in the Grand Hall. "I've been out West," Clancy called out to the redcaps. "I've seen 'em throw these beasts. Look out!"

The animal dodged the men, plunged into the drugstore and came back out. Clancy lunged in close, seized the steer's horns and twisted. The animal lost its footing on the polished floor and fell "with a grunting thud," according to a newspaper account. The steer kicked with his legs, but somebody got a rope and tied the legs together. The animal was soon on its way to the stockyards, and Clancy earned coast-to-coast headlines for something that would never happen at one of New York's beaux-arts stations.

THE MACHINE

In 1932, an event took place that symbolized boss Tom Pendergast's regime of corruption, then at its peak. Conrad Mann was returning by train as a convicted felon. Mann was a rotund, jovial person who, as the longtime president of the chamber of commerce, aided immensely in the business community's acquiescence toward Pendergast's stranglehold on City Hall jobs and civic improvements. But a federal judge in New York had found Mann guilty of violating federal interstate commerce laws. Mann had secretly pocketed $230,000 in an illegal national lottery for a charitable organization. Now fellow chamber officers and a city councilman, instead of distancing themselves from this swindler, organized a surprise welcome for him at Union Station when he came home December 5 before the court sentencing.

Mann

Several thousand people showed up. They packed the lobby, reaching out to shake his hand and holding up banners exclaiming, "Kansas City Has Faith in You," and, "Our Own Conrad H. Mann." One of the organizers stood on a platform put up in the Grand Hall and announced to Mann over a temporary loudspeaker: "There are not more persons here, because the station lobby will hold no more." As it was, "Kansas City was telling the world that it didn't consider gambling a crime," William M. Reddig concluded in *Tom's Town: Kansas City and the Pendergast Legend*. Eventually, Pendergast cashed in some political chits with President Franklin D. Roosevelt, and the president pardoned Mann a couple of hours after he started serving a five-month sentence.

PASSING OF A JAZZ LEGEND

In the 1940s, Kansas City became an unwitting focal point of the jazz world. Not at its famed 12th Street or 18th Street clubs, but at Union Station. Before dawn on a bitter cold morning in December 1943, the Santa Fe Chief pulled in under the station train sheds. The train was on its way from Los Angeles to New York, and on board one of its Pullman cars was Thomas "Fats" Waller, a 39-year-old pianist and composer, a jazz artist who had taught and influenced Bill "Count" Basie.

Just a few hours earlier, as the train had plowed through a howling Kansas blizzard, Ed Kirkeby, Waller's manager, had entered their shared Pullman sleeper. A burst of cold air blasted him. "Jesus, it's cold in here," Kirkeby recounted saying in his biography of Waller, which contained the only firsthand description of this night. "Yeah," Waller replied, "Hawkins is sure blowin' out there tonight."

Kirkeby recalled in his biography of Waller that he thought the wind reminded the musician of the blustery sax playing of his friend Coleman Hawkins. But jazz historians later noted that "Hawkins" was an African-

FATS WALLER DIES HERE

NOTED NEGRO PIANO PLAYER SUFFERS HEART ATTACK.

He Was on Train Going From West Coast to New York With Manager.

Waller

American slang term for a cold and icy wind — one potentially deadly. Any other night, Waller's offhand phrase would have been forgotten. But sadly the phrase took on deeper significance, the consequence of being someone's last words. For as his train pulled into Union Station, the jazz great lay dying of pneumonia brought on by influenza.

Kirkeby was asleep by then, but a "choking sound" coming from Waller woke him up about 5 a.m. He turned on the light and saw Waller shivering. Thinking Waller was having a bad dream, Kirkeby shook him to wake up. Waller didn't stir. Kirkeby called for a porter and then ran out of the compartment to find help. A doctor happened to be on board and probed Waller's now-motionless body with a stethoscope. The doctor looked up and quietly announced, "This man is dead."

For an hour the corpse stayed on the train, while word of the death immediately spread. It was 4 degrees below zero outside, a record low, yet a small crowd formed on the platform — African-American porters, janitors, cooks, even a few city folks who were alerted about the tragedy. They just stood outside the train, bundled up in the bitter cold, hardly moving. It was an impromptu wake for the entertainer. By a strange coincidence, another train sat on a siding at Union Station around the time of Waller's death. It contained another jazzman, Louis Armstrong. Upon hearing the news there, Armstrong supposedly cried for hours.

Hail to the chiefs

During all these years, trains remained the primary mode of cross-country and intercity travel, especially for dignitaries, who didn't yet trust airplane flights. So when a president of the United States made an occasional call on Kansas City in the first half of the century, he came through Union Station.

Woodrow Wilson was the first, stopping by in 1916 for a speech on military preparedness and then in 1919 to push popular support for the League of Nations — the trip on which he suffered the illness that eventually killed him. In 1923, Warren Harding also passed through on the trip in which he suffered a stroke and died. Calvin Coolidge came for the Liberty Memorial's opening in 1926. Herbert Hoover was nominated in Kansas City as the 1928 Republican presidential candidate and campaigned there in 1932.

Franklin D. Roosevelt had the longest term in office of any president, but he never set foot in the station. He was asleep when his train stopped in the middle of the night in 1935, while soldiers lined the tracks on both sides of the train and armed guards were stationed at every bridge. In his 1936 re-election campaign Roosevelt made two visits. The first time, in September, he merely appeared at the back of his bulletproof Pullman car. Bea Kronhart, a nursing student on Hospital Hill nearby, saw him from the Main Street bridge. "It was the first time we knew he was paralyzed," she remembered. "We could see the white of his knuckles from the strain of holding himself erect." Roosevelt returned a month later for the opening of Municipal Auditorium, which was one of the largest projects to use federal funds. But his train stopped in Kansas City, Kan., across the Kansas River. It's probable FDR went through Kansas City on secret defense inspection trips in World War II, but he never left his special blackened-out trains.

One of the last — and, in retrospect, historic — times a president went through the station was in 1948, during Harry S. Truman's election campaign.

This was the campaign no one thought he could win. Some in his party even tried to nominate someone else. It was the first postwar election. Inflation had raised prices. Soldiers came home to a housing shortage. Even meat was in short supply. But Truman embarked on a cross-country train trip to connect with the people. He left Washington in mid-September with this pledge: "I'm going to fight hard, and I'm going to give 'em hell." One of the first stops was for a major speech at a farm convention in Iowa. It set the tone for the campaign. He attacked the Republican-controlled Congress and the harm he said its policies caused to the average American.

The next night, Truman's train stopped at Union Station for his one-day stay at home in Independence. Harold Smith, then admissions director for Park College, was at the station picking up some out-of-town students. He was flabbergasted at how packed the Grand Hall was becoming. After all, everyone knew Truman didn't stand a chance. But Truman was the first local boy to become president. Smith and the students decided to stay and see the man.

Smith, who had worked at the station during Christmases in college, knew the building's innards and found the staircase to the balcony above the lobby. As Truman came up one of the new escalators and entered the lobby in a roped-off corridor, those gathered applauded, and some yelled out, "Harry, we're for you!" Truman smiled and waved his hat. Smith expected the leader of the free world to be head and shoulders above everyone else. But Truman merely blended into the crowd as he veered to the ropes to shake hands. Then the president disappeared into the dark outside, where another mass of supporters waited. As he climbed into a car, some in the crowd chanted, "Give 'em hell, Harry."

It was a gathering typical of his campaign — larger than anyone expected, more supportive than anyone thought possible. Truman passed through the station and was gone in a matter of minutes, but those who saw him witnessed a piece of history — a presidential candidate on the way to what's considered the greatest political upset in modern times. And it was fitting the night after the election, following thousands of miles of whistle stops, that Truman stood at the rear of his private railroad car in St. Louis and held up a copy of the famous journalistic mistake, the *Chicago Daily Tribune* headline blaring,

In the midst of his supposedly underdog race for re-election in 1948, President Truman walked past a crowd of supporters after leaving his train.

"Dewey Defeats Truman."

Truman was the last president for whom the train was the primary mode of campaigning. It was an era coinciding with Union Station's heyday, when it not only was the city's center, but also when its traditions and especially its legends were imprinting themselves into the city's psyche.

CHAPTER 5

THE STATION LEGENDS

A building's worth can be measured by more than its function or its aesthetic qualities or its occupants. Those merits may explain why a building gets built, but not always why it becomes an icon or a treasure or ultimately gets saved from the wrecking ball. Often it takes something more, something beyond utility or location or architectural integrity.

This something involves a building's intangibles, the unforeseen circumstances that, for better or for worse, connect it to history and give the building a personality or character. Whether as a result of popularity or notoriety or traditions, the intangibles can confer legendary status.

Consider the Empire State Building in New York City. Other skyscrapers were more architecturally dazzling, and its prestige as the world's tallest building lasted only a generation. But it endured as a singular piece of Americana. Its observation deck was not only a popular attraction, but it also became a romantic rendezvous immortalized in movies. The Empire State fed the public's fascination for the macabre with suicidal falls from the top and a fiery crash of a World War II bomber into the 78th floor.

Union Station also had a personality, one not at all staid or stoic like its stone facade. Rather, it was friendly and inviting and animated — and in one memorable sense infamous. These traits can be traced to Union Station's three chief intangibles. One, the popular Fred Harvey restaurant, served some of the best food in town and was remembered for its class and camaraderie. The second, the tradition of New Year's Eve "under the clock," endured for years as one of the city's largest parties. The third, the Union Station Massacre, was a crime so shocking that it changed federal police powers forever and so notorious that it drew curiosity seekers for decades. Through the years, these three intangibles became romanticized in the public's imagination. They became Union Station's legends.

Preceding page and above: The Fred Harvey lunch room in Union Station, inside and out.

Good food, good service, reasonable prices

In the midst of the Great Depression, Dollie Stephens graduated from high school. She needed a job, any job, to help keep her family in Kansas City, Kan., going. The woman next door worked in the bakery of the Fred Harvey restaurant in Union Station. She knew the restaurant needed waitresses. So Stephens took a streetcar to the station and applied. She was told to come back after she had turned 18 years old. Her birthday was that weekend, so she returned the next Monday, April 22, 1935, and was hired.

Stephens was sent to see "Miss Lena" downstairs in the Harvey linen room for a uniform. She received a white "Indian head" wraparound skirt, a white blouse with a starched collar, a white bib to go over the blouse, and then a black bow tie, black hose and black shoes. Miss Lena also included some strict instructions on Harvey decorum — wear the uniform with a good girdle, keep runs out of the hose, and make sure the shoes remain spotless. Oh, and Stephens had to wear a hair net, too. She was now a Harvey Girl, tall and lean and comely, representing the absolute finest tradition in railroad transportation dining.

If there was one institution that paralleled the growth of railroading from its adolescence to an American fixture, it was the Fred Harvey restaurant. Along the way, it created an entirely new form of business, contributed toward taming the West and made Kansas City's Union Station its flagship operation.

Fred Harvey got his start in the restaurant business as a dishwasher in a New York cafe. This was soon after he crossed the Atlantic from his native London in 1851. He moved to different restaurant jobs in different cities until the Civil War, which curbed the leisure business. In 1865, Harvey moved to Leavenworth, Kan., to become a western freight agent for the Burlington railroad. In those days eating on a long train trip required an iron stomach, as depicted by Dee Brown in *Hear that Lonesome Whistle Blow*. A "chicken stew of prairie dogs" was not uncommon, meat chops were "generally as tough as hanks of whipcord," biscuits were known as "sinkers," coffee was fresh once a week, and pie, if found, contained basically dried fruit and crust.

Fred Harvey and the depot in Topeka where he opened his first operation for the Santa Fe.

Illness had scarred Harvey's life, leaving him bedridden a couple of times and killing two of his children, so he was more averse than most travelers to this sordid service. He went to his railroad with an idea for opening restaurants where trains stopped for breaks along long-distance routes. The Burlington turned him down, so Harvey in the mid-1870s went to another railroad official he knew, Charles F. Morse, then general superintendent of the Santa Fe in Topeka. In a couple of years Morse would settle in Kansas City as Bostonian Charles Francis Adams' investment agent and a part-owner of the land where Union Station was later built.

Harvey's pitch to Morse: Better food could draw more travelers to the railroad, creating a competitive advantage over other western lines. The Santa Fe agreed to provide the restaurant space, and Fred Harvey opened his first restaurant in 1876 in Topeka's depot.

He immediately showed off what became his trademarks: Good, hearty food presented on tasteful linens and china, with courteous service, at reasonable prices. With that formula expanded in dozens of places all the way to California, the Harvey House became the first extended chain restaurant in America. Soon, Harvey became dissatisfied with male waiters in his western outposts. So he placed advertisements in the East and the Midwest for single "young women, 18 to 30 years of age, of good character, attractive and intelligent." The women were trained in rules of etiquette, received black-and-white uniforms befitting a nun and stayed in dormitories in the small towns.

At every Harvey outpost along the Santa Fe, waitresses dressed the same.

All this created a mythic figure of purity, the Harvey Girl. Humorist Will Rogers once said Harvey and his young waitresses "kept the West in food and wives." Indeed, one estimate put at 20,000 the number of Harvey Girls who wound up as brides of Western cowboys and railroad men. Four thousand babies in those marriages were supposedly named Fred or Harvey. "Harvey and the railroad took Anglo-American culture west, civilizing the territories of New Mexico, Arizona, Colorado, Texas and California with American language, food, dress, money and values," wrote Lesley Poling-Kempes in *The Harvey Girls: Women Who Opened the West*. The waitresses were later immortalized in a 1946 movie starring Judy Garland, "The Harvey Girls."

Like all Harvey Girls in Kansas City, Dollie Stephens started in the lunchroom. Quick service was expected there, because travelers stayed only 15 minutes for breakfast or lunch. The lunchroom was dominated by a long, U-shaped marble counter surrounded by swivel chairs. Tables were scattered around it and up on a balcony. A recessed skylight brightened the windowless room. Harvey operations, in fact, ended up occupying almost the entire east wing, from top to bottom. Next to the lunchroom on the main level was a small, more formal restaurant. It had glass chandeliers, a marble floor and tables covered with white tablecloths. Both rooms were decorated with richly detailed cornice moldings, and ornamental plasterwork created a paneled ef-

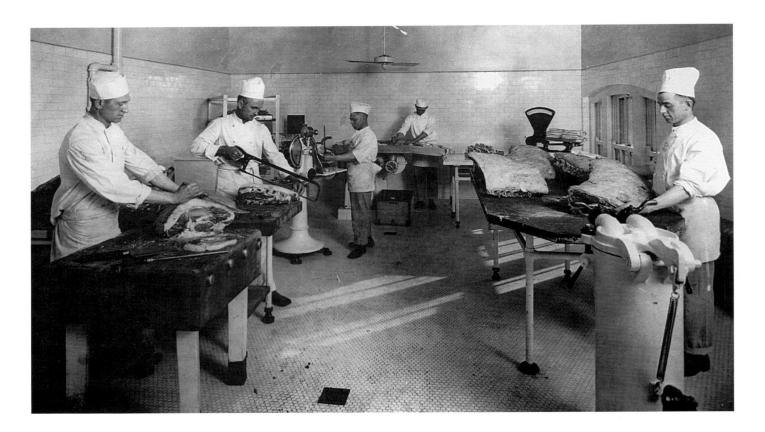

fect on the walls. A report later cataloging the architecture and the uses of Union Station called these rooms "the most elegant areas of the station building."

Upstairs were Harvey offices, including one in the southeast corner of the second floor with oak paneling and a limestone-faced fireplace — the station's only fireplace. This was the office of Ford Harvey, Fred's son and the company's top official in Kansas City after Fred Harvey died in 1901. Downstairs a commissary building extended east of the station. It contained a bakery, a butcher shop and a silver-cleaning room, plus other rooms where canned goods such as olives, pickles and peas were stacked. One floor below that, at track level, were individual rooms for fruits, vegetables, cheese and milk jugs, plus freezer rooms for pork, fish and poultry. Fish as long as a man's arm and twice as thick were stacked on shelves of one freezer room. There also were stockrooms for the various Harvey shops, including a huge humidor kept at 68 degrees that held up to 3 million cigars and 5 million cigarettes for all the Harvey depot outlets.

Back in the lunchroom, Dollie Stephens was responsible for three tables, a total of 10 seats. She had to set the tables just so. Silverware exactly one inch from the edge of the table. Water glass at the tip of the knife. Salt and pepper at the top of the plate. Napkins folded in a rectangle and placed right by the forks. Knife blades facing the plate. And a pitcher of cream filled to the top.

This pitcher typified Harvey's penchant for extravagance on even the smallest details. The story goes that as Union Station got ready to open, the

Facing page: Cup of coffee, coming up.

Today's Suggestion

1.—BROILED FILET OF BOSTON SCROD, Hoteliere	85
Saratoga Chips, Spring Salad	
2.—SCRAMBLED EGGS, Mixed Peppers, Mushrooms and Spinach	70
Fried Egg Plant, Shredded Celery Cabbage	
3.—FRIED CALF BRAINS, Tomato Sauce	70
New Corn, Saute, and Mashed Potatoes	
4.—BARBECUED PORK SPARE RIBS, Dressing	75
Candied Yams and Spring Salad	
5.—ROAST FRICANDEAU OF VEAL, Mashed Potatoes	75
Head Lettuce Salad	
6.—DICED CHICKEN and Mushrooms, a la King on Toast	80
Head Lettuce Salad	
7.—TERMINAL VEGETABLE LUNCHEON	85
Poached Egg Center	

INCLUDING ROLLS, BREAD OR CORN MUFFINS

Milk or Buttermilk 12

Coffee or Ice Tea 10

Desserts

Apple Pie	20	Old Fashion Strawberry	35
Blueberry Pie	25	Short Cake	20
Chocolate Crumb Pie	20	Raisin Cup Cakes	20
Sherbet	20	Apple Cobbler	20
Lemon Custard Ice Cream	25	Cheese Cake	20
Vanilla Ice Cream	20	Cup Custard	

FRUITS:—		CHEESE:—	
Half Grapefruit	25	Liederkranz Cheese	30
Honey Dew Melon	25	Argentine Blue Cheese	35
Sliced Oranges	25	Swiss Cheese	25
Persian Melon			

maitre d' was seen searching frantically for individual-sized cream pitchers. He couldn't find any dainty pitchers, only softball-size china pieces that held a pint. Finally the maitre d' sought out the manager. The manager told him: "There aren't going to be any individuals. If we served cream in a pitcher smaller than that they might think we were trying to economize."

Once the table was set, Stephens greeted customers — referred to as "guests" — with a "good morning," waited by their side until they ordered and then put in the order. Some five minutes later she was back, walking properly with her shoulders square, carrying four plates on her left arm — one under her thumb, one under her middle finger, one under her ring finger and the last one on her wrist. For breakfast the pancakes melted in your mouth. At lunch the hamburger was an inch thick and as round as a bagel, and it cost 25 cents.

In the 1930s celebrities streamed through. Stephens served Douglas Fairbanks Jr., Jimmy Durante, Jack Dempsey and Clark Gable. She, like many women of the day, was enamored of Gable, so she was particularly fastidious with him. When he got up to leave, the slick and mustached Hollywood movie star bent over and bowed to Stephens. She asked for his autograph, and Gable replied, "Of course I will, Dollie," remembering her name. It was fast-paced,

Top: An elegant upgrade for the rail traveler was the Harvey dining room, which adjoined the lunch room on the east side of Union Station. For decades, men were required to wear dinner jackets; alpaca coats were kept in a cloak room for jacketless diners. *Above:* Fred Harvey fare in the mid-1940s.

Decked out for Easter, this window promoted Fred Harvey products in its lobby shops — gifts, fruit and candy, cigars and toys.

fatiguing work, though. Early in her career, Stephens spent evenings after work with her feet in a pan of warm water. They hurt after walking all day on the marble and concrete floors.

In the Harvey company's first outposts out West, the rules were strict when it came to romance. The girls lived together in all-female dormitories, and they pledged not to marry for at least six months. But these rules were waived in the big city, and soon after Stephens started at Union Station, she was asked out by one of the men working in the basement commissary. They married two months later, and she became Dollie Stephens Martinson.

A few years before, another Harvey Girl, Ethel Whitlock, had married just two weeks after meeting her Union Station beau, redcap Jesse "Red" Jameson. To ensure their co-workers could make the wedding, they took their vows inside the Grand Hall, in the southeast corner near the Harvey entrance. It was one of only two weddings known to have taken place at Union Station. Ethel was 23 at the time, a brunette with short hair set in a side wave, the style of the times. She was a devout Christian whose parents had died when she was in grade school, causing her to quit the seventh grade to care for her younger brother and sister. Red was 27 and had gone to work as a redcap expecting to earn just enough money to take a train to New Orleans and catch a freighter to Spain, where he had hoped to spend his life listening to guitars and watching brunettes. But he ended up liking what he was doing.

Ethel later wrote briefly about the June 1927 wedding on a "Certificate of Marriage" page in one of her Bibles. Under witnesses, she put down "Mr. and Mrs. Ray Neely," really Roy, who was one of Red's fellow redcaps, and "a host of Union Station Friends." One small blurb in the *Kansas City Journal* noted that a throng of travelers stopped to gawk and cheer. The couple's first child arrived a year later, and Red stayed at the station 38 more years, during which part of his job was catching some of the troublesome pigeons that congregated on the window ledges. The couple's children remember Red coming home occasionally in the Great Depression with boxes of pigeons, which Ethel stuffed with dressing and then baked. They tasted like hens.

THE HARVEY SORORITY

In 1951, for only the second time since the station opened, Fred Harvey uniforms changed. A pink uniform with white apron and collar, *left*, replaced the white uniform with black bow tie. *Above:* Old-style uniforms were modeled by four Harvey girls in the late 1950s, among them Dollie Stephens Martinson at far right. *Below:* Uniforms had returned to an older style when the Westport Room closed in 1968.

In Union Station's early years, the two Harvey eateries mainly served railroad travelers passing through or departing. Kansas City wasn't much of an eating-out kind of town. Gradually, however, local diners made up for a steady erosion of railroad clientele. On weekend nights, couples looking for an elegant night out could choose from only a few hotel restaurants or the swanky Westport Room, the name of the Harvey dining room after a 1936 remodeling, in which red carpeting replaced the marble floor and three murals of Westport

Landing and stagecoach scenes replaced the ornamental walls. At weekday lunches, many of the city's legends became regulars: politician Harry S. Truman, underworld figure Johnny Lazia, City Manager L.P. Cookingham, *Kansas City Star* President Roy Roberts, real estate developer J. C. Nichols, who tipped a miserly quarter, and 400-pound Mayor H. Roe Bartle, who tipped the maitre d' a cigar.

Through the years, the restaurant developed its own legends. There was Verna Dennis, the coat checker who was so good at remembering names and faces that she didn't pass out hat tags, which amazed just about everyone when she invariably returned the right hat to the right owner. There was Joe Maciel Sr., the always-jovial maitre d' who greeted pretty women with "Good evening, Miss America" and who concocted special dishes, such as a sherry and curry chicken dish named Chicken Maciel, which, when ordered, prompted the banging of a big, brass gong. And there was a chef, Sylvester Bonani, who turned the cooking of a duck into a half-hour dining-room scene, complete with a 2-foot-tall duck press that crushed the cleaned duck but salvaged the blood, which was then mixed with various ingredients to form a sauce. In the book *Dining Out in America's Cities*, critic Raymond Ewell declared: "One of the most famous links in the Fred Harvey chain, the Westport Room, is one of the best railroad station restaurants in the country."

Harvey's heyday at Union Station coincided with the height of segregation in America, and the company operations practiced some of it, too. Although public spaces were not segregated, the Terminal Railway added room partitions to separate white employees from blacks within several occupations — ushers, train cleaners, even Harvey staffers. A separate rest room "for Harvey Company's colored help" was built in the basement, according to spending documents. Across the South and Kansas City, African-Americans weren't typically served in white dining establishments, either. So at Union Station, many African-Americans simply steered clear of the main dining facilities and ended up eating in what was considered the second-class cafeteria off the waiting room. In reality, however, the Harvey eateries were about the only major Kansas City restaurants that served African-Americans. Lucile Bluford, longtime editor and publisher of *The Call* newspaper, used to stop in the lunchroom after many long nights and was seated among tables where whites dined, although usually in the back. "You could eat at the station long before the regular restaurants," Bluford recalled decades later.

Meanwhile, Dollie Stephens Martinson eventually advanced to the Westport Room. The Harvey Girl uniform hadn't changed much since she started, except the skirt rose a little above the ankle and white replaced black for the shoes and hose. Dollie waited on some of the same customers lunch after lunch, even memorizing their favorite dishes. They could get Lake Superior whitefish or pork chops for $1.50 or an entire baby lobster dinner, including soup and a sundae, for $3.75. One business executive, Bill Etzbach, couldn't resist showing off his rapport with his waitress. He took out-of-towners there for lunch. One by one the others ordered. Then they noticed that their host didn't have a menu and complained. Not to worry, the executive crowed, "Dollie knows what I want to eat."

She developed such close ties with some of her regulars that when a flood swept away her house in the Armourdale district of Kansas City, Kan., they took up a collection and presented her $1,200 — worth more than $7,000 in late '90s dollars. Then there was the time a hardware entrepreneur and his wife, Conover and May Smith, who lunched together every Friday, invited their waitress to their Ward Parkway home for cocktails. The couple surprised the waitress with a gift of a Royal Worcester tea set. Dollie scolded the businessman: "That's too valuable." To which he replied, "My dear, you're valuable to us."

Celebrate! Celebrate!

The year Prohibition began, a curious thing happened at Union Station. On the last night of 1920, a few hundred people — a little more than was typically there at that time waiting for trains — gathered under the big clock between the Grand Hall and the waiting room. There they counted down the final seconds before midnight and ushered in the new year with whoops and whistles.

As the '20s progressed, a New Year's Eve tradition was born. The night's revelry began outside the station. The most popular place to celebrate the new year in Kansas City was at the intersection of 12th and Main streets downtown. Thousands filled the streets. Hawkers peddled noisemakers. A snake dance weaved by the burlesque houses. No cars could get through. Federal agents staked out downtown hotels and clubs, trying to make sure no one was imbibing, because alcohol was now illegal. After midnight struck, some partyers headed down to the station, which had one of the only restaurants in town open late at night. Lines stretched out Fred Harvey's doors, and waits for tables stretched more than an hour — even as late as 6 a.m., when the early-morning silence in the waiting room was interrupted by couples sprinting down the center aisle and sliding in their socks along the smooth marble floor. As the years went on, revelers kept arriving a little bit earlier to avoid that big line, so the crowd at the stroke of midnight kept getting bigger.

It beat being outside in the cold. There was ample room on the surrounding streets to park and even double-park. By the early 1930s upwards of 15,000 folks packed the Grand Hall and the waiting room, promenading around the lobby, holding balloons and blowing horns, until the big clock struck midnight and everyone erupted at once, blowing their horns more loudly, throwing hats into the air and letting their balloons go, and then watching those balloons bob and weave up, up, up all the way to the darkened maroon, blue and chestnut ceiling, almost as high as some of the buildings downtown. For one night Union Station was the center of the city's wide-open, party-till-dawn, swinging culture.

As a teen-ager then, Fred Jenkins and his high school buddies from Kansas City, Kan., headed there. It was a simpler time. Folks were friendlier. It

A BIG RUSH AT STATION.

Merrymakers Celebrate New Year With Noise and Liquor.

The New Year celebration ended at the union station at about 7 o'clock this morning. All night long the lobby was crowded with merrymakers. As far as could be determined only two fights took place.

The police understood the fights were among friends and so they did not make arrests. A participant in one of the fights left the union station in a taxicab, with the tail of his dress suit shredded. Another merrymaker lost one of his shoes in the scuffle and a friend gave him a shoe. But it was all among friends.

At 6 o'clock this morning the restaurants at the station were so crowded persons who desired to eat found it necessary to await their turn for table or stools.

The motor cars, too, had their share of difficulties at the station last night and early today. The pavement on the plaza was so slick motor cars frequently were seen sliding merrily around.

An account of the revelry from *The Star*, Jan. 1, 1929.

For one night Union Station was the center of the city's wide-open, party-till-dawn, swinging culture.

(THE *Morning* KANSAS CITY STAR)

The Kansas City Times.

** KANSAS CITY, JANUARY 1, 1954—FRIDAY—24 PAGES. **

UNDER THE CLOCK AT THE UNION STATION—As the New Year sweeps into Kansas City, hundreds of persons, many of them travelers, gather in the station to make the high-vaulted building ring with cheers, songs and New Year's greetings. Noise-makers and balloons on long strings were part of the decorations. The crowd waited expectantly for the large hands of the clock above them to reach straight-up midnight before touching off the welcome for 1954—(Kansas City Star photograph; other New Year's eve pictures on page 8).

Bowl Games on Radio and **HOLD A BANK WORKER** On Inside Pages.

RING IN NEW YEAR

Din by Celebrators Ushers In 1954 at Clubs and Private Parties.

MANY INTO THE STREETS

Crowd in Downtown Area Appears to Be Largest in Five Years.

Police Say the Throng Is Extremely Noisy, but Orderly.

The new year was greeted at midnight with an ear-shattering barrage of sound at Twelfth and Main streets, where about 6,000 persons packed the sidewalks and pavement, tooting horns, clanging cowbells or just shouting out the old year amidst a drumfire of exploding firecrackers and popping balloons.

There were gay gatherings in other sections of Kansas City, too, and some may have matched the Twelfth street crowd in spirit, but none could have approached it in volume of noise.

Throng Stretches Afar.

The crowd began forming by 11:30 o'clock at the intersection, and by midnight it stretched west to Baltimore avenue along the sidewalks and halfway up the block on the pavement. Police said it was a comparatively orderly group, although the size of some of the firecrackers caused concern for a while.

Observers who have watched the street crowd downtown for many years said they believe the number of persons at the intersection was the largest in the last five years. Mild weather encouraged many to join in the press of the celebration. Light jackets or topcoats, mingled with a few suit coats, were the prevailing apparel.

The crowd began to gather about 11 o'clock, and by 11:45 the throng was estimated at 3,000. In the last fifteen minutes of the old year the intersection became filled from corner to corner. The celebrators jammed Twelfth street from side to side for about half a block west of Main.

Wife Ju[...]
GI [...]

Tokyo, [...]
—The Ja[...]
Claude [...]
with joy [...]
that her [...]
back to [...]
nism. [...]
"I can [...]
said Ky[...]
body wa[...]
come ba[...]
She he[...]
Yuichi [...]
press ph[...]
not belie[...]
she saw [...]
Associat[...]
reau. [...]
She im[...]
the follo[...]
her hus[...]
thirty-on[...]
of-war c[...]
"I wa[...]
as possi[...]
re fina[...]
love you[...]
Kyoko [...]
had neve[...]
Batchelo[...]
know ho[...]
in touch [...]
"I do[...]
going to [...]
here." [...]
had time [...]
With a [...]
"I'm a v[...]
girl." [...]

GAIET[...]

Moscow [...]
Their [...]

ROAD

Some Co[...]
lice [...]
D [...]

New [...]
From M[...]
this was [...]
eve in his [...]
Champ [...]
capital tr[...]
In New [...]
were iss[...]
ing—the. [...]
bestowed [...]
The N [...]

New Year's doings, Jan. 1, 1954.

was like an all-city cocktail party. People milled around in groups, meeting and talking to folks they didn't know. Some sported coats and ties. Others had on overalls and cowboy boots. Jenkins wore his usual brown slacks and a cotton shirt that his mother had made out of the 100-pound sacks in which flour came. Balloons by the hundreds were sold in the toy shop. Families with smaller children arriving to catch a train took 20 minutes to move through the throng. In an era before public displays of affection became commonplace, dating couples pretended to be husband and wife. The girls sneaked into the midway and then came back out through the doors as if they had just arrived, greeting their "husbands" with hugs and kisses.

Jenkins and his buddies hung out by the cigar shop and lighted up cigars. Other teens made part of the lobby their playground. They formed line dances. They ran through crack-the-whip games, sometimes knocking down bystanders.

Time flashed by. Then the crowd counted down the last minute, and at midnight balloons popped, strangers hugged and hats were tossed high in the air — although Jenkins didn't throw his brown felt hat. He was afraid he wouldn't get it back. Punctuating the bedlam was the bark of firecrackers, which echoed like machine-gun fire off the walls in the cavernous hall. A few years later, teen-ager Laura Winkler joined the horde:

I remember my first New Year's Eve under the clock....One of the fellas in our group had a party and his Dad volunteered to drive the 'bunch' (about six couples in our group) down to the station. In order to try and keep from getting separated, we all tied long strings to our wrists with big green balloons tied on them (this was our school color). It was a good thing we had agreed on our meeting place to go home by 1 a.m. because when we got to the station all ballooned up, there were balloons everywhere, tied to vendor booths, in the Harvey restaurant and decorating the balcony that encircled the main lobby. 'Under the clock in Kansas City' was like Times Square in New York. Everyone hugged one another, stranger or not, and wishes for a New Year bounced from everyone's mouth. When the final tone of midnight struck, it was like 4th of July with many of the balloons bursting with the prick of a pin. Hot chocolate from the Harvey House brought us together, and just in time, for our ride was at the southwest entrance near the baggage handling department.

Often the carousing only picked up after midnight. One time a man with a few quart bottles sticking out of his overcoat picked a glass light off the station Christmas tree and threw it against a wall. The light shattered with a resounding pop. He did it again, and several others soon joined in. The lobby sounded as if it were under bombardment, until the tree was stripped. As the sun rose later that morning, young women carrying their high heels and men in wrinkled suits still roamed the lobby. The *Kansas City Journal-Post* reported: "Tradition has it that Kansas City's 'swanky' parties must terminate with breakfast at the station, just as New Orleans citizens clamber on stools at the city market for coffee and doughnuts. Apparently everyone obeyed tradition New Year's day, because Harvey's restaurant and the station lobby were crowded until late in the morning."

Broken glass, fallen bodies: The scene after the shootout in the station parking lot, June 17, 1933.

The Massacre

Nothing that ever happened at Union Station changed the nation more than a shootout the morning of June 17, 1933. Yet, separating fact from fiction has taken decades.

In the version that the federal government and various bystanders reported at the time, four federal agents, two Kansas City police detectives and a small-town Oklahoma police chief were there to escort gangster Frank Nash back to prison. Nash, a bank robber, had escaped from the penitentiary in Leavenworth, Kan., but was collared later in Arkansas. Now the escorts ex-

pected to collect Nash off a Missouri Pacific train from Arkansas, haul him into a waiting Chevrolet and drive the prisoner back to Leavenworth. After the train's arrival about 7:15 a.m., the group marched along the platform and up the midway stairs, just like all the other departing passengers from that train. Then they crossed the lobby in a V-formation, with the handcuffed Nash in the middle.

It was a typical Saturday morning. Many station employees were arriving to open up shops and booths. The morning rush of departing trains was just beginning. The squad of men, a few of them carrying shotguns, exited through the east front doors and headed for the Chevrolet parked straight ahead in the station's front driveway. The car's passenger door was opened, and Nash slid in up front, followed in back by two agents and the Oklahoma chief, who had chased Nash for years. Two other agents and the two Kansas City detectives stood outside the car.

Then a man wielding a machine gun appeared. He seemed to have emerged from a line of cars parked in front of and a little to the side of the Chevrolet. "Put 'em up. Up! Up!" the gunman shouted to the law officers. Suddenly a second gun-wielding man appeared beside the first, and a third approached from behind the Chevrolet. One of them shouted, "All right, let 'em have it."

They blasted the Chevrolet with machine-gun fire, rat-tat-tat, little balls of fire flickering out of the barrels with each shot. Bullets ripped into the two detectives beside the car, and they fell together on their backs, their straw hats flying off their heads. More bullets pierced one agent's head outside the car and shredded Nash's head inside the car. More bullets pummeled the backseat, raking another agent's back and hitting the Oklahoma chief from the front and the back. Still more bullets riddled holes in the Chevrolet's front and back, windows and side posts. Cabbies ducked onto the floors of their cars. Travelers dodged behind the cabs or hit the ground or ran for the east doors.

Another federal agent sprang to his feet behind the Chevrolet and dashed for the east doors, too. One of the gunmen turned and sprayed machine-gun

THE DEAD

Caffrey

Grooms

Hermanson

Reed

Nash

Adding to the legend of the massacre — and doing violence to several of the facts — was the 1959 movie "The FBI Story" starring James Stewart and Vera Miles. In this scene, photographed on a set, Pretty Boy Floyd shoots agents in the back. Some researchers believe it's doubtful that Floyd was anywhere near Union Station at the time.

fire in that direction. Bullets bounced off the polished granite facade, and one nicked the skin under the agent's arm before he disappeared from sight.

Inside the station, the gunfire echoed off the walls, sounding as if it came from indoors. Nancy Dixon and her mother, walking across the lobby, sprinted for the east doors. They pushed their way through the doors and sidled up against the polished granite facade outside, when a bullet whizzed two inches from Dixon's head and clanged off the granite. When all the shooting was done, five men were killed — Kansas City Detectives Frank Hermanson and Bill Grooms, federal agent Ray Caffrey, McAlester, Okla., Police Chief Otto Reed and Nash.

It was known as the Union Station Massacre. And much of this version proved to be fibs and fiction, except the actual deaths.

In those days the public was fascinated with gangsters as celebrities. It was the Depression, after all, and the banks those gangsters robbed had reputations for swallowing peoples' savings. And the gangsters kept getting away, adding to the Robin Hood-like allure of Bonnie Parker and Clyde Barrow, Ma Barker and her boys, John Dillinger, Baby Face Nelson, Pretty Boy Floyd,

Machine Gun Kelly and more. Federal law enforcement officers, meanwhile, had little power. Their crime-fighting duties were confined to interstate auto thefts, prostitution and federal bankruptcy violations.

Then the Massacre happened. It was savage. It was cold-blooded. It was gory. It was in public. J. Edgar Hoover, who headed a feeble federal police agency called the Bureau of Investigation, saw the Massacre as his springboard to power. Playing up the ruthlessness of the killings, Hoover begged Congress to act, and it did. Nine major anti-crime bills were passed less than a year after the Massacre. These bills, among other things, made it a federal offense to assault or kill a federal officer, to transport stolen property across state lines and to flee across state lines to avoid prosecution. Together the bills created a federal criminal code for the first time, and so was born an agency with the legendary initials FBI. One historian called the new laws "one of the most important, if least recognized, New Deal reforms."

As for the killers, an outraged country demanded action. And Hoover felt compelled to avenge the ambush of his agents at Union Station. This was no open-and-shut case, however. For one thing, the crime scene was looted. Once the shooting stopped, bystanders gathered to see the carnage, stepping into the blood forming puddles around the Chevrolet, leaving dozens of bloody footprints and pocketing almost all of the slugs and shell casings lying around. For another thing, the ambush happened so fast that most everyone's first reaction — even among the law officers who survived — was to bury their heads out of the line of fire. This made getting positive identification uncertain.

Witnesses ended up naming almost a who's who of American gangsters. Lottie West, one of the station's Travelers Aid Society attendants, swore she saw Pretty Boy Floyd sitting at her desk right before the shooting. The federal agent who had run back into the station thought the first machine-gunner was Bob Brady, part of the Harvey Bailey gang. Later he thought it was Machine Gun Kelly, and then Floyd. A local businessman who happened to be driving through the station parking lot before the Massacre saw Bailey's hat fall off as he got out of a car, revealing his distinctive curly hair. A redcap, Jesse Jameson, the one who had married a Harvey Girl in the station lobby, reported that Bailey had asked him what time the Missouri Pacific train arrived. Several days later, investigators traced a series of phone calls about Nash's arrival in Kansas City to the Brookside house where outlaw Verne Miller had harbored gangster fugitives, but the house was empty by then.

The Nash-Bailey-Miller connection made sense. All three were alumni of a St. Paul, Minn., gang. Also, one federal agent received a tip that Nash, from his prison cell, had orchestrated smuggling guns into the Lansing, Kan., prison for Bailey to use in his escape. So for the rest of 1933 and throughout 1934, Hoover's federal agents went on a sort of witch hunt, rounding up just about every gangster that witnesses claimed to have seen taking shots in front of the station. Bailey was caught and sent to prison for an unrelated kidnapping, while one of his sidekicks was riddled with gunshots. Miller was tracked, too, but he apparently angered the mob while on the lam and was slain in what ap-

In Hoover's zeal to have his agents solve the case, Richetti became the only man to go on trial for a Massacre killing. A combination of eyewitnesses, circumstantial evidence and a fingerprint convicted him. He died in Missouri's gas chamber.

Adam Richetti in the Jackson County Jail, photographed by Jack Wally of the *Kansas City Journal-Post*.

peared to be a gangland execution. Floyd was gunned down in an Ohio farm field, but sidekick Adam Richetti was captured. In Hoover's zeal to have his agents solve the case, Richetti became the only man to go on trial for a Massacre killing. A combination of eyewitnesses, circumstantial evidence and a fingerprint convicted him. He died in Missouri's gas chamber.

This roundup, though, didn't ease the mind of one law enforcement official. Mike Fanning, a Kansas City cop on regular duty at Union Station the morning of June 17, 1933, wasn't close enough to help when the shooting started. For a year afterward he worried that his colleagues blamed him for the deaths. Finally one night in November 1934, he got drunk and cracked. While off duty, he went into Union Station with a gun, threatened some station workers and made his way down to track level, where he killed another police officer on duty there. The Massacre, then, ended up being directly or indirectly responsible for even more deaths.

Blown out, not in: Bits of glass lay on the windshield of agent Ray Caffrey's car, a solid indication that a shot came from inside the vehicle, where agent Joe Lackey was seated in back, handling an unfamiliar weapon.

Actually, some pieces of the case and the FBI's tale just didn't fit together. The Chevrolet's windshield had been blown outward, not inward. One of the Kansas City detectives died from a shot that tore off much of his skull, consistent with a shotgun, not a machine gun. The murdered federal agent died from a ball bearing, not a gunshot, going through his head. Forensics experts could not match any of the few slugs or shells left at the scene with the guns of any known gangster. An independent forensics expert raised some of these discrepancies, but they were promptly shunted aside by federal authorities.

It wasn't until more than a half-century after the Massacre, in 1997, when newspaper reporter-turned-college professor Robert Unger pieced together an account closer to the truth. Acquiring an 89-volume, 20,000-page federal investigative file while with *The Kansas City Times*, Unger then took years to read it. He determined that the mayhem — and the killing — started inside the Chevrolet, not outside it.

According to this account, federal agent Joe Lackey and Police Chief Reed inadvertently switched weapons sometime that morning, leaving Lackey with Reed's unconventional Winchester Model 1897, sawed off short, without a safety switch and packed with a special load of ball bearings. Both men were sitting in the back seat of the Chevrolet when the gunmen approached. Lack-

Another car parked to the right of agent Caffrey's showed evidence that a shot coming from the rear seat of Caffrey's car had struck it.

ey fumbled with the unfamiliar gun, jammed it, and as he frantically pumped it and pulled the trigger, the gun fired, ripping ball bearings through Frank Nash's head and into the federal agent's head. The blast also blew an outward hole in the windshield and caused the gunmen to return fire. Then Lackey swung the shotgun toward the gunmen and pumped again, and more ball bearings blasted out, catching one of the Kansas City detectives in the side of the head. Lackey himself described this chain of events in a memorandum, and one eyewitness reported seeing Lackey struggling with a gun.

This federal agent, then, was responsible for three of the five deaths that day. He also made up the "Let 'em have it" dialogue. But the feds never admitted any of this publicly. And that was only the beginning of the deceptions. The court case against Richetti was riddled with lies, too. Federal agents testified that Floyd was one of the shooters, but those same agents had admitted in classified reports that they couldn't identify any shooters. Also, Richetti's fingerprint — unnoticed at first but eventually discovered on a dusty beer bottle from Verne Miller's house — was "at best highly suspicious and at worst a Bureau fake," wrote Unger.

Questions about the Massacre remain today. Who, for instance, were the actual gunmen? Unger's federal file doesn't say, except to discount that it was Richetti or Floyd or almost any other gangster. Unger believes Verne Miller organized the botched Nash-snatch and probably tapped a couple of local thugs he knew. Also, why didn't Lackey and Reed simply trade guns when they got into the car, at which point each surely knew he didn't have the right weapon? Unger doesn't hazard a guess.

Myths die hard, especially myths as repeated and ingrained as the Union Station Massacre. Even after Robert Unger virtually proved Pretty Boy Floyd had no role in the Massacre, *The New York Times* reported twice in 1998 that Floyd was one of the Massacre gunmen. Then there's the enduring story of the gangsters' bullet holes in the station's facade by the east doors. It has long been assumed that two round cavities high on the granite trim, one facing south toward the parking lot and another facing east, were remnants of the Massacre. Nancy Dixon, later Hiler, the child who ran with her mother outside after the shooting started, swears one of them was from the bullet that narrowly missed her head. "I have seen the bullet hole throughout the years," she once wrote a Union Station charity group. And for decades the first thing people off the street asked Union Station maintenance workers was where the bullet holes were. Then the people invariably stuck their fingers in them.

One day in the spring of 1999, at the urging of *The Kansas City Star*, the Kansas City Police Department tried to verify and authenticate the holes once and for all. Heat from a gunshot and its impact on granite would have vaporized a bullet's lead core and left some residue. This lead trace would be so impregnated in the hole that fingers or rainwater would not remove it, even after all the years. "If it was there, we would find it," said Gary Howell, director of the Police Department's crime lab.

So Bill Newhouse, a 52-year-old senior criminalist who became Montana's first firearms examiner before coming to Kansas City, carried a cardboard box to the front of the station. Inside the box were a nitric acid solution, cotton swabs and test tubes. Nitric acid can extract lead from any surface it touches. Newhouse took a dropper filled with the liquid acid solution and dribbled the solution onto a white cotton swab, rolling the swab in his fingers to wet it on all sides. Then he stood on a wood pallet against the polished, gray-colored granite containing sparkling quartz, feldspar and mica miner-

Using these weapons, John Cayton, a Kansas City police ballistics expert, fired .45-caliber shells into a slab of granite like that used at Union Station.

als. He reached up and dabbed the swab into the first hole. This was the south hole, about the size of a quarter, tapering inward about half an inch. Newhouse rolled the swab around the hole and against its rear, and then placed the swab upright in one of the test tubes to dry. He walked four steps around the corner of the protruding granite wall to its east face and the only other supposed bullet hole. This one was a little different, about the size of a marble. Newhouse stood at head level

with the hole and repeated his process. It was all over in a few minutes. Newhouse closed up his box and left.

A week later, the test tubes sat on a black examination table in the crime lab. Newhouse took a bottle of sodium rhodizonic acid, poured some into a tiny beaker and added water. The mixture turned a dark orange. It's commonly used for gunpowder tests, and when it comes in contact with lead, the orange turns to bright red. To make sure it worked, Newhouse took a new cotton swab, touched it to a known gun slug, and then poured the sodium rhodizonic mixture over the swab. Sure enough, the cotton tip turned red. Now he turned his attention to Union Station's test tubes. He plucked the swab used for the south-facing hole. If any lead had been in that hole, the acid-laced swab would have picked it up. Newhouse turned the swab in one hand and dripped droplets of the sodium rhodizonic mixture from an eye-dropper with the other hand, drenching the swab. The cotton stayed orange. Negative — no lead traces. Then he picked up the last swab, the one from the east-facing hole. Again he poured droplets all around the white cotton tip. Again negative, no change in color.

No one knows, of course, whether some souvenir hunter over the years scraped the lead out of the holes while trying to unearth a slug. Still, if the lead test were the one and only uncertainty with the holes, the bullet myth might endure as just another mystery of the Massacre. But it's not.

Additional incongruities are just as troubling. The Massacre criminals used machine guns that fired bullets in rapid succession, yet the holes on Union Station's facade are single indentations, not part of a string or circle of marks expected from such gunfire. Also, both holes were punctured straight in, while the criminals were shooting at an angle from where the holes are. Bullet holes, Newhouse explained, "have a pretty characteristic look from an angle, and these don't have it." Moreover, these two holes aren't the only ones on the station facade. Two more holes the size of a half-dollar are embedded in a piece of granite outside the station's west wing. This confirms that something else poked holes in the granite, although no one has any idea what could

Unlike the marks on the station wall — long thought to be bullet holes from the massacre in 1933 — 1999 tests left granite barely scuffed, above. The test marks were quite unlike the holes in the station granite, below

have caused them.

Beyond these quandaries, there's even more. The east hole, in particular, was not in the direct line of fire. It was around a corner from where the gunmen stood. If it were, indeed, a bullet hole from the Massacre, it would have had to be

caused by a ricochet. Yet the corresponding wall directly across from this hole is some 50 feet away, too far for a ricochet with enough speed to puncture the granite. As for the south hole, "it's bigger than a .45 would cause," John Cayton, a longtime ballistics expert with the crime lab who has studied the Massacre shootings, said in 1999. The hole's half-inch depth is more consistent with a bullet ripping into pine than granite.

Finally, Cayton conducted one other test. He obtained a slab of the same type of granite that's on Union Station, a Barre Vermont gray. He propped the 1-by-2-foot slab against a fence on his 80-acre farm north of Kansas City and, with a tape measure, marked off 75 feet — about the distance the Massacre gunmen were from the station. Then he loaded a .45-caliber, copper-jacketed bullet into a carbine similar to a submachine gun and shot at the granite slab.

The bullet bounced off, leaving a small, flattened clump of molten copper and lead. With a rag, Cayton wiped away the clump, revealing a small scuff, no wider than a tack. No indentation at all. And certainly no hole. Cayton reloaded, moved up closer to the granite, 50 feet this time, and shot again. Same small scuff. "It didn't knock any of the stone out," Cayton reported. Based on this test, Cayton believes a Massacre bullet "wouldn't cause the big chip that's there" on Union Station's facade.

Taking all these findings into account, then, the infamous bullet holes on the front of Union Station are not bullet holes at all.

Does the truth take anything away from the building's character? No. Now there's even more to Union Station's lore.

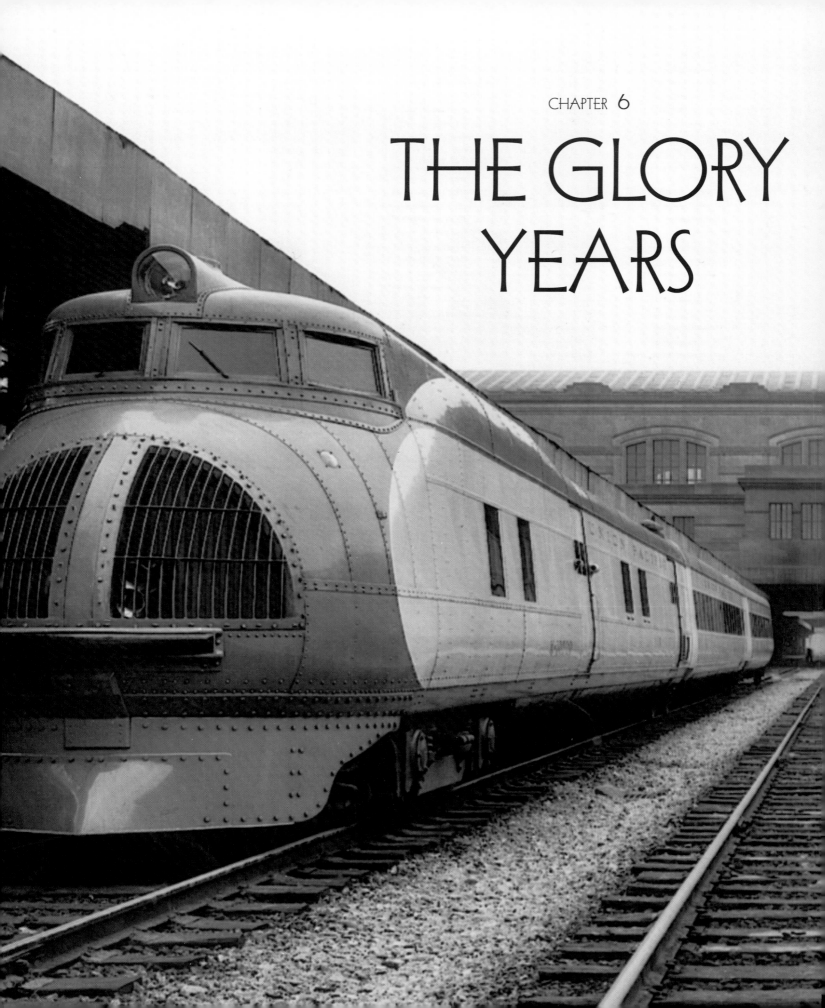

CHAPTER 6

THE GLORY YEARS

Preceding page: Boasting new shapes and a new mode of power — internal combustion — Union Pacific's M10000 and the Burlington's Zephyr were dual pioneers of a new era in railroading in the mid-1930s.

Within a year after the Union Station Massacre, something else happened at the station heralding change for the nation. A new kind of train rolled into the yard. The newspapers said it resembled a caterpillar. It had a smooth and rounded form and seamless metal sheathing over its three cars. No one had seen anything like it. It didn't even have a proper name. It was called the Union Pacific M10000. And it was the nation's first streamliner, representing a new age in passenger trains.

Streamlining was the rage in all sorts of equipment and kitchen appliances, characterized by rounded edges, smooth surfaces and low horizontal profiles. The ideal shape for penetrating the air with lower resistance and higher speed was considered a teardrop, which the M10000 copied. For the railroads, "the streamlined form came to symbolize progress and the promise of a better future," Donald J. Bush wrote in *The Streamlined Decade.*

So for three days in April 1934, thousands stood in long lines under Union Station's west-side train sheds, gawking at Union Pacific's futuristic marvel, which was on a nationwide tour. Trains just didn't change. That was one of life's constants. Trains had been the same for generations, going back before Union Station opened. But this — well, it was no old-fashioned locomotive. There was no bulky steam boiler or protruding bolts or exposed driving rods. Nor was everything black. Instead, this train had an aluminum surface, with some parts painted canary yellow. And its front resembled a modern-day airplane, with a humped nose and a band of windows set back atop the hump. Under this was a semicircular air-intake grate resembling a shark's gaping mouth.

Those in line gaped. They hadn't had much to get excited about during the Depression, and this was *something.* The procession was allowed on board. Railroad officials watched — and counted. Early on the second day of the M10000's stop at Union Station, the officials suddenly plucked a young college-going woman from the line. She was the 1 millionth person in the nation to visit the train, and photographers caught an early history-making moment in the streamlined era.

THE HEART OF AMERICA

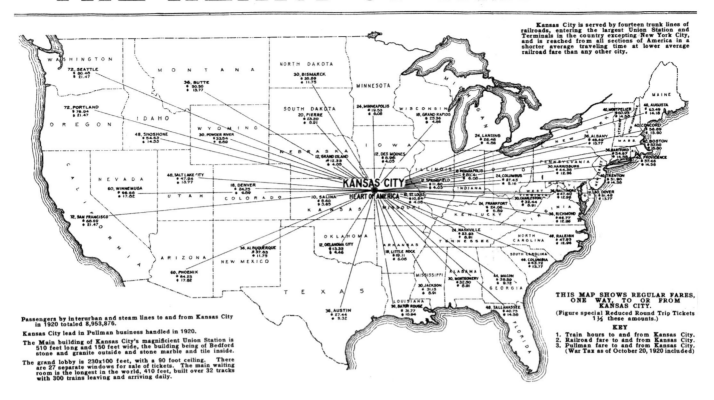

Kansas City is served by fourteen trunk lines of railroads, entering the largest Union Station and Terminals in the country excepting New York City, and is reached from all sections of America in a shorter average traveling time at lower average railroad fare than any other city.

Passengers by interurban and steam lines to and from Kansas City in 1920 totaled 8,953,876.

Kansas City lead in Pullman business handled in 1920.

The Main building of Kansas City's magnificient Union Station is 510 feet long and 150 feet wide, the building being of Bedford stone and granite outside and stone marble and tile inside.

The grand lobby is 230x100 feet, with a 90 foot ceiling. There are 27 separate windows for sale of tickets. The main waiting room is the longest in the world, 410 feet, built over 32 tracks with 300 trains leaving and arriving daily.

THIS MAP SHOWS REGULAR FARES, ONE WAY, TO OR FROM KANSAS CITY.

(Figure special Reduced Round Trip Tickets 1½ these amounts.)

KEY

1. Train hours to and from Kansas City.
2. Railroad fare to and from Kansas City.
3. Pullman fare to and from Kansas City.
(War Tax as of October 20, 1920 included)

In the early 1920s, Kansas City civic promoters boasted about their huge station, and about the short traveling times and low fares available to it from across the country.

That same month, the Burlington railroad christened the nation's second sleek streamliner train, later dubbed the Pioneer Zephyr. *Newsweek*, in writing about the streamliner phenomenon, declared, "In the new train, railroad men…see possible salvation." The route to that salvation passed right through Union Station.

Later in 1934 the Burlington put the Zephyr into regular passenger service on a route between Lincoln, Neb., and Kansas City's station. Meanwhile the Union Pacific renamed the M-10000 the City of Salina and put it into service in early 1935 between Kansas City and the Kansas town of Salina. Union Station became the epicenter of the railroad industry's new marketing blitz. But only after the railroads had been compelled to modernize by sheer desperation.

Fading glory

Union Station had opened at the end of what's considered the Golden Age of railroading. Just two years after trains began running there, the railroad industry reached its nonwar zenith in passenger travel and track mileage, with 35 billion passenger miles across the nation's 254,000 miles of track. The average citizen was riding a train 10 times a year, and trains handled 98 percent of all intercity travel.

Yet a little anxiety, a little pessimism soon crept into Union Station's administrative offices. Passenger business at the station hadn't even topped that of the Union Depot it replaced. The depot peaked with 81,300 trains in the 1911-12 fiscal year. Union Station's usage exceeded 79,000 trains in 1917 and then fell off. Likewise the new station's ticket sales, operating revenue and work force all started sagging after 1920. John Hanna, the Kansas City Terminal Railway's longtime chief engineer, wrote in a 1926 letter to a Milwaukee official lobbying for a new station there: "We are confronted with a constantly diminishing number of passengers....There is no prospect of increased revenue from increased travel. It is the common expectation that the inroads of the motor car and motor bus into the passenger business of the steam roads will continue."

But because trains still held a virtual monopoly on travel between cities, folks were stuck with the accommodations that railroads provided. Those accommodations ranged from deluxe quarters with swirling Victorian moldings to rickety wooden coaches on which pillows cost extra. For the wealthy, trains created, in the words of one historian, a "fantasy world," a world filled with servants intent on pampering. In 1926, Santa Fe introduced the Chief, a luxury train between Chicago and Los Angeles that charged a premium to ride it — $8 above the regular ticket price from Kansas City. The promotional brochure smugly boasted: "The Chief is frankly designed for people who want the best. It is for men who value the extra roaming space provided by spacious club cars and smokers; it is for women who love personal daintiness and immaculate surroundings." Its dining car often featured such dishes as jumbo whitefish, boneless perch and fresh lobster or shrimp salads. In an essay, "I Travel by Train," Rollo Walter Brown described life on a pricey Pullman sleeper. It had "cheerful people who seemed not to have a care in the world" — and this still during the devastating Depression.

Later railroad historians romanticized this era of train travel. In his 1989 book, *All Aboard! The Golden Age of American Rail Travel*, Bill Yenne made a train ride seem utterly peaceful and awe-inspiring: "The relaxing periodicity of the incessant clickety-clack of rails, the immediacy of scenery masquerading as something more itself than just an abstract, geometrically-shaped land mass, the utter determinism and variety of a fixed, impervious route through changing climates and seasons — all these conspired to lullaby one's will within and into its own private heaven."

The actual experience was somewhat different. Take the Pullman sleeper. It wasn't exactly cozy. The sleeping arrangements were like a dormitory, with double-bunk compartments squeezed together, with not enough room for a 6-foot-tall man to stretch out. At night there was the degrading spectacle of disrobing in the aisle, and the trip to the one rest room for each sex at the end of the car meant stumbling over shoes and bumping into beds. When a few passengers woke up early and talked and called porters to make their berths back into couches, all the noise awakened those nearby. Maverick rail executive Robert R. Young termed these sleepers "rolling tenements."

If this represented first-class accommodations, then regular coaches

Tickets sold

Year	Tickets sold
1915	1,560,638
1917	1,675,000
1920	2,010,000
1923	1,352,365
1926	1,029,108
1929	788,942
1932	306,897
1935	331,063
1938	376,955

Trains handled

Year	Trains handled
1915	78,928
1917	79,268
1920	75,939
1923	76,065
1926	76,736
1929	74,342
1932	55,330
1935	55,330
1938	58,536

Source: Kansas City Terminal Railway annual reports

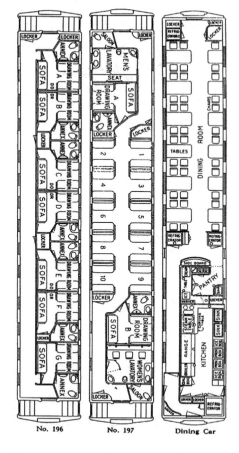

No. 196   No. 197   Dining Car

Passenger-car configuration on the Santa Fe's Chief, 1926.

Above: Pullman cars, which were like coaches in the daytime, were transformed into rows of sleeping berths at night.

might well have been warehouses on wheels: yellow straw over plain wood seats on day coaches. Workers with filthy hands placing ice in drinking-water containers. Constant clickety-click noises drowning out conversations. Side-to-side jerking making walking or eating perilous. Soot and coal dust blowing through open windows and collecting on clothes. C. Thomas Carr, who later became a lawyer and headed the Kansas City area branch of the National Railway Historical Society, remembered childhood vacations riding the Santa Fe to California during this time:

During the daytime my favorite place on the train was the back platform of the observation car. There I would spend most of the day sitting on the dark green folding director-type chairs. At lunch time and again at dinner time, my mother would appear at the platform door and remark how wind-blown and sooty I had become, and then pull me by the hand to the nearest women's room and there, with washcloth, hot water and soap, scrub my face, scalp and well into my ears to remove the cinders and other steam engine debris.

Despite the filth, this ride spawned a lifelong love of trains and Union Station for Carr.

For a young Arline Latham, the same ride to California opened her eyes to the wonders of America's scenery. The route rolled through flat western Kansas, then down into New Mexico and across Arizona. Latham was on a summer vacation, sharing coach seats with her mother and brother. Sometimes a porter set up a table between their facing benches to rest a book on or play cards. Her diary from age 14, in 1934, provided a glimpse of the train's tedium to a teen-ager: "Got up about 8 o'clock and stopped in Las Vegas (New Mexico) for 20 minutes. Then we had breakfast on the train. After breakfast and during the day I wrote letters and read the book, *The Vanity Case.*" Another day on the same trip she groused, "There wasn't much to do on the train." Most of the time she stared out the window. She saw fields of sunflowers and oil wells in Kansas, expanses of red soil in New Mexico, her first mountains and her first Indians, who were sitting on blankets selling pottery and jewelry along station platforms at lunch or dinner stops. "It was a geography lesson all the way," she recalled. But always from her seat. A wood seat with little padded upholstery. She couldn't escape it even at night. The coach lights dimmed, a porter came by renting pillows for pennies, and Latham went to sleep in her hard seat while leaning against her mother.

In those days railroads acted like the monopoly they were. Their idea of improvement was putting tissues in the Pullman rest rooms. Humorist Will Rogers joked that the only advance in railroading in a generation was the introduction of the razor-blade slot in the Pullman cars. Not only that, but train travel was slow. The trip between Chicago and Denver, for instance, averaged 40 mph for more than a day across cornfields and desolate plains. The trip between Kansas City and St. Louis took more than 12 hours in the first decades of the century, because the train stopped at almost every hamlet along the way.

Not surprisingly, then, when the populace found an exciting and independent alternative — the automobile — they jumped at it. In 1922 auto travel was one-quarter of annual railroad passenger mileage, but five years later those figures had reversed, although auto travel was still mostly local. Cars had been rolling off assembly lines for about two decades by the 1930s, but they finally were affordable to middle- and lower-class families. The railroads at first embraced a better-roads campaign across the country on the theory that more paving would allow farmers to reach stations easier. The highway

The Santa Fe used scenes of the American Southwest to create a romantic image and attract passengers for vacations by train.

Facing page: A Santa Fe streamlined steam locomotive waits to depart Union Station for points west.

lobby in Washington, too, maintained that highways would never compete against railroads. Such propaganda won the road and auto industries virtual freedom from government regulation.

But, of course, highways did compete against railroads. At Union Station, the number of trains passing through held steady for much of the 1920s but then fell off 25 percent by the late 1930s. For the Kansas City Southern Railway, one of the train companies operating out of the station, passenger revenue fell from $2.5 million to $650,000 from 1921 to 1931. This prompted a confidential company report to conclude that "passenger revenue has about diminished to the vanishing point" and that "such earnings as the above would not appear to justify any passenger service." To many railroad presidents, passenger traffic was a nuisance hardly worth the expense and headache for roughly 10 percent of annual revenue. So with declining usage and falling revenue, railroads lopped thousands of men off the payrolls, reduced the number of passenger routes and raised rates — much like an industry without a care about competition. In fact, the federal transportation coordinator in Washington, in 1935, investigated the decline of train travel and declared in a "Passenger Traffic Report": "Flight of passenger traffic from the railways is due to failure to keep pace with modern methods of marketing, servicing, pricing and selling."

Life at the station

Despite the trends, whenever cross-country specials or ordinary coach trains pulled into Kansas City, they set off a flurry of activity from several different quarters of Union Station and its grounds. Trains had to be assigned to tracks, track crossings had to be switched, baggage had be to unloaded, cars had to be serviced and passengers had to be cared for.

Of Union Station's 12 railroads, four accounted for more than half of all trains. These were the Burlington, the Santa Fe, the Missouri Pacific and the Rock Island. Five others provided steady but limited service — the Union Pacific, the Kansas City Southern, the Frisco, the Katy and the Wabash. The three lines struggling most were the Milwaukee Road, the Chicago Great Western and the Alton. An array of control towers guided the different railroads onto Kansas City Terminal tracks. The Santa Fe's line, for instance, rounded the Kansas River west of the station and entered Terminal tracks at the south end of the west bluff. Burlington and Wabash trains crossed the Hannibal Bridge, followed tracks through the West Bottoms and hooked up with Terminal tracks near where the Santa Fe did. Missouri Pacific and Kansas City Southern joined with Terminal tracks at junctions five to six miles east of the station by the Sheffield neighborhood and the Blue River.

Tokens of the automobile's inroads into railroad traffic. A metal plate showed the car's owner had paid the city fee, top, and a Convention Bureau road map showed travelers "highways in Kansas City territory...How to get in and out of Kansas City."

Inside this eastern signal tower and one like it on the west side of Union Station, switches were thrown to guide trains to their assigned tracks.

As a train neared Union Station, it came under the province of a signal tower, situated right where the four main tracks fanned out into 16 station tracks under the sheds. The signal-tower operator gave an order to clear one of the 16 tracks, and then a leverman pulled a 6-inch-long handle that opened the necessary track switches and closed that particular track to other trains. This was the automated, interlocking switch system. It was quite innovative when the station opened. Before then, switching required as much brawn as brains. A husky man threw all his weight toward or against a chest-high shaft to move it, which dragged a long wire to shift a track switch. The man had to move several shafts to close any stretch of track. With this manual operation in use during the first years of the 20th century, some 10,000 people died in railroad accidents nationwide each year, mostly in track-crossing crashes and accidents when a stretch of track wasn't entirely closed off. With interlocking switches, however, a single handle powered all necessary track crossings and locked them into place, preventing more than one train from merging onto the same track. This ability to automate several tasks made the actual interlocking switching machines, as long as a conference table, "the nation's first large-scale computers," concluded railroad historian John R. Stilgoe.

A train slid under Union Station's train sheds once every eight minutes or so. If it was passing through Kansas City, it typically stopped only 10 to 20 minutes, resulting in bedlam like a race-car pit stop. Crews from the baggage

Kansas City Terminal Railway's operations extended along Southwest Bouldevard to the roundhouse and yards where locomotives and cars were repaired, cleaned and stored.

department in the basement hustled up and down wrought-iron baggage elevators in the middle of the passenger platforms. Mail and parcel workers drove package trucks on the platforms, weaving around travelers and columns, to load and unload sacks. Fred Harvey attendants shoved food aboard the diner. Inspectors from the station's car department walked the length of the train, shining a flashlight into the undercarriage and looking for problems like damaged springs or low pressure in the air brakes.

If something was found, a handyman mechanic was called. Jim Cain, a strong and stout man with arms like telephone poles, was one of those "car men," in charge of what was termed "running repairs" during a short layover. He drove a tractor loaded with tools and parts to the end of one passenger platform, crossed the wooden planks over the tracks and turned onto the platform where the wounded train waited. The 80-inch wheels of steam locomotives loomed almost as tall as he was. Sometimes the brake shoes burned up and had to be replaced right there. Sometimes the heavy metal door on a baggage car came off its roller and had to be jacked into place. And sometimes the steam heating pipes outside each car froze in winter and had to be sprayed with a steam hose until they thawed. The steam and the electricity for many of these tasks, along with the water and the heat for the entire station, came from a battery of coal boilers, turbine generators, refrigeration plants and air compressors in a separate powerhouse building near the Broadway viaduct.

Steam locomotives, boasting huge drive wheels, required continual maintenance.

Meanwhile, another cluster of uniformed men waited on the train platform to greet passengers getting off. There were redcaps to get their luggage, passenger agents to help them find their way around, vendors to sell them ice

HANDLING FREIGHT, FROM LOBSTERS TO LOOT

While all the passenger activity occupied the center of Union Station and Harvey food facilities filled the east wing, an adjoining west-end building was reserved for special cargoes. This was the Express Building, which handled shipping services that were the precursor to today's United Parcel Service.

The building extended about one-fifth of a mile, mostly below street level, making it the largest such facility in the country when the station opened. Nine stub-end tracks terminated in front of it for loading and unloading light freight. These were the kinds of things making Kansas City's economy hum, like steaks packed in dry ice, or the kinds of things making up everyday life, like mop handles and car tires and hats.

But sometimes exotic shipments passed through, like crates of gray minks, or fresh lobsters or millions of bees, packed one hive per case, with swarms of stray bees around each case to stay near their queen. Crates of roosters on their way to Hawaii, where rooster fighting was legal, could not be unloaded too closely together, because invariably one rooster poked its head out of the crate and began pecking at a foe in another crate, and soon the floor was a bloody mess. One time a circus passed through and handlers let an elephant out of her car to switch cars, but she wouldn't get back in. The elephant strolled around the train for more than two hours, poking her trunk inquisitively at the train's brakes and air cylinders.

Also, because Kansas City had a Federal Reserve Bank, shipments of coins arrived regularly. The coins were stuffed in white bags the size of a small pillow, weighing about 50 pounds each, and then packed in boxes so big that the express workers could not lift them. They had to open the boxes under the watchful eyes of a security guard, remove the coin sacks and load them into different boxes on a wagon. When merchandise like this traveled on train cars, messengers accompanied it. "Lots of times," said James "Chief"

Miniature trains of wagons hauled light cargo along platforms to and from their big siblings on the tracks.

These Railway Express Agency drivers in the 1930s picked up and delivered cargo at the low-slung building extending from the west end of Union Station.

Williams, one of those long-ago messengers, "when we would have only a hundred or so bags of halves (half-dollar coins) from the mint, they would be carried in the express car in open boxes. I always tried to keep my eye on them when the train stopped. But I never worried too much, because I knew a man couldn't pick up more than two bags and run."

cream and magazines, even a Western Union messenger to take their messages. All these workers were white. African-Americans in the 1920s and '30s weren't hired as redcaps or sales clerks or mechanics or electricians or even ticket sellers. About the only job open to African-Americans at the station were janitor and washroom attendant, so they often became porters on trains.

Union Station had strict rules governing how employees dressed and acted. They could not solicit tips. They could not sit on waiting-room benches. They could never pull their caps down over their eyes. And they had to pick up any trash they saw. "Civil and gentlemanly deportment is required of all employees in their intercourse with passengers, with the public and with each other. Rudeness or incivility will not be excused," the station rule book stated. In 1932, Union Station's first stationmaster, Vinton Bell, told a newspaper reporter: "Sometimes we hire a man who just can't be courteous, and if a man doesn't possess the quality of courtesy, you can't put it in him, so we have to let him go."

The redcaps were easily identifiable. They wore a blue shirt with a detachable white collar with a black tie, plus a cylindrical red cap with a short black bill — the bill being exactly a thumb length from the nose. They worked out of a small room called the "cabin" off the Grand Hall, where a machine called a teleautograph was installed. A teleautograph resembled a stock-market ticker, with a tape constantly moving across it. The teleautograph tape contained the signal-tower operator's scribbled handwriting telling which track an incoming train had been slotted into. Then the redcaps, having already jockeyed for the most crowded cars or Pullmans, rushed downstairs to meet the train cars. Steam spurted from under the cars, brakes squealed, engines hissed, and bells clanged. The conductor or a chair-car attendant leaned out the coach-car doors handing out luggage, and the redcaps set each bag on the platform. When passengers got off, they either picked up their own bags or told the redcap where to meet them upstairs.

Kansas City's Union Station was known for its efficient operation. In the early 1930s, for instance, Chicago's union station averaged two-dozen luggage mix-ups everyday, in which one traveler's luggage was misplaced or carried off by someone else. In Kansas City, that many mix-ups occurred only every six months.

Back then redcaps didn't have carts or dollies, so they lifted the luggage themselves, holding one piece in each hand and tucking a couple of other pieces under each arm, before climbing the 44 steps upstairs. Redcaps quickly learned to avoid salesmen with big black sample bags, although they couldn't avoid folks in wheelchairs, who had to be carried up the stairs on stretchers. In those days redcaps didn't receive a salary. They depended on tips. During the Depression, however, many travelers skimped on the standard 10-cent tip. "We did a lot of charity work," Bob Blowers, a tall and lanky redcap from that time, recalled. "But it wasn't backbreaking work, at least to a young guy."

After handling all the passengers getting off and getting on, redcaps headed back to the "cabin," where they were joined by other passenger service

Magazines, apples, cookies and candies filled the platform shops on wheels.

crews and Fred Harvey cart vendors, such as Maurice Rubin. Rubin was just ending his teen-age years in the Depression, but Union Station felt like a second home to him. During his school years, Rubin had taken a streetcar every afternoon to the station, where his mother worked an evening shift in one of the Harvey shops. Union Station became his neighborhood, his playground. He played with the toys in the toy store. He took naps on the waiting-room benches. He watched Harvey chefs prepare ice cream in the commissary. And the girls at the soda fountain occasionally slipped him a free soda. The Harvey managers told the slight, scrawny youngster he could start working once he turned 12 years old, and the first summer after that birthday, Rubin was hired to push an ice-cream cart.

This was one of several vending carts the Harvey company used for passengers on pass-through trains who wouldn't go upstairs for a snack, a smoke or a book. Rubin stayed with the redcaps in the cabin until the teleautograph machine delivered the next train alert, and he then joined everyone else in rushing to the platform, amid the bells of moving locomotives and switch engines, the grinding of drive rods and the clanking of cars being coupled and uncoupled. Rubin, in his white jacket and white cap, perched under a train car's open windows and delivered ice-cream cones for 5 cents. A few years later he graduated to the big cart, the one with books, magazines, tobacco and toiletries. This cart was so bulky he simply parked in one spot on the platform. Passengers got off the train to see his selection.

One day a dapper, portly fellow ambled up to his cart. It was Babe Ruth. Rubin happened to have a slip of paper, and he borrowed a pencil from the Western Union messenger to get the home-run hitter's autograph. After that, Rubin took to carrying a notepad and a pencil in the front pocket of his navy suit. His favorite train was Santa Fe's Chief, because that's what the movie stars rode in their coast-to-coast travels. Laurel and Hardy signed his pad. So did Jean Harlow and Ginger Rogers and Mary Pickford. Usually they wore ordinary clothes and no makeup. Rubin looked at some and thought, "She's not nearly as pretty as on the screen."

Once, though, he wasn't disappointed. It was late morning, the Chief had come and gone, and the a.m. rush was over. Only a smattering of people roamed the Grand Hall or the station shops, but Rubin spied someone familiar. Clark Gable was browsing in the bookstore, picking up books and turning the pages. Rubin had seen Gable get off the Chief, and the train had pulled out before the movie star got back on. Now he was killing time before hopping another train. Rubin approached and asked for an autograph. Gable looked muscular and trim, his mustache short and his hair slicked back — just the way he appeared in movies. And he didn't come off as prissy or particularly perturbed about missing his train. Rubin added another star to his collection, and Gable went back to browsing. Just another day in the heyday of Union Station, during the age of steam.

Streamlining means speed

It was during the Depression that Averell Harriman made a long trip out West. Harriman was the son of railroad baron Edward Harriman and had followed his father in becoming chairman of the Union Pacific. His private car was hitched to a regular train, and at one point Harriman left his car and walked through the coaches. They were so empty "you could shoot a cannonball through the train and not hit anybody," as one of his associates described it. After returning to his car, Harriman asked his company president why Union Pacific couldn't just get out of the passenger business. The president described the federal government's regulatory straitjacket, which basically required railroads to continue serving small towns along major routes, because town folk along the routes still depended on the railroads for supplies, mail

Film star Jean Harlow on a visit to her home town in the 1930s.

Director Cecil B. DeMille and an unidentified woman next to a passenger car.

Dancer and actress Ginger Rogers (left) buying a magazine from vendor Maurice Rubin.

Helen Hayes in the Fred Harvey restaurant

CELEBRITIES
AT THE STATION

Newspapers made it a habit to assign staffers to Union Station, where celebrities often stopped on their way in and out of town or across country. These photos were taken by Jack Wally and other photographers for the *Kansas City Journal-Post*.

JACK WALLY

JACK WALLY

Comedian Fred Allen mugged for the camera with his wife at the station toy store, above. Not so eager to be photographed was singer Jeanette MacDonald, right, who rushed along the platform with her husband, Gene Raymond.

JACK WALLY

JACK WALLY

Ventriloquist Edgar Bergen stepped from the train in 1937, left, a trip he made to Kansas City with precious cargo — dummies Charlie Mc-Carthy and Mortimer Snerd, who were photographed at Municipal Auditorium.

Notre Dame football coach Knute Rockne (center) arrived at Union Station in March 1931, then climbed aboard the airplane that crashed in the Kansas countryside, killing him.

PROGRESS

"THE LAUREL WREATH FOR TRANSPORTATION PROGRESS
MUST GO TO THE UNION PACIFIC RAILROAD"
—George Creel in Collier's, August 5, 1933

UNION
PACIFIC

and transportation. In that case, Harriman retorted, their company had better do something to get people back on trains. In fact, that "something" was already being studied: slick, shiny streamliners, powered by diesel-electric engines.

Streamlining adopted the design principles of absorption, the merging of one form into another with transitional curves, plus reductionism, the elimination of extraneous details. Diesel-electric power permitted this design innovation because its parts were more compact and efficient than steam at turning heat into mechanical energy. A wind-tunnel test at Westinghouse Laboratories in 1931 concluded that streamlining could ease a train's power output by one-third at 75 mph. Two years later, Martin Stevers' book, *Steel Rails: The Epic of the Railroads,* speculated: "In the matter of speed, the prospects for matching the airplane are by no means so hopeless as they appear. In fact, the railroads could have gone far toward accomplishing this long ago, had they not clung so conservatively to their nineteenth-century equipment. Just one thing

Union Pacific was proud of its streamliners, beginning with the M10000, as the latest advance in ground transportation history.

was needed — streamlining their trains — for surprising though it may seem, air resistance is what limits present-day train speeds."

Averell Harriman soon realized this himself. He later related in a speech to the American Association of Advertising Agencies: "It seemed to us that speed and lower costs, leading to lower rates, in combination were the two ways to recapture the public imagination and, incidentally, our lost passenger business. But this meant going to a new form of power with lighter equipment. So the streamline train, diesel driven, with cars designed of lighter metals, was developed by our engineers." Union Pacific's own wind-tunnel tests resulted in wheel units being shrouded, gaps between cars being covered, doors and windows being pressed flat against car bodies, and those bodies being lowered closer to the ground.

The company's revolutionary M10000 was delivered in February 1934. It could reach higher speeds, such as 80 and 90 mph, with less power — and less noise and jostling than steam. As the train's nationwide tour approached Kansas City, Union Pacific sent dozens of invitations for civic leaders to meet the new train in Lawrence, Kan., and ride it into Union Station. On that ride, the lightweight train hugged the rails like a car hugging the road, a mere nine inches above them, and the reduction in noise made it seem as if travelers were touring in a car with the windows closed instead of open. One of the riders, a reporter for *The Star*, wrote: "The quiet within the cars at high speed is noticeable, particularly to one who just has left an older type of train to board the new one.…High speed in the new train does not seem so noticeable as in the old, probably because the new creation makes much less fuss in accomplishing the result."

Meanwhile, the Burlington was introducing its own streamliner, and to draw some publicity away from the M10000, the company proposed making a world-record jaunt. Its train would make a dawn-to-dusk trip from Denver to Chicago, with an arrival at that city's Century of Progress World's Fair. This seemed unfathomable in the age of steam. Regular Denver-Chicago service took 26 hours. Never before had a train gone 1,000 miles so fast without stopping. The previous long-distance record was 56 mph set over just 401 miles between London and Edinburgh in Great Britain. Newspapers and radio built up intense interest in the American feat. "Probably no comparable performance in modern times has had more advance publicity and at the same time less experience on which to predicate a successful outcome," Richard C. Overton wrote before the space age in his *Burlington Route: A History of the Burlington Lines*.

The train attempting this was called the Zephyr, after a god of the west wind who signified renaissance. The name was inspired by Burlington President Ralph Budd's rereading of Geoffrey Chaucer's *The Canterbury Tales* from the Middle Ages. Its prologue was about a spring pilgrimage to Canterbury. The middle passage went like this, translated into modern English:

When April with his showers sweet with fruit

The drought of March has pierced unto the root
And bathed each vein with liquor that has power
To generate therein and sire the flower;
When Zephyr also has, with his sweet breath,
Quickened again, in every holt and heath,
The tender shoots and buds...

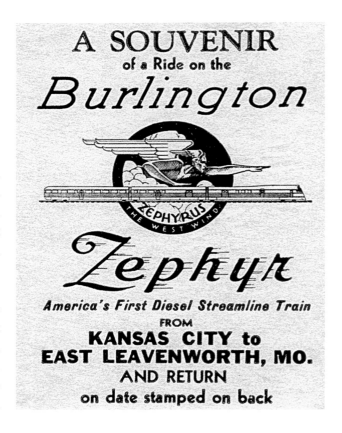

The Zephyr, like the M10000, was a three-car unit with a rounded front resembling a medieval armored helmet visor and a tapered rear. Compared with the ornate, Victorian-like Pullman cars of the day, the Zephyr's interior was simple and unadorned. It was decorated in pale green and cool blue and had no overhead baggage racks to disrupt the cabin's uniform appearance.

The train set off from Denver on May 26, 1934, at 6:04 a.m. Chicago time with 84 passengers, including a little Rocky Mountain donkey given to the Zephyr crew as a mascot. Within the first hour, disaster struck. There was an explosion in the power car. A door had slammed on a temporary cable from the power section, stripping the wires and causing a short-circuit. The engineer instinctively shut off the engine, but the short-circuit had burned out the starting mechanism. The train couldn't be restarted.

If the world-record attempt ended here, it would be a public-relations embarrassment for the new technology.

Fortunately, though, the train had just crested a hill at 80 mph and had 42 miles to coast downhill. This provided a little time to attempt repairs. But only a little.

The crew searched frantically for some replacement wire. None was found. The air-pressure reserve was falling almost to the point where the brakes set automatically. Finally, one newsman aboard found a piece of cable. One end was spliced to the broken cable. Then a General Motors diesel-engine specialist along for the ride jammed the remaining cable ends together.

A brilliant spark shot up, burning the man's hands. But the engine roared to life.

The trip continued, with the train racing around curves to make up for lost time, toppling over the crate containing the mascot donkey. All along the route north of Kansas City, "it seemed like the entire population was lined up at every town, city and village to cheer us along," J.S. Ford, an assistant mechanic on the Zephyr, told the press later. "Even the farmers in the fields got a big kick out of it." Just past 7 p.m., the Zephyr broke the finish-line tape in Chicago after a 13-hour trip. Its long-distance, nonstop speed of 77.6 mph broke the world's record by more than 20 mph.

Before 1934 was done, Burlington's Zephyr and Union Pacific's M10000 toured hundreds of cities and attracted nearly 15 million curiosity seekers — more than the number of people who attended major-league baseball games that summer.

Zephyr tickets showed the railroad artist's conception of the winged god, Zephyrus. Silver matchbooks issued by the railroad evoked the look of stainless steel skin on the shovel-nosed trains.

In 1939 the Rock Island advertised stewardess-nurses on its Rocket streamliner between Kansas City and Dallas-Fort Worth. Of them, it said: "Being a graduate nurse and registered in her profession, she naturally can think correctly and act quickly."

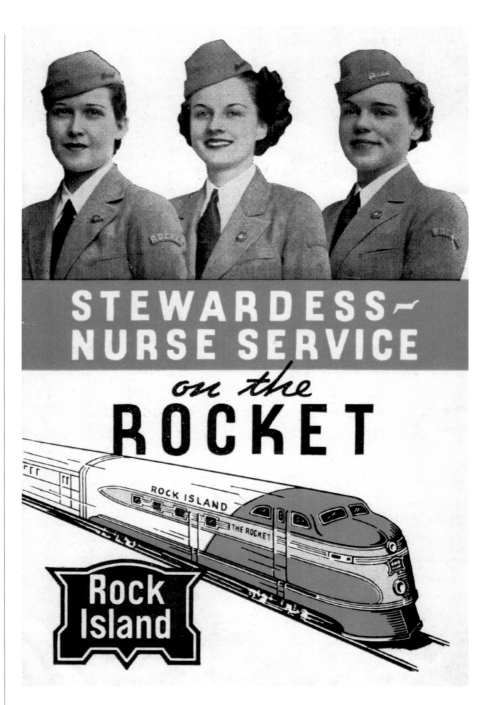

When it came to deciding where the first two streamliners should operate, both the Burlington and the Union Pacific set nearly identical criteria. First, the train had to make a round trip everyday, because it had only one maintenance crew, and that crew could be stationed only at one place. Also, the route could not be too popular, because the train had no standard couplers, so it couldn't add extra cars. In the Zephyr's case, the Burlington added one more dictum: The new train should replace an existing train that was losing money. The Burlington chose the 195-mile run between Kansas City and Omaha, Neb., with an additional 55 miles added to Lincoln. "The route traverses one of the finest local territories in the United States," Burlington President Budd

Colorful and ubiquitous matchbooks advertised the railroads, trains and routes of the Missouri Pacific, above, the M-K-T, below, and the Frisco, bottom.

wrote in *The Traffic World* magazine, "but, sad to relate, the people there have ceased to ride on railroad trains to any great extent. With the idea of tempting them back to the rails, this latest innovation is offered for their approval."

The Zephyr officially went into regular service Nov. 11, 1934. As the train left Lincoln, some automobile drivers tried to race it on adjoining roads, but the streamliner quickly pulled away on the way to 80 mph. In Kansas City the Zephyr stopped in the station yard next to its predecessor, old engine No. 35, the Pride of the Prairie. The 20th century machine towered over its 19th century vestige like a son who eventually outgrows his father. In its first year on that Lincoln-Kansas City run, the Zephyr drew 50 percent more passengers than the two steam locomotives it replaced, and it cost about half as much to operate per mile partly because it weighed three-quarters as much.

Two months after the Zephyr began operating through Union Station, Union Pacific's M10000 made its home there. It was rechristened the City of Salina for its 187-mile trip between Kansas City and Salina, Kan., with cities like Topeka in between. Soon, a fascinated Charles Yancey and his cousin Bill Gilliat just had to ride it. The trouble was, they were merely teen-agers who had never ridden a train without their parents. Gilliat lived in Kansas City, and Yancey's family visited every June after school was out. The two cousins were inseparable during those visits, roaming the city, seeing ball games and sitting by the signal tower just west of Union Station, not far from the Gilliat home at 36th and Summit streets. On one visit the two boys scrounged up a couple of dollars and headed out one morning for the train station. They were leaving home, just for the day. They bought two round-trip tickets on the City of Salina just to Topeka. In Kansas City's June heat the train's air conditioning felt like a cool dip in a swimming pool. The coach had a nice, fresh aroma, too, not unlike today's new-car smell. When the train headed west, it felt as if they were gliding. There was no chug-chug of a steam engine, no blast of the steam whistle and no whoosh of hot air from an open window. To two young boys on an adventure, it was like a Buck Rogers fantasy, only in real life.

One by one, most of the other railroads operating out of Union Station tried to catch up with the Union Pacific and the Burlington, spawning a new speed war. The Rock Island entered the streamline diesel age with its Rockets, the Milwaukee added its Hiawatha line, and the Missouri Pacific introduced its bold, blue Eagles, all while the Burlington kept rolling out a few more Zephyrs. By 1940 at least a dozen streamliners passed through Kansas City. Union Station, in the Heart of America, became the hub of the streamliner. The Wabash later named a new train after this capital of the streamliner, the City of Kansas City. The Kansas City-St. Louis corridor became a particular hotbed. The running time between those two cities was 7 hours in 1935. Two years later it was down to 5 1/2 hours. As soon as one line announced a faster time, others quickly matched it.

All of them offered reclining chairs, circulated air, wide windows and what one newspaper writer of the era termed a "more cheerful atmosphere." Another writer explained: "No longer does the passenger ride in uncomfortable

"Meeting of the Chiefs" — an illustration for one of the Santa Fe's famed calendars — associated the native tribes and landscape of the American Southwest with the railroad's Chief and Super Chief streamliners.

chair cars and wearily try to put up the window to obtain a breath of cool air, only to be pelted with cinders and dust and smoke. He rides in air-conditioned cars, the windows of which are sealed shut, while relaxing in upholstered seats that can be moved to one's liking."

No train through Union Station was as luxurious as the Santa Fe's Super Chief. It was one of a handful of trains charging an extra fare just for its speed and comfort. It featured only Pullman sleepers with wood paneling from the Ivory Coast. Because the train's western route ran through Indian territory, the decor applied Indian names, colors and motifs. The observation car was named the Navajo and had a turquoise ceiling, goatskin lampshades, sand paintings under glass and zig-zagging patterns on the upholstery. In the book *Luxury Trains of the World*, train historian Geoffrey Freeman Allen asserted that the Super Chief "had only to contend with New York Central's Twentieth

Century Limited for the title of America's most prestigious."

The Kansas City Southern attempted to enter this top-of-the-line niche with its Southern Belle between Kansas City and New Orleans. The train consisted of a diesel locomotive, a mail-baggage car, a chair car with separate seats for white and "colored" passengers, a Pullman sleeper with private bedrooms instead of open berths, and an observation-parlor-dining car with a couch. Kansas City Southern spent almost $70,000 on each new coach. All the cars were painted a deep green on the outside, with continuous red and yellow stripes across the sides, "giving an impression of speed and power," wrote a 1940 review in *Railway Age* magazine. "Southern Belle" was chosen as the name over such alternatives as "Aluminum Arrow" and "Casino" (which phonetically expressed the initials KC for Kansas City and NO for New Orleans) because, as one company committee reported, the name Belle "injects the possibility of feminine charm into the plans — and beauty has sold more mattresses, gasoline, automobiles and other commodities than any other one element."

That Christmas season, Don Campbell took his first ride on the Belle. He

YOU ARE INVITED
to attend a Private Preview of the
Southern Belle
"SWEETHEART OF AMERICAN TRAINS"

STREAMLINED - ALUMINUM - DIESEL POWERED
The "last word" in Comfort, Safety and Speed
Built by
PULLMAN-STANDARD CAR MANUFACTURING COMPANY
★
KANSAS CITY - TWENTIETH & McGEE
Ten A. M. to Eight P. M.
THURSDAY, AUGUST 22, 1940
Public Showing - Union Station
Monday, September 2

KANSAS CITY SOUTHERN - LOUISIANA & ARKANSAS LINES

Kansas City Southern's first diesel streamliner, above, parked at Union Station in 1939. It was the leading unit of the railroad's Flying Crow. The next year, the railroad introduced its top streamliner, the Southern Belle, as the "Sweetheart of American Trains."

was a railroad man, just like his father before him. Campbell was spending the fall digging ditches for cables and mixing concrete foundations, all for adding signals along the Southern's lines. So when the 22-year-old boarded the Belle for a ride from Louisiana to his native Neosho, Mo., after a full week of digging, he was tired. For a while he sat in the observation car, with its unbroken series of windows. It made the rolling, Ozarks landscape unfurl in a panorama. Kansas City Southern advertised its route as "straight as the crow flies," but in reality the line curved much of the way through the hills. One of the Belle's hostesses came through, asking travelers for their names so they could be broadcast over the train's radio later.

Later, Campbell found a seat in coach. The headrest was covered by a white cotton cloth with a belle in formal dress embroidered on it. It had been hard for him to sleep on steam trains. Too much noise, too much motion, too little comfort. But the Belle had shock absorbers and stabilizers instead of a spring plank, so it moved without jerky bumps or side-to-side lurches. It also had sound-deadening materials on body side bearings and plates. And his seat had softer upholstering than he was used to. Now Campbell reclined and stretched out. He closed his eyes. In a matter of minutes, he was asleep.

'...of travel and faraway places'

There was enough going on at the station all the time to keep train watchers busy.

One place from which to watch was Hospital Hill. As a boy visiting his grandfather's drugstore nearby, Walter Cronkite sat there enthralled by the action in the station yard. He later remembered in his autobiography: "You could lie up on that hill in the daytime and watch the trains, 10 or so at a time, being shunted through the yards, and the sleek expresses puffing into the bays of the passenger terminal. At night the fireboxes of their steam engines and the bright headlights patterned the tracks." In an interview, he recalled something else: the scent. "It smelled like burning coal. It had a heavy redolence of railroad yards. It wasn't unpleasant. It spoke of travel and faraway places."

Other favorite viewing spots were on the Broadway and the Grand viaducts, with views of the station's 16 tracks. There were other places, of course. One was the office of the Ready-Mixed Concrete Co., the business Tom Pendergast ran. After the political boss got out of prison in 1940, he remained on probation. It was virtual exile. He was not permitted to visit his old headquarters. His wife had left him, so he lived alone in his Ward Parkway mansion. And he carried a tube in his side from poor health. He didn't have many places to go or much to do to lessen his loneliness and pass into his 70s. But the Ready-Mixed building at 25th and Summit streets bordered the west-end station track approaches.

Many an afternoon, the one-time most-powerful man in Kansas City sat in his office, hearing the whistles of steam locomotives, sniffing the coal fumes and watching the trains pull in and out, carrying soldiers to a new world war.

CHAPTER 7

WARTIME

The way World War II greeted Union Station wasn't captured in photographs or on film. No newspaper or radio reporters were on the scene. So the moment, because of the emotion attached to Dec. 7, 1941, lent itself to melodrama, even fiction. That's how this fable arose:

Union Station was tranquil that Sunday afternoon. It was still hours before the transcontinentals passed through. Only a few hundred passengers lounged in the main waiting room or the men's smoking room, biding time before their departures. Occasionally the next train was called out. Some travelers kept reading or smoking, ignoring the announcements drifting through the wide halls, while others cocked their heads, anticipating their train, hoping it wasn't running behind like everything else.

As the story goes, the station's loudspeaker crackled close to 2 p.m. "Attention please, attention please," it began, an overture whose grave tone immediately set it apart from its predecessors. "The United States government has just announced..." That morning Japanese bombers had attacked the U.S. naval base at Pearl Harbor, Hawaii. The war going on in Europe and Asia was now dragging in the United States.

The voice stopped, but the station remained almost frozen. Some travelers stared at nothing, still numb at the gravity of the situation. Others exchanged whispers, trying to absorb what they had just heard. A few began weeping, knowing that loved ones would be going off to fight and possibly die. In this somber stillness, an African-American woman stood up from one of the waiting-room benches. She was young, with flowing black hair and wearing a long print dress. She started singing, "God Bless America, land that I love...." Her voice blazed through the room, echoing off the walls, slicing around corners and into the men's smoking room, the baggage counter, the ticket booth. Travelers turned their heads toward the singer. Those outside the waiting room headed under the clock to see who she was and to join the swelling of American pride.

It was a magical moment at a dire point in the nation's history, and it was

Throughout World War II, Union Station was the scene of emotional moments as members of the armed services left for war and returned. On Oct. 3, 1944, Staff Sgt. Lynn S. Chinn returned from a German prison camp in Romania, where he was sent after his B-24 Liberator bomber was shot down. Years later, his wife, Midge Proctor Chinn, recalled the day he came home...

"I received two dozen beautiful red roses and a telegram saying Lynn would be arriving at the station at 9:15 p.m. The family was there, and at 9:20 p.m. he was there. I was very excited....All those who had been praying and sending notes of encouragement were calling and writing us and we were happier than ever you can imagine."

The Chinns, who retired to Bella Vista, Ark., kept a photo of their reunion at the station, facing page.

a story that soon became part of Union Station lore. Lottie West, the Travelers Aid Society attendant known for her fanciful imagination, recounted this tale for years and identified the woman as Marian Anderson, the celebrated contralto. Decades later, station buffs repeated the tale with Pearl Bailey as the singer.

Yet neither woman mentioned the event in her autobiography, and local newspaper interviews with the singers when they came through town on concert tours never mentioned it, either. Besides, the station's loudspeakers weren't even installed until 1944.

Then there's the recollection of Jack Deveney. The 19-year-old railroad worker had been at the Midland theater that afternoon when the "B" movie suddenly stopped, the lights came on and the manager announced the Pearl Harbor bombing. Deveney quickly headed to Union Station to catch a train back to Neosho, Mo., where he worked. He found the station hushed, a few people whispering and most everyone looking shell-shocked. Deveney's train didn't leave for hours, so he walked around the station and ended up talking to a few clerks and other travelers. No one said anything to him about a woman singing "God Bless America."

Nevertheless, the tale, fanciful or not, embodied the melodrama and the melancholy that engulfed Union Station during wartime.

The war years

With the start of World War II, Kansas City's station experienced a huge upswing in travel. With gasoline and rubber-tire rationing, trains were the only long-distance travel option. The number of trains passing through the station annually jumped from 59,474 in 1940 to 72,302 by war's end. The number of tickets sold skyrocketed from 365,780 to 1,168,995. This happened despite posters everywhere asking, "Is this trip really necessary?" and a national Office of Defense Transportation edict that passenger trains filled less than 40 percent would be discontinued.

All the traffic created hurried, bustling scenes at Union Station every day. New stationmaster Charles Clancy looked down from his mezzanine office overlooking the waiting room and hardly saw a speck of marble flooring, so thick were the travelers. Any seat vacated by someone leaving was quickly filled by someone else standing around. Often the waiting room and the Grand Hall resembled an army camp more than a railroad station. Bands of servicemen dressed in khaki or white uniforms milled about. Sometimes a sergeant led a group of recruits to a train gate, and the waiting civilians applauded as they passed. At night the soldiers stretched out anywhere on the floor or on the wooden waiting-room benches, their heads on top of their duffel bags.

When it came time to board trains, military personnel always received

WISHING YOU THE BEST OF EVERYTHING THIS HOLIDAY SEASON AND THROUGHOUT A VICTORIOUS NEW YEAR

1943

SIEGRIST ENGRAVING COMPANY

KANSAS CITY, MO.

A wartime Christmas card from Siegrist Engraving Co. depicted servicemen and their loved ones coming and going.

M. Brenton

War-time travel - Kansas City - 1942

Stationmaster Charles Clancy at the war
bond booth in Union Station, 1943.

first preference, along with their spouses, and then everyone else, until the
coaches were filled to standing-room capacity. This spawned a temporary
mating ritual known as the "marriage factory." In the crowd at the gates, a soldier and a woman traveling alone locked eyes. The soldier knew the woman's
predicament: little chance of getting on board. Without a word spoken, he mo-
tioned to the woman and let her walk through the military police checkpoint
with him. Of course, the soldier then flirted with her on the train. But eventually they went their separate ways.

Back in the station, stranded or wayward travelers stood in line at the
Travelers Aid Society desk by the Grand Hall's east entrance doors. Every day,
the desk handled nearly 1,000 requests, mostly for directions. But sometimes

These uniformed men posed at the servicemen's information booth outside the baggage room.

soldiers had no place to stay, or runaway youths ran out of money. One time, 10 shipyard workers going from the Gulf of Mexico to the Pacific got off at Union Station, broke. They asked Travelers Aid for money for food the rest of the way. Right away it was determined that all their money had gone for booze. So Travelers Aid provided them one meal and then wired the shipyard telling what happened. A shipyard official wrote back, thanked Travelers Aid, paid for the meals and explained that responsible men were scarce.

Across the lobby at the Harvey restaurant, a line stretched out the doors, bags stood stacked up at the entrance and waitresses scurried around with hardly any rest. One morning, a woman lingered around the doors, not in line. Inside the restaurant, a man and his son were served waffles, and the man got up to take off his overcoat and hang it on the coatrack. Suddenly the woman dashed over to the man's table, took his seat and proceeded to shove bits of the waffle into her mouth. The man came back and politely told her she was eating his dinner, but she didn't even look up, except to take a drink of his coffee. Then his waitress came over and told the woman to leave. The interloper finally looked up, mumbled that she was hungry and had to make a train, and turned back to finish the waffle. The waitress wrote out a bill and handed it to the woman, who got up, smiled and paid it. The man, meanwhile, got a new waffle.

Elsewhere in the station, the scenes were more somber and poignant: parents giving good-bye hugs; little girls crying and tugging at an older brother going off to war; sweethearts huddling together, afraid to part. These were the wartime spectacles etched indelibly into the minds of a few Kansas Citians.

Bill Lawrence

After the war started, I was 21 and I talked to some of my friends who had joined the Army earlier on, and some of them had joined the Navy. A good buddy of mine came home; he had been in the Navy about a year. He told me he liked the Navy, and the ocean sounded intriguing to me, to see all the ports. I went downtown and enlisted. They examined me, I took my shots, and I was all ready to go. It was just after the Fourth of July. Both my mother and father came from large families with many relatives. On my departure date, the whole clan gathered at the base of the Liberty Memorial. There were maybe 15 or 20 of us; then we went inside Union Station.

My train was supposed to leave at 6 o'clock, and we got over there about 4 o'clock. There was a big crowd, people milling around, carrying suitcases. They'd drop their suitcases, or drop something, and the noise would magnify. There'd be phones ringing in the ticket booths, and the guys would be hollering, and all this would come together, muffled. And there was a smell of soot or smoke from all those engines. Just imagine, trains coming and going, steam engines, and whenever they got started all that smoke came up, but it was pretty well diffused.

I remember the Navy recruiting guy was there at the gate with his clipboard, and all of us men gathered together. There must have been a hundred men from all over — Kansas City, the small towns, a lot of farm boys. We were all waiting to get on the train to leave at the same time to go to Chicago, then the Great Lakes (Naval Training Center). My family, they were all concerned, and I was just sort of in a quandary myself because I knew I was leaving, and I knew it was going to be a different life, didn't know what was going to be ahead. And, of course, they were getting kind of mushy, and that kind of bothered me because I felt the same way, but I didn't want to express myself in front of all those other people. They all gave me

Lawrence and some of his relatives at the Liberty Memorial in 1942, just before his departure from the station.

> "... I was looking out, and I thought, 'Well, it's a new world. I'm on an adventure.' "
>
> — *Bill Lawrence*

hugs and goodbyes, like a million other mothers and fathers with their son going off to war.

Like I said, there were about a hundred men, and we were all looking at each other. We didn't know each other, and we were all in the same boat. At the same time, I felt alone. I felt I was all by myself, and I know all the rest of these fellas felt the same way, too. Some of them were joking around, but they were joking because they didn't know what else to say. Then they pushed us on the train.

I remember the sun as we pulled out of the yards here as we headed east toward Chicago. The sun was getting real low, so it must have been close to 8 o'clock for that time of year, and it was shining across the landscape and I was looking out, and I thought: "Well, it's a

new world. I'm on an adventure." It was exciting — and scary, the unknown, what's going to happen? I had already had some buddies killed over there — Jack Murphy and a high school friend, Ed Reddig. They had already been killed right after the war had started. So you kind of think of those things. Will I get through? What's the future going to be? How long's it going to be? That was one of the things during the war: How long's it going to last? How much longer?

Lawrence spent time on ship convoys in the Atlantic, and his ship was credited with sinking one German submarine. Then he served on a destroyer as a fire controlman, adjusting the guns to hit different targets, in the Pacific. After the war he co-owned a grocery in the Argentine district of Kansas City, Kan., un-

Lawrence in 1999.

*til his store was bought out for an ur-
ban renewal project, and then he was a*

*passport officer for the U.S. Postal Ser-
vice. He retired in Lenexa.*

Sally Martin Rice

I lived five miles outside of Lowry City, Missouri, about 100 miles from Kansas City. It was during the Depression, and we had a hundred-acre farm. My oldest brother from (my father's) first marriage...lived in Deepwater, which was nine miles away. So when this brother came to visit, it was like, "Boy, somebody really special is coming." There was just enough years between us that I'm sure he looked down on me, but I was just enthralled with him.

I was the baby of the family, really spoiled, a real daddy's girl. My father got killed in March 1941. I was 8 years old at the time. He had been out in the fields all day. He had just bought a new Ford pickup, and in those days tires weren't like they are now. A tire blew out on the way home, and he got thrown from the truck, and his head hit a bridge abutment. It was really emotionally draining, and I felt kind of lost.

My oldest brother was already in the Army. In those days that was a way of making an income. When my father got killed, the Army sent my brother home by rail. All I remember is he appeared, and he was wearing this wool Army uniform. We had to take him back to catch the train. We had to take him to Union Station. It was real exciting to me. A mile away from where we lived was a little post office with a little store in it. That's where you got your everyday stuff. For Christmas shopping, you went to Clinton, which was a big town. But to go to Kansas City to take our brother to Union Station, that was really a big deal.

I was just enthralled with the lights and the station and all the people coming and going. I just couldn't imagine people really lived like that, the gorgeous ceiling and the clock and the guy calling out which train, and just seeing all those people. It was a big deal, so all of us were there. My brother was scheduled to get out in December, but there were rumors of war. We were depending on him now, and I felt like I was losing him forever. I can remember the females of the family standing around. He picked me up, and it seemed like I was hanging onto him. I could feel his scratchy wool uniform as he hugged me, and I can still feel those big Army brass buttons that were pressing up against me. I was boo-hooing and carrying on to high heaven. It was like your whole support system was leaving. I was this 8-year-old daddy's girl clinging to her handsome older brother going off to who knows where and terrified he'd never come back.

Somehow amid all those tears and fears, I looked over my brother's shoulder and the Union Station was a beacon and an anchor in this changing, bewildering world.

Rice's oldest brother, Arleigh Martin, was scheduled to be released from the Army on December 8, 1941, but with the Japanese attack the day before, all discharges were canceled. Martin stayed in

"Union Station was a beacon and an anchor in this changing, bewildering world."

— *Sally Martin Rice*

the service four more years, going overseas, participating in the Battle of the Bulge and surviving the war. Afterward, Martin became a Baptist preacher, presiding over a string of country churches around Missouri. He died in 1991. Sally, meanwhile, graduated from high school in May of 1949, went to Kansas City to find work and that September married Sam Rice, who managed drive-in restau-

Sally Martin and her brother Arleigh after the war. Below: Sally Martin Rice in 1999.

rants. The Rices raised five daughters and for years operated Sam and Sally's Fish & Chips in Kansas City.

Inside the waiting room, 1999: "…we were sitting in the Union Station…and I just decided I wanted to marry her."

David Pence

It was January 1943, and I was in the Union Station along with 15-20 other enlistees, waiting for a train to take us to the Great Lakes Naval Training Center up through Chicago. I was a farm boy from Kearney, Missouri. A good friend of mine, David Carey, who had graduated with me the previous spring from Kearney High School, and I joined the United States Navy for what we thought was our patriotic duty. Being 18 years old, you know. I wanted in. I wanted in bad. Everyone else was going. I wanted to do my part. We knew when we were leaving, and I had invited my girlfriend, who lived in Kansas City at the time and who also had been a classmate, Joellen Evans. She came down to see us off.

We had been dating, oh, probably the last part of our senior year. At this particular moment we were sitting in the Union Station, on one of those benches at the far end of the waiting room. We were sitting there talking, sitting pretty close together, holding hands. I guess I had the thought of leaving and all of that. I had never been away from home, to speak of, at all.

I had been going with her steady for at least six months or maybe a little more, maybe about a year. And she was a very beautiful blonde. I was in love with her, really deeply in love with her, and that all had an effect on me, I guess, and I just decided I wanted to marry her. I don't know as I gave it a lot of thought before I got there, but something of the moment just did it. So I asked her. I was probably a little nervous, mumbling a bit. It's not something you do everyday. But I know she smiled and said yes, and we kissed.

That old Union Station wasn't real

David and Joellen Pence.

warm and friendly. It was enormous and looked something like a barn. But it was romantic that night, at least to me.

Pence's stay in the Navy was short, nine days to be exact, because of bad vision in one eye. But 90 days later he got drafted by the Army. That July, while he was stationed at Fort Leavenworth, he and Evans eloped and got married on a judge's porch in Kansas City, Kan., without telling her mother. In 1944, Pence was sent overseas and served as a clerk in an Army hospital in Europe. After the war he became a city manager for several towns in Missouri and Oklahoma. He and Joellen had two sons and were married 43 years until her death in 1986. Pence retired in 1990 and returned to Kearney, where he was elected mayor.

HONEYMOONERS

He had a 25-day leave while his battleship, the USS North Carolina, was being repaired, so Seaman First Class Raymond L. Bauer returned home to Iola, Kan., aiming to marry his sweetheart. It was August 1944; he was 22 and Nellie F. Moss 18. Both were from farming backgrounds. As Moss left work, Bauer surprised her with a marriage proposal. Soon they were wed, rode the Santa Fe to Kansas City for their honeymoon, and took these pictures of each other outside Union Station. Later, Bauer reboarded his battleship in the Seattle area, and in September 1944 it sailed back to the South Pacific. He served on it as allied forces advanced through the islands to Tokyo Bay. After the Japanese surrender, he returned home in October 1945. The Bauers eventually retired and lived in Overland Park.

Changing times

As the comings and goings of war surged through Union Station, the building's appearance remained remarkably detached from the ongoing crisis. It wasn't exactly dressed up for war. The grave-looking, gray-bearded, top-hatted Uncle Sam poster was hardly seen in the Grand Hall. It wasn't like downtown, where Sam pointed his finger out of nearly every shop window, wanting you. It wasn't like Washington's station either, where a larger-than-life banner booming, "Americans will always fight for liberty," hung down from the vaulted ceiling. And it certainly wasn't like auto plants and shipyards that were adapted for war production, although station shipping crews did handle airplane motors and 2,000-pound bombs.

About the only alteration in Union Station's look was the addition of a couple of extra booths, one of which was topped with a sign reading, "Buy War Bonds." The only patriotic trimmings were a few American flags, one at each end of the semicircular ticket counter and another pair hanging from window ledges under the big clock. This was nothing like the last war. In World War I, a display booth and two display windows by the Harvey restaurant contained Liberty bond posters two stories tall. One, for instance, depicted a massive sailing vessel beside the message, "No Port But Victory." Also, little flags with the crests of Allied nations hung over balcony railings.

The Second World War couldn't help being different, however. There was just more of it — more years, more trains and more headaches for Union Station's management. The headaches mostly had to do with manpower, espe-

Cater-cornered from Union Station lay Signboard Hill, at the foot of which stood restaurants, a hotel and in World War II the Service Men's Club. In this wartime photo, two members of the armed services are standing on the raised median.

cially the lack of it.

Redcaps, for instance, seemed nonexistent. Travelers and soldiers usually lugged their own bags up the stairs from the train platforms, and *The Star* reported "instances" of people collapsing at the top of the stairs. The uproar reached City Hall, where politicians reminded the Terminal Railway of a clause in its 1909 franchise agreement with the city to provide "adequate facilities." In this case that meant adding escalators. The company promised to do so at war's end.

Down in the station's basement, the problem was just as acute. There weren't enough hired hands to unload and sort the mail, which was Union Station's largest cargo business. Mail handling occupied a long, continuous room in the farthest depths of the Express Building. The room was dominated by a conveyor of tubs, each tub as big as a truck, running between the unloading and sorting operations and a post office built in the early 1930s across Pershing Road. Working down there was a thankless, physical job, up and down the elevators under the tracks, lifting and throwing 100-pound sacks on and off trains, all under rigid discipline in which eating, washing up and changing work clothes weren't allowed on company time. In a typical week, mail clerks sorted 2 million cubic feet of catalogs and letters, enough to fill the interior of the 10-story Business Men's Assurance Co. building across the street. During the Christmas season it was worse, with unsorted mail and boxes piling up in 10-foot stacks on the basement floor. Christmas Day in 1943 was particularly bad. Seven dozen boxcars stuffed with holiday greetings sat on sidings around the station grounds, still waiting to be unloaded. Three dozen more cars had

been emptied, but the mail had not been sorted for delivery yet.

As elsewhere on the nation's home front, women stepped into this void, taking over what had been men-only jobs. At Union Station, women wearing pants and low-heeled shoes sorted mail, drove baggage tractors, even loaded or unloaded boxcars of express packages, enduring aching muscles in the process. Upstairs in the Grand Hall, women also were put behind ticket counters for the first time, and customers tried to take advantage of them. One male traveler vying for a sleeper berth at the Pullman reservation desk asked one of the female ticket takers, "I guess a pair of nylon stockings for you would end this Pullman shortage for me, wouldn't it?" To which she replied, "It would only make your famine permanent."

It all finally came to an end in 1945. First, Germany surrendered. When that announcement came over Union Station's loudspeakers, soldiers threw their hats into the air as if it were New Year's Eve and whooped and yelled. But that was only a prelude. A few months later, when Japan signed a peace accord and President Truman proclaimed the war over, the city popped its cork. Downtown, revelers tossed pillow feathers out hotel windows, while inside Union Station, they littered the floor with confetti and paper streamers. Others arrived with cowbells and pots and pans, and the racket drowned out train announcements. Women pranced around kissing men, and one lipstick-smeared GI beamed, "The war news was terrific, but this is out of this world." Smiles finally replaced tears at Union Station. Soon the station took on a new meaning from the war. It meant home.

On Aug. 15, 1945, after fighting with Japan ended , businesses took a holiday across the city — among them restaurants and groceries. Unprepared, Kansas Citians flocked to the few eating places that remained open; the largest crowd gathered at the Fred Harvey restaurant in Union Station. The line outside averaged 60 to 100 people through much of the day.

At the station where he was a military policeman half a century before, Walter Lewis held a picture of himself and his old key to the station gate, below.

Walter "Buck" Lewis

After high school in Carrollton, Missouri, a town about 70 miles east of Kansas City, I came to the city to live with my aunt and uncle. My aunt's sister's husband was with the railroad. He was with the Union Pacific railroad, and he got me a job with the mail and baggage department for the Terminal Railway at Union Station.

It was September 1942, and I was taken on as Christmas help, because it was a mess. Clear down in the basement, mail and parcels would come in by the (train) carload, and we probably had a pile of parcels there, I'd say, a block long, maybe 20 feet wide and 10 feet high. And we'd have a load, put it on one end, come up on the other end and take it out. They were that far behind. People sent everything. They even sent raw chickens. Nobody understood what the mail department was. We'd get cakes that would have just cellophane on them. Generally they

got through, because we all knew they were for some soldier, and we all took care to get it through. As I said, I was hired as Christmas help, but it was such a big volume that I went on past Christmas. It was all outside work, and in the extreme cold it got down to 17 below zero working out there. You had trunks and big baggage, and any remains that came through, you handled those too. You called them remains. You didn't say "that stiff" or "that body" or anything like that, and if anything happened, you didn't see it.

In April (1943), I was drafted into the Army. They sent me to Nevada, Missouri, for an MPEG company. That's "Military Police Escort Guard." We made trips overseas; then I was assigned to Kansas City. When I reported in, one of the first questions they asked me was, "Where did you work before you came into the service?" I said the Union Station, and they said, "Well, we know where you'll be; you'll be a sergeant at the Union Station." Our office was clear to the southwest corner of the main room (the Grand Hall), in a little vestibule. I had a desk right in there, and we had a closed-up elevator that was our lock-up room. Generally I had four men and myself. A lot of our job was getting troop movements through the station. The station was busy, people all the time, everywhere. I had my own key to the gates. We had that because if we were taking a bunch of soldiers down (to the trains), there was a great crowd by the gates. It was standing-room only, and, of course, soldiers got to go on first.

You had all kinds of people in the service, and you'd get some mean ones, you know. One time we had a lieutenant colonel down by the tracks, and he was very obstreperous, and I finally had to use some force and get him into the lock-up room, the elevator. I called the (outside military police), and they came in, really funny like, "Couldn't handle this fella, huh?" and I said, "Well, you all go in and get him." They went in, "Yes, sir, may we help you?" and he kicked one of them and hit the other one, and that was it for him.

Lewis in uniform.

He was just a drunk.

I was on duty on both V-E Day and V-J Day. V-E Day, there really wasn't much to it, because you still had the war in the Pacific. There really wasn't a lot of celebration. People were happy about it, but they didn't celebrate like they did on V-J Day. V-J Day, we, the soldiers, knew it was coming. If I remember right, it was in the evening when we finally heard the word, 5:30 or 6 o'clock, and I happened to be on duty, and within an hour it was people just solid in that station. Union Station had always been a meeting place when anything happened, like New Year's. It wasn't so much during the war, but it had been. And it filled up again, wall to wall, and it was wild. People just exploded, screaming, hollering, yelling. It was worse than a football game. There wasn't anything you could do except go along with it and keep people from killing themselves. We were the only ones in uniforms and dressed up, and of course all these gals would come up and

give you a big hug and a kiss, you know. Never was I kissed and hugged by so many strangers. They just let loose. They'd been tied up for years. Everyone was carrying a bottle of booze and wanted to give you a drink, though, of course, we couldn't have one. And that went on from 6 or 7 o'clock to after midnight, and it finally broke up. The next day there was a line at Fred Harvey's all day long, because everything in the city ceased. There were no grocery stores open; there was nothing. The city was at a standstill. A lot of people came down there to eat because there was nothing else. It was something.

Lewis stayed at his station post until April 1946, went to college on the GI bill, and then went back to Carrollton. He ran a shoe store and went on to work at a bank on the town square and to lead some of Carrollton's local service clubs, such as the Kiwanis. He married and had one daughter. Decades later, after that daughter had married and the station had closed, its doors were reopened briefly for a few open houses. Lewis' son-in-law had heard all his stories and wanted to see whether Lewis' MP key still opened the train gates. So they drove to the station and went in. The gates were roped off, and some of the locks had been changed. But Lewis reached past the rope toward one older-looking gate and fit the key in. Sure enough, it worked.

Edna Sutton

My husband and I both grew up around northwest Missouri, around Maryville. We started going together when I was probably 16, something like that. He was my first boyfriend, first major one. We got married in June of '41. I was 19, he was 21. When the war started, it was pretty rough. You never knew when you were going to be called. We didn't know what kind of plans to make or anything. I went ahead and taught school. He was drafted and left in December; that was 1942.

I tried to write almost every day. We tried to make plans for the future. One of the things we wanted was a home of our

Edna Sutton across from the station in 1999.

own. A lot of his letters I didn't get. In England they came through pretty well, but when he went to France, there was just no way you could get them. Lots of times they were censored and things would be crossed out on them. I know he got more of my letters than I got of his. After he left, I went back to school and got my degree, because I didn't know at that time whether he'd come back or not; you just didn't know. Overseas, my husband was in the ground crew of the air force. I knew he wasn't doing hand-to-hand like a lot of them were, but I knew he was in danger. But you didn't think too much about it. You just knew it was happening and everyone was in the same boat. It was a constant thing. You didn't know what was going on.

Edna and Donald Sutton: When he returned, "we hugged and kissed and hugged some more."

I finally got letters that they were supposed to get ready to leave. In May 1945 there were rumors that they'd be coming back and that went on all summer. Then he finally called me when he got to the States. He called me one night, kind of late, and said he'd be in the next evening

in Kansas City. I had the car, of course, but I'd never driven by myself down there. We'd been down there a number of times, but I thought, "Well, I knew where it was; I could surely find it." So I just got on ol' 71 (highway) and came right on down, found Main Street and went right down Main. My heart was racing. They had the arrivals posted up, so I'd go check by the doors they were coming in, or stand where I thought he could see me if he did come in. You didn't know which train he was going to come in on. How slowly the time passed. I tried to sit down, but the benches were so hard. So I'd get up and move around a little bit. I must have looked at the clock a thousand times to see what time it was. It was very, very,

very slow.

Of course, half the family wanted to come with me, and I didn't want them to. We hadn't seen each other for a long time, and I wanted that to be a special time. I was afraid to wander very far away from the arriving doors. If he came in, he wouldn't know I was there. And I was too excited to eat. Finally, it was about 11:15; he had just gotten through the doors when I saw him. There were a lot of people between us, and I just worked my way over there. I don't think he saw me at first. We hugged and kissed and hugged some more. It was just such a relief that he was there.

After their reunion, Sutton's husband, Donald, went to work in St. Joseph driving a gasoline truck, and then worked for a few auto garages, including one in the Waldo section of Kansas City. Later the Suttons had a carrier route for The Kansas City Star and Times for 23 years. Donald did the delivering, and Edna did the bookkeeping. They raised two boys and a girl in Kansas City. Donald died in 1998.

Isak Federman

I was born in a small, little town in Poland. Half of the population probably was Jewish. I was away from home going to school, and I came home just a couple of weeks before the war broke out, when the Germans invaded Poland in September 1939. I was 17 at the time. We lived very close to the German border, so three days later the Army moved into my little town, occupying it. Around December sometime, I went to a grocery store to pick up some sugar and some groceries for my mother, and I was stopped by six SS people. I got kicked all over, and they told me to get on this truck. And I haven't seen my family since. I wound up in roughly 17 different concentration camps. I was transferred from one place to another, building barracks and building roads and fixing the railroad tracks as the Germans headed east.

I had a couple, three breaks in my 5 1/2 years. On the way back west from the east, we stopped at Plaszow, which is where "Schindler's List" was made. I was there for three to four months, not too long. But when we got transferred from one place to another, we already were kind of pros. The first thing in a camp when you come in, they take you through the dogs and the beatings and all that, and finally you wind up in a barrack. And when you get in that barrack, you go find out where you're at and what's going on. So you kind of go around the block at the camp, and you kind of look around and see where's the closest kitchen and the closest place where you could get killed

With friends in Poland after the German invasion in 1939. Federman (right) recalls playing cards to beat the boredom of curfews.

and so forth. I ran into a kid from my hometown, and he saw me walking between these barracks, and he said: "Let me give you a tip over here. Don't walk between the barracks by yourself."

I said, "Why not?"

He said: "There's a guy out there, the commander, Goethe, who has a habit of taking shooting practice, and he has just the biggest time when he sees a single prisoner walking. He just knocks them down."

Things were so bad, you took chances to get out of there. In Bergen-Belsen in Germany, we took a chance and we went under the fence. Out of the 11, three of us survived. I was shot three times. We hung around for about 10-11 days outside. We managed to get to Hamburg, Germany. The Germans found out where we were, and they captured us. They were taking us to headquarters, and there was a big alarm. The Americans were bombing the hell out of Hamburg, and they dumped us

in jail. Several days later we were put on a train with POWs, for 11 days, without food, without water. Every morning, they would open the door, and the SS man would come with a bucket of water, and he'd just dump it in there. And whoever was close enough to get a splash, you got it, or otherwise you didn't get any. Practically half of the people died. From there I went to another camp, Sand-Posten, from where I was liberated.

When I was liberated, I remember seeing a tank going through the fence, and from there on I don't remember one thing. I just remember waking up in a bed, cleaned up and hooked up to IVs. I had typhus, and I weighed 80 pounds. The time came I was being released from the hospital, and they took me to a displaced-person camp. Every displaced person had to register. I found out there my family was murdered by the Nazis. That's also where I met Ann. We went to the American side, and there I heard President Truman speak on Christmas Eve 1945. He spoke to the nation, and they broadcast it in Europe and translated it. President Truman said that he was going to ask Congress to let 100,000 refugees into the United States. In March they opened a consulate in Frankfurt to register people to go to the United States. We went and registered. And in June we came to the United States. The Jewish agency in New York was responsible for any Jewish immigrants that come to the United States without money, and they placed them. They picked us up at the ship and took us to a hotel. They had social workers talk to us, and they told us, 10 of us, including

Isak and Ann Federman at their wedding in 1946 .

"It looked like such a big place, with so many people. And it seemed like everybody was much friendlier than Chicago or New York. The Station looked so big and so beautiful. — *Isak Federman*

The Federmans in the waiting room of Union Station in 1999.

Ann's sister and brother, "You should go to Kansas City."

We're like, "Where the hell is Kansas City?"

They said: "It's a wonderful place. We sent people there before the war and never heard from them, so it must be OK." They also said: "We want you out of New York, because you'll never Americanize properly. You go to Kansas City and you'll be an American."

We didn't care, so we said, OK. We had no relations, no one we knew. So we got on a train in New York. We arrived on a Friday morning. It was June 24, 1946, and the first thing we saw was the Union Station. It looked like such a big place, with so many people. And it seemed like everybody was much more friendlier than Chicago or New York. The station looked so big and so beautiful. The Union Station made a tremendous impression on us, because of its vastness somehow, and the friendliness. People recognized we were foreigners, and some people wanted to talk to us, and we didn't know what they wanted, but they had smiles. The Union Station had something. It seemed like so many soldiers and GIs were coming off the trains, and people were meeting them, parents, you know, and sisters and brothers. We were scared, but I felt at home somehow. We lost that scaredness. After that, the Union Station, we were attached to it.

Federman and Ann married. They built a new family — two daughters, one son and five grandchildren. Federman put his perseverance to work in business. He started working in a furniture plant by the City Market and eventually went into the furniture-making business on his own. Then he branched out with a fabric company, became a bank chairman in Lenexa and later went into the investment business. As long as Union Station remained open, "we always went there," he said.

CHAPTER 8

THE LONG DECLINE

T he week before Christmas 1947, the affable Charles Clancy couldn't have been much prouder of that longtime home of his, Union Station.

Clancy had been there since the beginning, first as a train caller, then as assistant stationmaster and now as stationmaster. He had been there for the station's first days, when every Kansas Citian rushed to see the new industrial palace. He had been there in the late teens and '20s, too, when the place was packed and he had wrestled a steer to the marble floor. He had been there during the Depression, when the crowds dwindled, and during the Second World War, when they re-emerged. And now he watched again as the postwar holiday seemed to signal a return to peacetime prominence.

Masses swarmed around the midway doors to greet arrivals. Departing travelers occupied almost every space on the waiting-room benches. Shoppers waited in lines inside Harvey stores to order Christmas gifts. Yes, the station was humming, back to normal, back to the way it used to be. That old adage that you couldn't go to Union Station without seeing someone you knew still held true.

Sure, train traffic had dipped from the war years, but who didn't expect that? War rationing had ended, troop movements had slowed to a trickle, and car sales had bounced back after being all but nil during the war. Yet people were still riding the rails. Better yet, they were riding more than during the Depression, more at least at Union Station than any year since 1930.

And look at the station. The majestic ceilings had been washed this past spring for the first time, unearthing the original reds and blues and tans sullied by smoke. This past summer, escalators finally had been installed between the tracks and the main floor. And now,

Above, left: Escalators were finally installed to ease arriving travelers' ascent from the track platforms to street level.

Left: A ticket from the 1960s.

Preceding page: As travel by rail declined, Union Station's waiting room grew ever emptier.

Hoping to increase sales, the station management built new glass-wall space for shops in the lobby in the late 1950s.

this week before Christmas, the station's loudspeakers broadcast "Silent Night," Bing Crosby singing "White Christmas" and other yuletide songs. It was another station innovation that turned heads, as people tried to see where the music came from.

So it was with more than the usual holiday cheer that Clancy reported: "It looks like old times, except better, of course, with bigger than prewar crowds, the station cleaned and this music. This is going to be a real Christmas."

Who could have guessed all this would change so fast, that train travel soon would be dropped from so many lives like the habit of wearing hats, that

Heady years after World War II masked the oncoming decrease in rail passenger travel.

Union Station would seldom again see such crowds as those the week of Christmas 1947? Who could have guessed this actually was the beginning of the end? Not the heads of the nation's railroads, who were ordering and buying more new locomotives and train cars than at any time in nearly two decades. And certainly not some travelers still enthralled by Union Station.

Around this time, budding architectural historian George Ehrlich came to town for the first time for a job interview at the old University of Kansas City. He arrived at the station early in the morning, marveled at the vastness of the Grand Hall and was immediately impressed by the city. Another day, Carolyn McMasters was returning from a nine-week trip in Europe, tired and glum like most travelers coming home after the time of their lives. Seeing the station perked her up. "Never had the Union Station looked better," she thought. Still another day, little Charles Pitcher gathered with other children of Kansas City Southern employees around the railroad's president, who patted their heads, posed for pictures and handed out souvenirs before sending them off for a ride on the Southern Belle.

Ehrlich, McMasters and Pitcher would each play a role later in the station's life, but now they were merely three persons bucking a trend. They were not flocking aboard airplanes or onto new highways for their journeys.

Kansas City Southern's Southern Belle, ready to leave for New Orleans in 1949.

The passenger train business was shriveling up. The postwar slowdown that was inevitable after trains' wartime dominance turned out to be the start of a precipitous decline. The number of passengers nationally dropped 13 straight years, to about one-third of the wartime peak. During this period, too,

Battling to hold on to the passenger market — or at least stem its decline — railroads introduced new trains. These Burlington trains followed a new, shorter rail route between Kansas City and Chicago.

New, even more streamlined trains couldn't save the rail passenger business. The "Jet Rocket" visited Union Station about 1950.

the city of Kansas City suffered its own slide, plunging from the ranks of America's top 20 metropolises as its urban neighborhoods hollowed out.

These were ominous signs for Kansas City's beloved train depot. For, if there was one constant in its life, it was this: As go the railroads and the city, so goes Union Station.

Prospects for profit

The leaders of the nation's railroads emerged from the war flush with cash and stuck on their prewar strategy for attracting passengers. They pinned their profitability hopes on diesel-powered streamliners. Instead of hauling 50 passengers on a 500-seat train, they expected to turn a profit by hauling the same number on a 100-seat train. As *Fortune* magazine reported: "The new approach thus emphasized carrying small numbers of people in large numbers of short trains."

So the Santa Fe launched a new streamliner out of Kansas City, the Kansas City Chief, with overnight service between Union Station and Chicago. The Kansas City Southern, too, re-equipped its Southern Belle and cut the running time to New Orleans by 14 percent. By the summer of 1948, more than 250 streamliners traveled the country, and some sported another innovation, the Vista Dome, a glassed-in upper compartment on coaches for sightseeing. The strategy appeared to work. The Burlington's two primary Zephyrs, for instance, earned a 72 percent profit margin in two postwar years, and the industry's passenger revenue increased in 1948 from the year before. "By whatever standard the streamliners are judged," *Fortune* magazine followed up in 1950, "most of them seem highly successful."

These bright spots, however, became momentary blips in an otherwise bleak business. From the wartime peak of nearly 1 billion passengers, the number of train travelers nationwide fell below 800 million in 1946, below 600 million in 1949 and below 400 million in 1957. Yet, instead of reducing fares or trying to out-hustle the competition, the railroads reacted by downgrading their services to save money. Paper headrests on the back of coach seats replaced cotton on some trains, and window washing ended at the halfway point of many runs, as did the vacuuming of coach interiors en route. The Rock Island in 1952 introduced what many felt was the most outrageous development yet — the pre-cooked, pre-planned, frozen meal instead of fresh cooking. By 1958 the Interstate Commerce Commission's Howard Hosmer investigated the railroad passenger system and found that trains no longer served significant demand. His conclusion became legendary: "At the present time the inescapable fact — and certainly to many people an unpleasant one — seems to be that in a decade or so this time-honored vehicle may take its place in the transportation museum along with the stagecoach, the sidewheeler and the steam locomotive."

For sure, this wasn't entirely the railroads' fault. They couldn't match the speed of airplanes. Plus, Americans after the war hit the road with a renewed infatuation with the automobile. Cars on new interstate highways could make better time than trains, without waits and delays at stations. And drivers could go whenever they pleased, not captive to somebody else's schedule. Then there was the issue of government aid. The federal government tended to help aspiring transportation industries. The railroads, of course, had gotten money and free land grants in the last century. Now the handouts went to motor vehicles. Roadways for cars and buses were built at public expense, while railroads paid taxes for their roadbeds.

Still, many of the railroads were unprepared, money-wise and service-wise, for competition. They were bloated, archaic companies. Railroads were notorious for poor promotion and customer service, such as prospective passengers getting all-day busy signals at ticket offices because clerks took the phones off the hook. Railroads also were burdened by rising union wages and labor rules, such as one forcing trains to carry coal-stoking firemen even after they switched to diesel. In a 1960 speech, Burlington President William Quinn graphically illustrated the railroads' competitive disadvantage. Comparing his Zephyr with a Boeing jetliner traveling between Chicago and Denver, he noted that the jet took less than two hours to the train's 18. If that wasn't bad enough, the jet turned a profit while the train lost $334 because the train required 47 crew members in different shifts; the jet used six pilots and stewardesses combined. About the same time, the U.S. Senate's Commerce Committee faulted the railroad industry, in a 732-page report, for failing "to compete aggressively for business by use of modernized equipment, by adjustments in plants and financial structures, as well as a failure to adjust rates to compete effectively for traffic."

At Union Station the train traffic declined every year after the war, except for a brief early-1950s period, when it stabilized. By the end of the decade, a few railroads jettisoned the passenger business altogether. The Milwaukee Road pulled out of the station in 1958, followed by the merged Alton/Gulf, Mobile & Ohio in 1960 and the Chicago Great Western in 1962. In 1960 alone, the station's main railroads shed eight major passenger routes, including the Wabash's run to St. Louis and the Burlington's run to Lincoln, Neb., the path of the first streamliner. And if it wasn't some train or route biting the dust, it was some type of convenience, whether sleeping cars or checking baggage.

One spring in the early '60s, Charles Boring went to Union Station for a Boy Scout trip. He and his buddies passed the time awaiting their train by seeing who could toss a wooden nickel high enough to touch the waiting-room ceiling some 60 feet above. Up, up, up the wooden nickel soared, disappearing from sight. Then it landed on the floor several yards from where the thrower stood. Only in a waiting area as barren as a park could they do this without hitting anyone.

Throughout the 1960s, some railroads valiantly kept up their passenger

Tickets sold

1941	406,214
1943	1,036,370
1945	1,168,995
1947	734,929
1949	578,722
1951	502,795
1953	498,382
1955	415,062
1957	368,384
1959	350,529
1961	318,305
1963	285,716
1965	277,205
1967	219,554
1969	136,972
1971	54,160

Trains handled

1941	60,121
1943	68,107
1945	72,302
1947	63,647
1949	58,714
1951	53,757
1953	53,907
1955	51,316
1957	48,485
1959	39,793
1961	35,215
1963	33,992
1965	32,422
1967	27,009
1969	13,321
1971	5,290

Source: Kansas City Terminal Railway annual reports

The station as a draw: A crowd waited for a tour in 1949.

service, subsidized in no small part by mail-car revenue. But the bottom finally fell out in 1967 when the postal service pulled its staffed railway post office cars off the rails. Soon after that, all the famed transcontinentals were abandoned. And in the summer of 1968, the president of the Association of American Railroads told a congressional subcommittee: "There just isn't any future or need for passenger trains."

These were desolate times not just for the railroads but also for the city. In 1968, too, a riot added Kansas City's name to the ignominious list of places scarred by urban unrest. Urban sections of Kansas City, like those in every big city across the country, already suffered from rampant suburbanization. The core of the city was being abandoned for — literally — greener pastures. Families were fleeing as part of a vicious cycle of expanding wealth, real estate capitalism, racism and government policies.

The cycle worked like this: The postwar housing shortage led to a new building boom on the outskirts of cities, where land was plentiful. The primary way middle-class people afforded these new homes was with low-interest, federal-guaranteed loans through the Federal Housing Administration and the Veterans Administration. But early loan requirements and some early subdivision deeds prohibited black people. So they stayed behind in the city, moving into the homes vacated by whites. More whites fled those neighborhoods, which caused more business for the suburban builders and government loan officers. As the new suburban towns mushroomed, the federal government gave grants to build sewers and roads to accommodate all the growth.

For Kansas City, this translated into a smaller, poorer, more-fractured and less-spirited city. The grand city of 2 million people envisioned by Union Station's planners didn't materialize. At the end of the '60s, Kansas City was reaching its highest population ever, just past 500,000, but this was the result of extensive annexations that more than tripled the city's land area. While Kansas City proper contained 60 percent of the five-county region's residents in 1920, that percentage slipped to 42 percent at the end of the '60s and would eventually sink to below one-third. A group of local bankers, real estate professionals, educators and others comprising an urban-core committee later studied the situation and reported: "A key factor behind the exodus from the core to the suburbs was human nature. People migrating to the suburbs generally found that the housing and the other facilities in emerging communities were more modern and more spacious than those in the core….As more and more resources were shifted from the core to the suburbs, the perception that the suburbs offered a better place to live and raise a family would eventually become a reality."

Of course, this suburban growth meant people were getting farther and farther from Union Station, making it less convenient and less part of their lives. Dorothy Early, for one, arrived in Kansas City in 1936 as a nursing student and spent many of her early New Year's Eves under the clock, joining the line dances, counting down the final seconds and watching the hats flung into the air. But after the birth of her first child, she and her husband left their Country Club Plaza apartment to build a home in Merriam, with a loan guaranteed by one of Uncle Sam's housing programs. After that, New Year's Eves were celebrated at a friend's house in the neighborhood, with toddlers crawling around. Without Early, a few thousand still congregated in the Grand Hall and waiting room in the early 1950s, blowing horns, letting go of balloons, starting conga lines and making so much noise the last half-hour before midnight that train information being read over the public address system could not be heard. But the gathering was dwindling. Only a few hundred were there to usher in the next decade. By the mid-'60s the New Year's Eve scene was down to, as one ticket clerk described it, "a few toots on horns."

An eyeopener becomes an eyesore

Amid all this going on within it and around it, Union Station faced, in the eyes of various experts and managers, its own midlife crisis. Everything looked dated. Everything looked drab. It needed a little pizazz. It needed a little neon. This was an era, after all, when new-car body styles changed every year. The station, though, hadn't changed for decades.

So in came consultants. They were from the Sessions Engineering Co. in

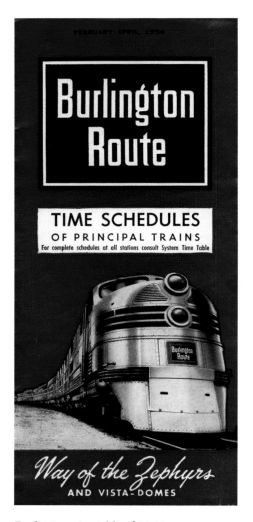

Burlington timetable of 1954.

The '51 flood didn't reach the upper floors of Union Station (far right), but inundated lower levels and flooded outlying rail approaches.

An old nemesis of Kansas City railroads paid a return visit in July 1951 — flooding. This one exceeded even the legendary 1903 deluge, which had played a key part in the eventual location of Union Station. On July 13-14, 1951, the rising Kansas River again inundated the West Bottoms livestock and railroad district, derailing and overturning freight cars. Water crept to within four blocks of Union Station at street level but filled its lowest basement 10 feet high along the walls, cutting off the power.

Station management had a back-up plan in place, though — candles. They had purchased hundreds of them earlier in the day. So candlelight illuminated the Travelers Aid desk and the Harvey restaurant, where the menu was reduced to coffee, doughnuts and rolls. Meanwhile, the station bulletin boards all displayed "No Trains" signs. The Kansas City Southern's report to stockhold-ers about the flood noted: "Northbound trains were turned back south of Grandview on the southern outskirts of Kansas City, and passengers, mail, express and baggage were handled between that point and the Union Station by bus and truck."

It was a month before the restaurant could offer its full menu again, and it took more than a month for all train routes to resume.

Chicago. They arrived in 1949 to study the Fred Harvey operations. Restaurant revenue was down one-third since the war, Sessions reported, and the eateries no longer turned a profit. The reason appeared simple to the consultants: The facilities were old-fashioned. Consider the U-shaped lunch counter. "Counters are obsolete and counter seats are painfully uncomfortable....The room belongs unmistakably to a bygone era," Sessions advised.

The company recommended a complete overhaul. It urged more space for shops and a cocktail bar. "Failure to modernize will be accompanied by the risk of gradual deterioration of the remarkably high prestige which Fred Harvey enjoys in Kansas City," the consultants concluded. Union Station's managers took this to heart, not only in the Harvey operations but with the rest of the public spaces. After studying the situation more, the Terminal Railway went ahead with the remodeling in 1957-58. The Westport Room was refurbished with, oddly enough, Victorian decor — crimson carpet, brass lamps, fringed drapes. The lunch counter was removed and replaced with a space-age-looking cocktail lounge. The old marble floor was covered with tile. The east-wing Harvey entrances were sheathed in glass, topped by a neon sign. Out in the lobby, glass walls were added outside the candy store west of the big clock and the bookstore east of the clock. These newly enlarged shops protruded so far into the Grand Hall that the semicircular ticket counter had to be scrapped. It was replaced with a rectangular-shaped, open-air counter. The ultimate in modern kitsch convenience — vending machines — were installed along the walls under the clock.

The new, squared-off ticket counter in 1959.

"Failure to modernize will be accompanied by the risk of gradual deterioration of the remarkably high prestige which Fred Harvey enjoys in Kansas City."

— 1949 study by consultants

Lobby shops and passers-by in the late 1950s.

Now Union Station didn't look like some mausoleum of a dying king. It looked like a nondescript airport or bus terminal. What would Charles Clancy, the old stationmaster and chronicler of the station's traditions, have thought? Probably not much, but he was retired by then. As it was, the makeover didn't help much. Neither did a later futile attempt to keep up with the times — the conversion from traditional wooden benches to bright, multicolored plastic chairs in the waiting room. The number of trains per day spiraled downward from the 130s to the 100s to the 70s, and Harvey restaurant revenue slumped below the $1 million mark for the first time since the Depression.

The end for the restaurant came in 1968. The Fred Harvey Co. was sold to Amfac Inc., and railroad eateries like Union Station's were shut down while the company concentrated on roadside stops and airports. Barney Allen — a Harvey vice president who had started his career with the company in Kansas City, married a Harvey Girl here and held his wedding dinner in the Westport Room — flew in from Chicago to deliver the news. "If I'd have guessed," he related that day, "that I would start here in 1935 as a storeroom man and 33 years later be the man to bring the news that we are closing, well…." After the last meals were served December 31, former President Harry S. Truman wrote Harvey coat-check legend Verna Dennis: "Along with others, who enjoyed your hospitality at the Westport Room, we were sorry to see it pass as a casualty to progress."

Union Station still drew excitement of one form or another. One night in

January 1962, Suzanne Messer and a friend entered the station to pick up Messer's mother, who was arriving on a midnight train. Her friend noticed a tall man in a long coat strolling in the lobby and munching on a bag of popcorn. "That's him," the friend whispered, "the guy from that TV show." Messer wasn't sure, so the two of them stood and stared, trying to decide whether the man was or wasn't on TV. Suddenly the man looked over at them, as if he knew what they were doing, shook his head up and down and smiled. The two approached him, and the man said, "Yes, it's me." He was best known for TV appearances. The women asked what brought him to Kansas City, and he told them something about politics. Then Messer got his autograph: Ronald Reagan.

Scenes like that, however, became fewer and fewer, while more and more the Terminal Railway branched out into nonrailroad endeavors. It got into the rental business, leasing out parts of the building. The Harvey cafeteria at the north end of the waiting room was emptied first for a Circle Theater stage and later a cinema, which turned out to show X-rated flicks. The waiting room itself was cleared out for special events, too. There were antique car exhibits and even a cat show.

Union Station also was the scene of society galas, such as the Bacchus Ball benefit in Spring 1972. The theme was the 1930s, and the waiting room was dressed up as a basement supper club, art-deco style, with silver-and-black columns between train gates and fountains of silver paper on each table, while cigarette girls roamed about. Before dinner, women in slinky, sequined dresses and men sporting gangsterlike white sport coats and white fedoras took their cocktail drinks down to track 10 and lounged inside one of the Burlington's first Zephyrs, on display. After dinner, the 740 guests saw 68-year-old Sally Rand come out of retirement and perform the same fan dance with pink ostrich feathers as she had at the 1933-34 World's Fair in Chicago.

The ball catered to hundreds of couples in their 20s and 30s, too young to have seen the station in the 1930s, when it bustled as a little city. But they knew the cruel passage of time had reduced Union Station from a twinkle in the city's eye to something of an eyesore. As they mingled, some of them paid homage to its role in their lives. Sharon Hoffman, for one, reminisced about going there as a 1950s kid to catch a train for camp, going to the Westport Room for special dinners and hearing the gong whenever Chicken Maciel was ordered, and then learning from her parents how they used to go there on dates just as subsequent generations went to the Plaza. She and others lamented what a waste it was, this gargantuan space with seemingly no use. They wondered whether the station would ever hold a crowd like this again. It would — only one more time.

The last great gathering in Union Station occurred later in 1972, when presidential candidate George McGovern stumped there. A stage was set up in the waiting room, and the audience — a melting pot of businessmen in suits and youths in jeans, long hair and Afros — stood jammed together, bumping, jostling, stepping on toes. The shoulder-to-shoulder pack filled the waiting

Terminal Railway workers at play and at work. Hazel Odessa Surratt, second from left, in top photo, was an employee from 1946 to 1977. In the 1940s and 1950s, she cleaned trains at the Terminal Railway repair and cleaning facilities about a mile southwest of Union Station and beside Southwest Boulevard.

Democratic presidential candidate George McGovern packed the waiting room Oct. 6, 1972, top. His opponent that year, Richard Nixon, had appeared at the station Oct. 16, 1968, above.

room, filled the lobby and extended into the parking lot. Janet Mathes, then a 25-year-old teacher and an environmental activist, stood in the midst of this in the Grand Hall, trying to get into the waiting room, trying to see, with literally no room to turn her body. The pack surged, taking her along with it. She tried to get away, but she couldn't get free. The pack surged toward the waiting room, and then back away from it again, like waves hitting a shore and an undertow carrying the water back out. People were falling, people were yelling, and the pack kept surging back and forth.

If McGovern noticed any of this, he didn't say. As signs with his slogan, "Come Home America," bobbed and weaved in front of him, the candidate told the crowd he could not remember "any place in America where I walked in on a scene any more inspiring." An estimated 25,000 people were there, as many as the building supposedly could hold. *The Star* called the event the largest at the station since its opening, which it very well might have been. It didn't help McGovern much, though; he lost the election in a landslide. Notably, the station's swan-song events had nothing to do with railroad transportation. The society gala used the waiting room like a hotel ballroom, while presidential aspirants like McGovern and Richard M. Nixon before him didn't arrive by train. As all presidential incumbents and challengers had done since 1952, they flew into town.

In the early 1970s, Union Station was still technically a train station — barely. Congress finally bowed to calls for a nationalized passenger train service. In 1971, Amtrak took over. It inherited the railroads' dirty coaches, cut more routes and left Kansas City with just five or six trains a day. This culminated a 96 percent decline in train traffic in a mere quarter-century for Union Station.

Most hours of the day or the night, there were more cat-sized rats scurrying around the garbage and men hanging out in the main-floor rest room than actual travelers waiting. That rest room, in fact, had become a regular stop on Kansas City vice cops' tour of the city. They hit downtown streets and a Plaza hotel for prostitutes, a few gambling joints on the East Side and Union Station. There, the plainclothes officers strolled into a partitioned-off part of the giant men's rest room. They usually found all of the doorless stalls occupied, even in the wee hours of the night. A couple of times a week they arrested men for lewd acts and indecent exposure.

Meanwhile, the waiting room was closed and its departure gates locked up. What few travelers there were sat on their luggage or on the garish plastic chairs in the Grand Hall, and then entered the east midway to go down to the tracks. The majestic lobby was

After it took over most of the country's passenger service in the early 1970s, Amtrak scaled back the number of trains. Amenities were fewer for the traveler, too. These passengers boarded in the rain in September 1978. *Below:* In 1975, Amtrak employees used a makeshift counter to check tickets. For a while passengers were led to their trains.

Multicolored plastic chairs replaced the heavy wooden benches in the waiting room in 1967. When the waiting room was closed for other uses, the chairs were placed in the lobby, right.

still. The scrape of a chair screeched in the emptiness. The rumble of a radiator beat like a drum's cadence. The sound of a man's cough exploded against the walls. The squeaky wheels of a cart being pushed across the floor echoed through the vast chamber. This is what had become of Jarvis Hunt's monument.

Around this time, Carolyn McMasters and her husband, Pete, began riding trains again. Their journeys were more tranquil this way. Carolyn had grown up in Kansas City and ridden trains during the station's heyday to college in Lawrence, Kan., and later on vacations. It had been some years since she last stepped inside the station, and she didn't expect what she saw. "It was pitiful," she remembered. "I had known it when it was so busy and so active, and now it was so empty. It was a sad thing to see." Union Station's usefulness, its very reason for being, was nearly gone.

Emerging visions

Kansas Citians' views of the station had by then undergone a metamorphosis. It was caught in the time-warp of decline, no longer the place to go but still an endearing relic, a family member in need of nursing care, with death seemingly on the horizon. Discussion of its afterlife had already become a community topic. At the beginning of the 1960s, the city manager asked the chamber of commerce to study turning the station into an office and transportation center, with the Grand Hall converted into multistory floor space. Nothing came of it. The Kansas City Terminal Railway in 1968 hired a new president, Vernon Coe, and one of the first things he did was suggest the company pursue a new course, one based on real estate development.

Why not? Despite its urban woes, Kansas City was embarking on another of its once-a-generation, reach-for-the-stars, building binges. A sprawling international airport was being built. So were the country's first twin sports stadiums. Plus, a momentous urban redevelopment, the Crown Center office-retail-apartment complex, was on the drawing board. And it happened to be

THE STATION BECOMES AN EXHIBITION HALL

No longer needed for passengers, the waiting room was converted to a special events area. Programs ranged from displays of antiques in 1978, left, to vintage automobiles, below, to a cat show.

cater-cornered from Union Station, on the billboard-infested Signboard Hill.

The Terminal Railway hired another Chicago-based consultant, and in 1971 that consultant publicly unveiled a wildly ambitious design to woo potential developers. It followed in Crown Center's footsteps, with 20 apartment and office high-rises. It even mimicked Crown Center by including a shopping mall in the middle of the project, right on the station grounds. That is, right where the station stood. The station wasn't shown. It was nowhere to be seen on the project map. In fact, the project included a small, new Amtrak station.

Union Station was to be demolished. A project brochure even stated: "Before present station facilities can be removed, a new station must be provided." In a press release, Coe explained that the old building's operation costs, amounting to half a million dollars a year, were "no longer justified by its use."

This announcement immediately set off alarm bells. Normally unflappable Kansas Citians were stunned. Veteran *Star* writer and city historian Henry Haskell Jr. reported about "the sense of civic shock" and opined: "Ours may be a city notoriously careless about salvaging the monuments of the past. But the Union Station? That was manifestly something else, again. A repository of so much recent history and so many personal associations, surely nothing could happen to take it away from us after all these years!" But that's what

Union Station was to be demolished. A project brochure even stated: "Before present station facilities can be removed, a new station must be provided."

The 1971 apartment and high-rise plan for the Union Station area — absent the station building.

New Yorkers thought, too, a decade before when the wrecking ball started swinging into Pennsylvania Station. Its razing actually spurred the nation's first federal preservation act in 1966. But the movement hadn't caught on much in Kansas City yet.

What little interest there was in saving history here was mostly confined to Independence, part of the Santa Fe Trail and home of Harry Truman. In 1968, when demolition was scheduled for downtown's Romanesque-style Board of Trade building, considered the finest design in the city from Daniel Burnham's architectural firm, the handful of people who cared did not have enough clout or power to stop the destruction. But two years later the city government responded by creating the Landmarks Commission to document historic buildings. Against this background of apathy and inaction, Haskell wondered in his newspaper column about Union Station: "Can we, as a community, summon to this task the same type of effective voluntary collaboration that brought the railroads here in the first place a hundred years back?"

So with the Terminal Railway's announcement, the new Landmarks Commission met its first test. In a matter of months commission staffers researched the station's history and asked for quick federal action to include it on the National Register of Historic Places. That came in February 1972. Federal protection did not prohibit demolition but made it more difficult.

At the same time, George Ehrlich stirred up local architectural circles. Ehrlich was the architectural historian who had arrived by train years before to interview for a university professorship. He, in fact, landed that job at what was now the University of Missouri-Kansas City and became the city's most respected connoisseur of old buildings. After the Union Station bombshell, Ehrlich helped form the Heritage and Preservation Council of Greater Kansas City. He also organized a station preservation symposium at the university, building momentum against the Terminal Railway's plan. Other residents launched a Save Our Station letter-writing campaign, the city established a commission to suggest economically practical uses for the building, and Mayor Charles Wheeler held meetings and wrote letters pressuring the railroads to reconsider demolition. All this talk also provoked a flurry of other ideas to keep the station intact, among them banker R. Crosby Kemper's notion to use the headhouse as an entrance to a combination sports and American Royal arena. In 1973 the Terminal Railway showed how serious it was in jettisoning Union Station. The company began dismantling train sheds, taking out the escalators and concreting over the doorways. The building's fate seemed sealed.

On the first day of July 1974, some 340 business and political leaders filed into one of Crown Center's new hotel ballrooms. Missouri Gov. Kit Bond was there, as were Wheeler and the various banking and investment Kempers. Several out-of-towners had invited them there. The word was they were going to save Union Station. Ivan Himmel stepped to the lectern. Himmel headed a development firm that was half-owned by a huge Canadian real estate conglomerate, Trizec Corp. Ltd. The development firm had agreed to take on the Terminal Railway's project. Himmel stood in front of Kansas City's elite and introduced a repackaged redevelopment plan.

It was gargantuan, totaling a half-billion dollars, with some three dozen separate buildings, from high-rises to hotels, from retail shopping to residential town houses. It was much like the original design from three years before. Except smack in the middle of an artist's rendering of the new project, hemmed in on three sides by a skyline that resembled New York City, was the station building itself. The Terminal Railway had, in the words of Vernon Coe later, "backed off" its original design. "Union Station has lived one full life serving the people of Kansas City. Now it will be the focal point for new growth and rebirth within the city," Himmel announced. It was another way Kansas City could stem the flight to the suburbs. Inside the station, the waiting room would be converted into a shopping center, flanked by adjoining retail additions, while the headhouse was reserved for a science museum developed by the Kansas City Museum.

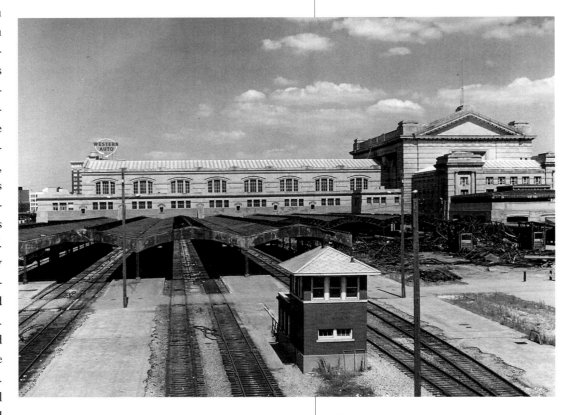

The train sheds coming down.

As might be expected, the Kansas City crowd applauded politely. Never mind that the developers didn't have any tenants for the shopping center. Or that the science museum didn't have a plan or its own development money yet. Eventually this plan would haunt the city. But for now, the preservationists had won. Union Station got a second chance. Later that year the plan slid through the City Council with hardly an objection. George Ehrlich, in his definitive book on the subject, *Kansas City, Missouri: An Architectural History, 1826-1976*, summed up this saga: "In many ways it was the Union Station crisis, and the involvement of the new Landmarks Commission and other groups in the struggle to save the station, that marks the beginning of a major preservation movement in Kansas City."

Out with the old

With a redevelopment plan in place and new uses for the building on the

horizon, everything left from its bygone days had to go. No longer were the ticket counter's date stamps needed. No longer were Fred Harvey's furnishings needed. No longer were train crews' bunk beds needed. So in the Bicentennial summer of 1976, the Great Union Station Liquidation Sale was on.

The waiting room was converted into the city's largest bazaar, jammed with a couple of thousand things already replaced or rendered obsolete. Things like oak rocking chairs from the women's silent room, brass rails and bar stools from the old Harvey restaurant, assorted marble slabs, railroad signs and maps and pictures, an old green sign used to post Kansas City Athletics baseball scores, even paneling stripped from some of the office walls. "This will be a once in a lifetime offering," stated a bulletin announcing the event. Kansas Citians sensed this and showed up by the thousands, milling around mail carts that held what were seen as souvenir mementos.

Auctioneer Jerry Hertzog opened the frenzy by warming up the hordes. "You'll be buying a piece of history," he told them. Then he launched into bidding, and away it went. He started an oak roll-top desk at $100, knowing they usually went for $500. "Do I hear 150?" Hertzog belted out. Someone raised a white index card signaling a bid. "Would you give me 200?" Hertzog continued. "Do I hear 250? Would you give me 300? Now the quarter, 325?" On and on it went. Past the $500 mark. Past $750. Finally the last raised index card got it at $1,000. This went on all day for two days. One by one, the mail carts were rolled in front of the stage, and each item on them sold in a minute. Wells Fargo metal strongboxes. Harvey linens. Even chairs missing an arm or a leg.

Charles Pitcher stood in the crowd, trying to get something of value, amazed that most things were going for more money than he imagined, or had. Pitcher was a train buff whose earliest memory of Union Station went back a couple of decades to the day he rode on the Southern Belle with the children of Kansas City Southern employees. Now he worked for KC Southern himself, as a clerk in the general manager's office, and he already had started his own collection of artifacts, things like train pictures, brochures and timetables. He knew this was an opportunity he couldn't pass up to add to his collection. He had raised his index card on several items but saw them zip past his budget.

Auctioneer Hertzog kept going from table to table. Finally, the bids slowed on an office chair, light in wood, with armrests but not on wheels or swivels, just a chair from an upper-floor desk, probably some bookkeeper's. Pitcher raised his index card at $50. "Do I hear 55?" bellowed Hertzog. There was no answer. "Would you give me 55?" Again, no answer. His gavel pounded, and the chair was Pitcher's. And nearly every last vestige of Union Station's heyday scattered like ashes in the wind.

Union Station lobby, late winter, 1980.

CHAPTER 9

MONUMENT TO FAILURE

T he rain started Sunday night and continued past midnight, when Loyd Dillinger's shift began at Union Station. It was one of Kansas City's monsoonlike deluges, driving and cascading in sheets, pounding the pavement like a herd of buffalo in full stampede. Already around the city in the wee hours of this Monday, Sept. 12, 1977, the rain had clogged creeks and closed streets, stranding some motorists and knocking out power to some 10,000 electric customers. But that wasn't Dillinger's concern right now. He was alone in Union Station, the night-shift maintenance man, and all this rain meant work.

It meant he had to climb stairs, 10 stories high, to the attic. And once there, it meant he had to empty the barrels catching the water leaking from Union Station's miserable roof. Dillinger was a man with thick hands and a ruddy face. He had started with the Terminal Railway in 1964 in maintenance, and then loaded and unloaded mail and baggage. By the mid-'70s he had enough seniority to avoid the pink slip when the U.S. Postal Service canceled its mail-sorting contract at the station and the latest mass of station workers was let go. But he didn't have enough seniority to avoid maintenance and the lonely midnight shift. And what a maintenance job it was. The building was being left to rot.

The amount of money the Terminal Railway spent on "station operating expenses" had fallen from more than $300,000 in 1951 to roughly $120,000 in the late 1970s, without factoring in inflation. Signs of disrepair were everywhere. A manager of the Lobster Pot and Colony Steakhouse restaurant, which had taken over the old Fred Harvey space, was walking on the sidewalk in front of the station one day when the concrete gave out under him. If he hadn't landed with his legs straddling an I-beam, he would have tumbled some 25 feet, possibly to his death. Then there was the roof. It was a sieve. The 4-foot concrete tiles that topped the headhouse looked durable enough, but they were cracked, and the joints between them weren't sealed, and the thin, wa-

Loyd Dillinger

Facing page: Beneath the porous roof, chunks of the lobby ceiling gave way.

terproof fabric underneath had long since disintegrated. The Terminal Railway had stopped fiddling with it. But the water leaking in under the tiles and trickling off the roof beams had to be controlled somehow.

So the expansive attic above the Grand Hall was outfitted with more than a dozen barrels. Troughs made of tarpaper ran from known leaks to the barrels, two troughs to a barrel. Without maintenance men to empty them, the barrels could fill up and spill into the Grand Hall ceiling, loosening the plaster and dripping down to the floor. That's why Dillinger had to go up there.

In the early hours of that Monday — the beginning of 11 inches of rain that day, the beginning of the great Plaza flood, when a saturated Brush Creek rose and filled the streets and tossed around cars and gushed through dozens of stores — Dillinger was climbing Union Station's stairs, bucket in hand. Thunder crackled above him, rain lashed the roof, and dozens of streams of water surged down the tarpaper troughs. It sounded as if he were standing in the middle of a city fountain. He went to work. He ducked under some troughs, stepped over others, reached into a barrel and filled his bucket. Then it was back through that room, under and over the troughs, carrying that bucket, until he walked out onto the roof ledge and threw the water into a roof drain. Dillinger spent hours going from barrel to barrel. His arms ached. He banged his head. He splashed water on himself. And the rain just kept coming.

Dillinger thought this was one of the all-time silly jobs. He didn't like it, being all by himself, the middle of the night, hardly any light, in the midst of booming thunder and flashes of lightning. He was like a hospital orderly. Only his dying patient was Union Station.

'Nobody knows what to do about it'

On Oct. 30, 1977, Union Station's 63rd anniversary of its opening, crowds returned to the venerable building. For a circus.

Under the big tops of the Grand Hall and the waiting room, there were animals — squirrels, skunks, beavers, in the form of costumed volunteers. There were balloons — hundreds of them handed out to children. There were stunts — a Hula-Hoop-size gyroscope twirling in a man's hand and a wizard revving up a gas turbine engine.

Karen McCarthy, who at the time was married and went by the last name Benson, stayed all afternoon. She wasn't dressed in costume but did wear a train conductor's cap. To her, this wasn't just fun and games. The Kansas City Museum was trying to raise money for its piece of the Trizec-affiliated station redevelopment. The new Museum of Science and History was going to cost $25 million, so the Kansas City Museum was seeking a city property tax increase. The election was 10 days away. This was the campaign's one-time, blowout event to inspire the voters. This was McCarthy's one chance to do what she did best — meet the people, mingle and persuade, work a crowd.

McCarthy

A rising star of local politics, she had just been elected a Missouri legislator the year before, at age 29. Later she would go to Congress. Now she was the science museum's campaign coordinator, responsible for getting the word

At the station's 63rd anniversary open house, General Motors sponsored an exhibit, "Previews of Progress." Demonstrated here were the principles of the gyroscope.

out. But how?

The election strategy aimed at rich, white, frequent voters and almost ignored everyone else. It sent brochures only to the Westport and Ward Parkway corridors. It courted their social clubs with wine-and-cheese parties at the station. That's what the campaign managers had set out to do. These were the older, supposedly wiser heads above her. How could McCarthy, a grass-roots specialist, work with only one-third of the city?

Not only that, she had to bring the Kansas City Museum along with her. The museum had always been a sort of neglected stepchild of Kansas City's cultural offerings. Its local history displays were chronically underfunded and lacking in thrills. It wanted desperately to grow up. In December 1969, $2 million toward the museum's dream of a science center at Union Station was included on a city ballot listing 17 propositions to be paid for through general obligation bonds. In addition, the ballot contained city charter amendments and taxes issues, 24 measures in all. Everything lost in a textbook case of taxpayer revolt. The widest margin of defeat was the money for the Kansas City Museum.

Eight years later the science center was back in the station's future plans. Again, the museum decided to seek public funding. It conducted polls. They showed the tax increase losing. That's why the election strategy was tailored to the traditional tax-increase supporters, those along the city's tonier Southwest Corridor, stretching from the state line to the traditional black-white dividing line, Troost Avenue.

But what about the rest of the city? Predictably, that's where McCarthy ran into trouble. Opposition groups formed in the city north of the Missouri River. They didn't understand how the science museum would benefit them. After all, no brochures were mailed there. South of the river, the dominant black political organization, Freedom Inc., also felt ignored. The campaign didn't have money to contribute to Freedom's get-out-the-vote effort. So Freedom's president, Harold Holliday Jr., blasted the Kansas City Museum, calling its 32-member board "patently racist" because half were from Johnson County in Kansas and only one was a minority. Freedom's politicking broke McCarthy's novice political heart. On Election Day, the science museum garnered just 43 percent of the vote.

The rising star couldn't fix Union Station.

Afterward, some new re-use ideas popped up nearly every year. In April 1978, U.S. Sen. Tom Eagleton of Missouri announced that the federal government's General Services Administration wanted to put federal offices in the station and build a new Internal Revenue Service regional center next to it.

Yet one of Eagleton's fellow Senate heavyweights, Bob Dole of Kansas, was already trying to steer the IRS building to the Kansas side of the state line.

With Union Station, Dole milked the government's propensity for procrastination. General Services had studies to conduct. While Eagleton kept indicating the Kansas City deal was sailing along, Dole kept working the channels of Washington and whipping up the folks of Kansas City, Kan.

One year went by, and then another. Then Ronald Reagan won control of the White House. Republicans won control of the Senate. Dole became majority leader. He gained more power. He signed a letter, with a couple of fellow Kansans in Congress, lobbying a Senate committee to put the IRS building in their state. The Senate committee chairman soon labeled the Union Station project "increasingly controversial." The IRS scuttled its plans and never moved. "Once Senator Dole intervened," Eagleton explained later, "that was it. It was dead."

Meanwhile, the Terminal Railway's redevelopment partner kept trolling for tenants. Ivan Himmel, who had headed the redevelopment firm, was out of the picture by now, and Trizec assumed the lead role. Its point man in Kansas City became Garold Osborne. He kept busy. He had plans drawn up for the Stouffer hotel chain to move into the station. He discussed ideas with the Rouse Co., which had turned Boston's Faneuil Hall into an urban shopping destination. He conducted an office-market study, because the Jerde Partnership was looking at the station for offices. He listened to proposals for a jazz hall of fame and an aquarium. He even welcomed a bill in the Missouri legislature allowing Union Station to become the state's first and only casino. On and on this continued throughout the early and mid-1980s. Nothing ever panned out.

Osborne's job was a joint vice presidency of a Trizec subsidiary and of Pershing Square Redevelopment Corp., a shell corporation created to receive tax breaks under Missouri law. It was Trizec that pumped roughly $2 million a

The news was bad on Nov. 9, 1977, for backers of the science museum at Union Station. From that day's morning *Times*, top, and afternoon *Star* bottom.

Osborne

Lonely times: The station's communication hub of long ago sat in late-century disuse.

Berkley

year into studies, operations and salaries of Pershing Square. But Osborne didn't know this job entailed trying to fit a round peg into a square hole.

The station was a casualty of capitalism: The building cost too much to modify, and no private firm wanted to absorb an up-front monetary drain without a big, guaranteed cash flow. As all this failure piled up, Trizec's interest waned. Osborne in a 1980 memo scolded his Trizec boss for the company's "image of procrastination." What was he supposed to do?

Osborne had something in mind. One way around the station problem was to demolish part of it. After all, the main building worth saving was the headhouse, and the biggest headache to potential tenants was what to do with the long north-south waiting room. So Trizec planned a glass office tower right next to the waiting room on the east-side tracks. In late 1983, Osborne and his leasing agent took Mark Shapiro of the Historic Kansas City Foundation on a tour of the site. The construction, Osborne explained, would cause vibrations and stress on the waiting room's columns. Who knows, the columns might buckle. Bottom line: The waiting room needed to be torn down. Shapiro contacted the mayor's office. Mayor Richard Berkley "was outraged when informed of the demolition plans and told Osborne in so many words that it would happen over his dead body," Shapiro chronicled in a memo around that time. Trizec dropped the demolition idea. But it went ahead with the office tower. City officials never realized until too late that the building would practically touch Union Station.

Where train sheds and platforms once stood, a glass-walled office structure and parking garage began rising adjacent to Union Station in October 1984. The structure, called Two Pershing Square, was built by Trizec's subsidiaries. Included in the project was a small new station for Amtrak, with a drive-up entrance at street level and a long descent to the trackside ticket office.

As the steel frame began jutting out of the ground, Berkley called some Trizec and Pershing Square officials to his office. When the door closed, he railed at them, pounding his fist on his desk. He screamed, "You never told me it was going to be that close to the station." The office tower eventually blocked the northern and eastern views of the landmark.

In a 1984 *Corporate Report* magazine article headlined "Deathwatch at Union Station," Tom Nelson, a respected local architect, summed up the station's saga best: "Nobody knows what to do about it." Soon, Osborne resigned and returned to the housing side of real estate.

At the same time, Union Station's influential neighbor, Hallmark Cards Inc., had an interest in the station's well-being. This interest was a combination of proximity and benevolence. The company had a huge investment to protect in Crown Center. And as one of the city's leading corporate citizens, it would be counted on to donate some large sum toward any community-backed station re-use.

Bill Hall, who wasn't related to the Hall family, was as close to a Mr. Fix-It as there was in Kansas City. He handled civic challenges, such as restarting a symphony orchestra, for company Chairman Donald J. Hall. With Union Station, Donald Hall told his right-hand man that the company should keep abreast of re-use ideas and encourage good ones.

Bill Hall brought in his own consultants. He helped interest the Walt Disney Co. in considering an indoor theme park. He served as a sounding board for various special city Union Station committees. Yet Hall never felt any of the ideas worked. The right use hadn't been found yet.

Then in 1987 he thought he had found the right use. Emilio Ambasz, a for-

Donald Hoffmann, Kansas City Star architectural critic, shocked the city by making a cogent argument for the unspeakable — tearing down the station. "Union Station stands as a memorial to failure," Hoffmann wrote in December 1983, "failure of this nation's unsavory imperialistic ambitions, failure of Kansas City's dream of growing into the great metropolis of the prairies, failure of the nation's railroads to survive as a vital system of public transportation and, in all these later years, failure in finding any new public use." Hoffmann was right — and wrong.

Hoffmann

Yes, some of those failures were true. Yet Hoffmann's reasoning for dismissing the station relied largely on architectural historian Carroll L.V. Meeks' writings. Stations like Kansas City's, Meeks believed, were overblown and pompous, buildings not worth saving because of architecture alone. It was a popular view among those, such as Meeks and Hoffmann, who favored the minimalistic simplicity of modern architecture.

Throughout history, architects disdained the styles preceding theirs. Even Meeks understood this. In the same book in which he characterized stations of Union Station's era as "megalomania," he also acknowledged their merits. "As a matter of fact, however, the vocabulary, though classic, was varied and infused with the spirit of creative eclecticism," he wrote.

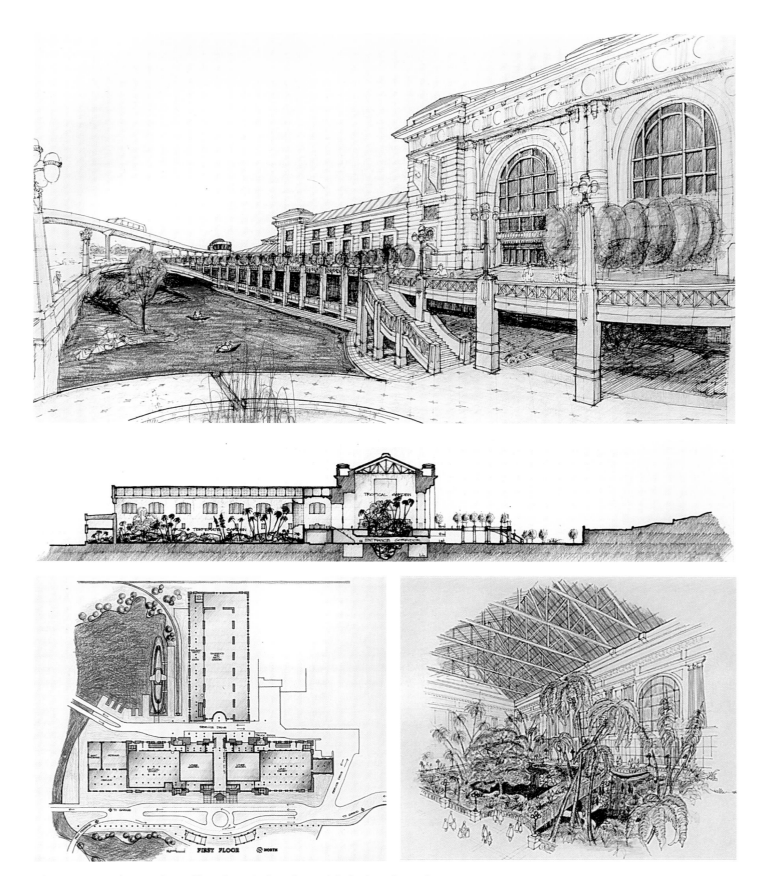

These 1987 renderings showed how botanical gardens might look at the station.

mer curator of design at New York's Museum of Modern Art and a man with a glittering resume of projects around the world, was the Joyce C. Hall distinguished professor of design for the 1986-87 academic year at the Kansas City Art Institute. Bill Hall tapped him to take a crack, as had Charles Eames a decade before, at Union Station. Ambasz proposed something really wild: a botanical garden in the Grand Hall, flanked by a planetarium in one wing and an aquarium in the other wing. "I had heard 50-odd ideas," Bill Hall remembered. "Ambasz made sense to me, and he had these incredible credentials."

Hall just had to convince everyone. The company paid much of Ambasz's bill. The company also flew local officials on the corporate jet to Wilmington, Del., to see similar indoor gardens. By raising its profile on this plan, Hallmark also entered the nasty realm of politics. Both the city and the county were preparing separate ballot issues totaling $35 million for the station. The money needed a use. Jackson County Executive Bill Waris told Hall he liked Ambasz's conception, and then turned around and brought in a Chicago shopping center developer to counter Ambasz's plan.

The ballot issues went to the electorate without any specified use. Both failed in 1988. Bill Hall was another Union Station casualty. He was one of many who started with the best of intentions but saw the chances spin out of control, slam against a wall of political egos and come to rest as a mangled wreck.

Pigeons, paint chips, plaster and puddles

In the late 1980s, Loyd Dillinger, the maintenance man, still made his rounds inside the station. He worked days now, and the only tenant left in the building was the Lobster Pot and Colony Steakhouse restaurant in the east wing. The restaurant's access to the Grand Hall was blocked by a plywood wall, so the rest of the station sat deserted. The maintenance crew was down to just a few men and a handful of janitors. The station didn't have to be cleaned or maintained for anyone. So it wasn't.

Dillinger walked through the station by himself, in and out of rooms above the Grand Hall, up and down the hallways upstairs, making sure doors were locked and broken windows got boarded up. Outside, from a distance, Union Station's profile was as grand as ever. But up close, it was now falling apart. A chain-link fence surrounded it in front, and grass and weeds poked through the broken concrete. Blistered paint hung from the undersides of the entrance canopies, and the two sets of front doors were entirely boarded up. Inside, the air turned musty and moldy. Plaster clumps fell from the lobby ceiling, and puddles formed on the floor. When it rained, roof leaks still flowed over the troughs into the barrels above the Grand Hall. But Dillinger and his fellow maintenance men had long since stopped emptying those barrels. They didn't have to. Those barrels just overflowed now. The water ran down the walls in the lovely lobby and just remained in puddles for weeks. In winter the puddles turned into sheets of ice. No one mopped them up.

During the station's painful decline, the estimated cost to renovate it had jumped tenfold, from $4 million to $40 million. Still, Dillinger kept at his daily

In other cities, stations were returning to life in what railroad station historian Janet Greenstein Potter called the "golden age" of renovations. These began around 1980 and lasted to the turn of the century. The Nashville, Tenn., station became a hotel. Stations in Washington, Indianapolis and St. Louis were turned into urban malls. Stations in Jacksonville, Fla., Chattanooga, Tenn., and Philadelphia were converted into convention centers. Cincinnati's reopened as a museum.

Many of these projects followed a similar pattern: The station declined in use, was abandoned, became filled with pigeon droppings and faced demolition in some cases, then a partnership of public and private leaders came to the rescue for the sake of a civic jewel and downtown revitalization.

The key, though, was some government's willingness to do something. In Nashville and Washington, it was with federal money. In Indianapolis, Cincinnati and Jacksonville, it was with city ownership.

Damaged and obsolete, the remaining arti-facts of the railroads sat untouched in the mostly deserted station.

Inside Amtrak's money-saving bubble.

rounds. "It was a lonely place," Dillinger said. But he would soon lose his job. The last tenant was finally being kicked out.

The last day had been a long time in the making. Early in the decade, the station's heating bill alone ran to $600,000 for a winter, and Terminal Railway gave Trizec an ultimatum: Either help pay the station's exorbitant utility expenses, or the railroads would close the station. Trizec refused. So in 1983 the Terminal Railway created an accounting file for "the closing of Union Station." Soon thereafter, the owners turned off the heat. Amtrak was forced to install a white polyester bubble 30 feet high inside the Grand Hall — an ignominious mask of Jarvis Hunt's architecture. This lasted barely a year before Amtrak moved out altogether in 1985, leaving only the restaurant.

One by one, tenant leases were not renewed — the office of Smaks restaurants, a commodity newspaper, Morey Associates audiovisuals. Many others had long since left, like the Custom Watch Co., Ginny Lee Gifts and a city government housing department office. Finally, when the restaurant lease was up, it, too, was not renewed. The Terminal Railway's president wrote restaurant owner Robert Gaines, "I wonder if Union Station is nothing but a bottomless pit in which money can be poured into." On his last day there, March 31, 1989, Gaines took his video camera. His lens captured the beginnings of chalky streaks down the Grand Hall's stone walls. Downstairs, the camera panned the basement. Tools were strewn on tables. A few undelivered letters, postmarked in 1975, were scattered on the floor. A 1954 book of Missouri post offices and train schedules sat on a shelf. It looked as if a siren had gone off and everyone left what they were doing, never to return.

Back upstairs, lime-green paint chips curled off the walls of the men's smoking room. Gaines' 6-year-old daughter took a pencil and drew a round face on a wall. Instead of a smile it had a frown. In the center of everything, the heart of Kansas City's Times Square, the place where people met and celebrated for generations, the great clock had stopped. The camera slowly zoomed in on the clock face. Time stood still at 12:40.

The battle in the courts

By this time city leaders had had enough. Enough of the broken promises to fix up the station. Enough of the long-expected progress. In 1988 the city government hired a law firm headed by civic leader Edward A. Smith to study legal retribution against the Terminal Railway and its partners. This would be the payback for all that had happened, or had not happened. This would be Union Station's Armageddon.

Smith

Politically it was a popular move. Legally, however, it was a quagmire. Trizec, the station's would-be savior and the moneybags from which the city would seek damages, hadn't signed the city's original redevelopment contract back in 1974. In fact, an assistant city attorney, Richard Ward, had asked Trizec representatives repeatedly to sign. They had refused. The City Council had approved the project anyway. After all, Trizec executives were telling business leaders they would see the project through. And hadn't Crown Center gotten done without Hallmark officials signing the contract? So the contract was signed only by representatives from Pershing Square Redevelopment Corp., a shell corporation with no income, no assets and no chance to get the project done without Trizec's money.

Without a contract to pin blame on Trizec, Smith's firm studied a legal strategy to "pierce the corporate veil." That is, the city would have to prove that Pershing Square and its related redevelopment firms were bankrolled, controlled and ultimately run by Trizec. The council bit on the idea. Trizec hadn't made good on its obligation. It had put up two tax-abated, income-producing office buildings near the station but hadn't touched the station itself. A lawsuit was filed in the fall of 1988. It sought $91 million in damages from the Terminal Railway and its redevelopment partners, including Trizec.

Edward Smith was, in the words of colleague David Oliver, "a deal-doer." And he saw the Union Station lawsuit as a way to finally force Trizec to act, ei-

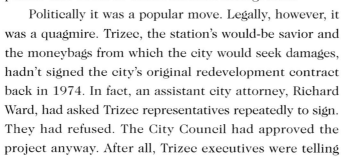

"I wonder if Union Station is nothing but a bottomless pit in which money can be poured into."

— George Thompson, Terminal Railway president

Hockaday

"I could see a train wreck coming."

— Irvine Hockaday

Cleaver

Shinn

ther with a new use or with a cash divorce settlement. The lawsuit was simply a poker hand to call Trizec's bluff.

Smith, a Harvard law graduate, had a reputation as a hard-nosed, combative, even emotional negotiator. He regularly socialized with Henry Bloch, the tax-preparation magnate, and Donald Hall and Irvine O. Hockaday Jr. of Hallmark. It was at one of these social gatherings that Hockaday heard Smith talking about the lawsuit in the early 1990s. Hockaday had more than a passing interest in it. He had once been an executive with Kansas City Southern, one of the members of the Terminal Railway, and Hallmark, of course, wanted the blight removed from its neighbor. Plus, Hockaday was one of those rare civic leaders who waded into the thorniest issues dragging down his town.

Hockaday listened to Smith describe how Trizec had neglected its duty and taken the city for a ride. Smith was going to make Trizec pay. Hockaday, as head of an international corporation himself, thought Trizec wasn't likely to back down. He wasn't the only one. The city's development director before the lawsuit was filed, John Laney — the same John Laney who now worked for Hallmark — had written memos to Mayor Berkley and the city manager arguing against a court case. He didn't think it would force Trizec into action.

Hockaday thought the city should get whatever it could from Trizec, cut its ties and move on. "I could see a train wreck coming," he remembered. He told Smith what he thought. "You're not seeing this objectively," Hockaday politely scolded his friend. Smith wouldn't hear it.

Smith continued his hardball approach, even as the stakes heightened. The city's new mayor elected in 1991, Emanuel Cleaver, had promised in his campaign to settle the lawsuit. Smith and Cleaver began meeting secretly with Trizec officials. Both sides were entrenched. There were cursory settlement discussions, but the city clung to its $91 million in damages, based on its rehab estimate and its lost tax revenue resulting from Trizec's alleged fraud, conspiracy and breach of contract. Trizec, meanwhile, offered less than $20 million. Smith sat at these meetings, glared at the Trizec representatives, raised his voice and said, "You're insulting us."

As the case neared trial in 1992, the trial judge, Jackson County Circuit Judge David Shinn, sliced off one-third of the city's damages. The judge ruled that the city could not seek money to rehab a building it did not own. Then, as the two sides arrived in the courtroom in June 1992, station preservationist Phelps Murdock interceded behind the scenes and ironed out what he thought was an acceptable settlement.

Murdock had served on one of the city's many station commissions and now led a nonprofit corporation trying to determine the right re-use and raise funds for it. In his behind-the-scenes role, Murdock had the blessing of both Cleaver and Hallmark's Bill Hall. They each had set nearly identical settlement conditions. Hall wanted at least $17 million, which included the station land. Cleaver wanted $20 million. The mayor by this time was hearing from several civic leaders he met with regularly — folks such as Kansas City Power & Light Chairman Drue Jennings, Sprint Chief Executive Officer William T. Esrey and

The chairman of Trizec Corp. Ltd. (right, with hand on wall) and company lawyers.

Allied-Signal Aerospace President Lou Smith — that the city should settle. Murdock talked with Trizec's side and got the best terms yet: $13 million cash, plus the station and surrounding land worth an estimated $10 million. This $23 million total would be conveyed to a new nonprofit corporation. "I thought it was done," Murdock recalled.

Upon hearing Murdock's terms, Cleaver was all for it — until he had lunch with Smith. The attorney told the mayor, "You're settling too cheap." Smith, in Murdock's view, was "determined to get the big bucks."

The weekend after opening arguments, Smith and his main litigator in the case, William Levi, got together in Levi's living room. Levi by now was having his doubts about this case. He knew he faced a tough task in court, what with this being the first lawsuit in Missouri history in which a city was seeking damages for breach of redevelopment. Plus, the city had already lost part of its damage claim, and now Trizec had beefed up its offer. Levi felt Smith should communicate this scenario to the entire City Council, not just the mayor and a committee of a few council members overseeing the case. "I think you've forgotten who the client is here," Levi told him.

Smith got huffy. He figured Trizec's last offer wouldn't even fix the station's roof, let alone the interior halls. Levi offered to step down as the case's trial attorney. Smith agreed. The next week Levi suddenly disappeared from the courtroom. And Smith never spoke to his 18-year partner again, not even to say "hi" in an elevator.

Once the trial got going, all the city did was lose some more. Shinn made a series of rulings rejecting the city's claims, including the pivotal argument to "pierce the corporate veil" and collect from Trizec. This defeated the whole point of the lawsuit. Piercing cases typically revolved around situations in which bigger corporations stripped the assets from shell corporations. In this case, though, Pershing Square had been created legitimately under Missouri law and hardly had any assets that Trizec didn't give it.

Judge Shinn, like most Kansas Citians, had followed Union Station's saga through the years, and when he first got the lawsuit, he was inclined to believe the city had been swindled. But when he pored over the details — facts like Trizec's never signing the contract — he thought, "This is 180 degrees different than what we were led to believe." Later, Shinn recapped the city's case in an interview: "Sometimes you have things that aren't right, but you don't have a legal recourse. I think that (the lawsuit) may be one of those things."

In the end, in August 1992, the city still won a $9.9 million judgment against Pershing Square. But even in victory, the city couldn't win. Pershing Square had less than $1,000 in its bank account, making the likelihood of collecting the judgment remote. The lawsuit was, as one council member put it, an "embarrassment."

Edward Smith's refusal to take an early settlement, when almost everyone around him preferred it, delayed eventual redevelopment planning by two years, at a time when the station remained closed and its condition worsened with each passing season. In the end, this delay cost the eventual station redevelopers millions of dollars — somewhere between $5 million and $13 million, maybe more, based on an HNTB Corp. study that estimated the "cost of inaction."

COMING TOGETHER

One winter day in January 1996, some of those responsible for the success of Kansas City's suburbs assembled around a conference table. They represented a who's who of civic leadership in booming Johnson County, Kan., across the state line from Kansas City. Some headed governments — Ed Eilert, Annabeth Surbaugh. Some held state offices — Dick Bond, Audrey Langworthy. And the rest served on education and chamber boards — Larry Winn III, Mary Birch, Fred Logan, David Westbrook.

They all knew each other, of course. They had worked together in the past. On committees promoting the county's growth. Or in election campaigns for school bonds. But this time was different. They had been called to this meeting by Steve Rose, publisher of *The Sun* newspapers in Johnson County. Rose had an unusual issue for them to consider. He wanted them to judge the merits of a first-of-its-kind sales tax bridging the state line. It would pool tax money from both the city and the suburbs. It was devised to fund regional cultural attractions like art galleries, theater companies — and Union Station's possible science museum.

Rose seemed an unlikely suburbanite to tackle this subject. His opinion of Kansas City was well-known from his twice-weekly newspaper columns. Boiled down, it was this: Kansas City was a cesspool, and the suburbs didn't need it. Just recently he had labeled Kansas City the "Tower of Babel" for all its political discord. A couple of years before, he had written: "Johnson County has become and will become less attached to Kansas City." He had even quit the Greater Kansas City Chamber of Commerce, because he thought it was too downtown-oriented.

Despite these qualms, Rose in fall 1995 accepted an invitation to breakfast with three Kansas City chamber leaders. To them, Rose was the perfect suburbanite to tackle a chamber priority — the two-state sales tax, dubbed "bistate." If the idea passed his muster — that is, if a city basher endorsed it — then much of Johnson County might follow.

The object of the bistate push: Union Station, its stone exterior reflected in the 1980s office tower that now blocked its eastern side. Inside, its plaster ceilings continued to crumble.

They asked him to lead the campaign to sell bistate to the Kansas-side suburbs. Rose said he would think about it. The group got up to leave. The four of them stood near the door at the First Watch restaurant off Mission Road. Suddenly, Betsey Solberg, a gutsy public relations executive who had just finished her term as the chamber's first woman leader, took hold of the lapels on Rose's overcoat. She implored him, "Steve, you need to do this for you and for Johnson County." Rose stood shell-shocked. He knew they were desperate. But he didn't want to stick out his neck if bistate didn't stand a chance.

So he called the meeting of his fellow Johnson County honchos, the government heads, the state officeholders, the education and chamber leaders. They gathered at Rose's newspaper office. He explained Kansas City's courtship. The bistate tax, according to its enabling legislation, had to pass in at least Jackson and Johnson counties to take effect. So Johnson County basically held veto power. That made Rose's role — and risk — monumental. The first question he asked his brain trust was, "Should I do this?" Whether these suburban leaders realized it or not, the fate of Kansas City's landmark lay in their hands.

Exit the Trizec quagmire

Getting from a Kansas City courtroom to Steve Rose's conference room had been no easy trek.

Emanuel Cleaver wasn't about to take the blame as the mayor who squandered Union Station. Cleaver was a politician who saw development as a tonic for whatever ailed the city. He followed the formula used for invigorating other big cities such as Baltimore, Cleveland and St. Louis — attractions and jobs. He felt he had something to prove. Cleaver's bid to become the city's first African-American mayor had been spurned by much of the city's business elite. They had bankrolled a white community college administrator instead.

Taking the issue of Union Station's salvation under his wing, Mayor Emanuel Cleaver encouraged a settlement with Trizec and then supported the bistate tax to renovate the building.

One member of the businessmen's Civic Council had been brazen about it, telling Cleaver he thought the city's first minority mayor would be under so much pressure from fellow African-Americans to produce pork and perks that he couldn't possibly succeed. Cleaver had told this executive: "You're wrong, and when I end my term as mayor, you will be able to see all over this city the ubiquitous work we will have done." Union Station represented as juicy a target as anything for Cleaver's affirmation.

So after the embarrassing outcome in court with Trizec, the Canadian company primarily responsible for finding a use for the station, Cleaver resurrected settlement talks instead of continuing a court appeal. Those talks dragged and went nowhere, however. The city wanted $5 million in cash, while Trizec offered $1 million. It got so bad that Trizec attorneys weren't even returning phone calls from city officials.

Yet the city had to deal with Trizec, because in 1990 an affiliate of the company had bought the station from the Kansas City Terminal Railway. Any attempt to save the building had to go through the defiant Canadians.

In September 1993, the mayor brought on Andy Scott from the city's economic development agency as a part-time chief of staff. Scott added a fresh perspective to the standoff. The city, to him, was being stubborn just to save face. It was holding out for a few million dollars when that amount wouldn't even fix the roof, let alone all the crumbling concrete, broken plaster and stained stone inside. Also, Trizec was in trouble financially, teetering on bankruptcy, so it probably didn't have $5 million to spare. Scott thought the city should salvage whatever it could and move on, for the good of the station, for the good of Kansas City. He told Cleaver this. Cleaver agreed.

Soon, with Hallmark head Irvine O. Hockaday Jr. acting as a go-between,

Andy Scott, the mayor's hand-picked man for the job, encouraged compromise.

the city and Trizec came to an agreement — Trizec would pay $1.5 million in cash and hand over ownership of Union Station grounds to a new nonprofit group, the Union Station Assistance Corp. In early January 1994, the deal was announced publicly. Cleaver had done it. He had delivered.

Now, with the community still searching for a home for a science center, once again the building was handed to the Kansas City Museum. And once again, the Kansas City Museum didn't have enough money. But this time something was different. This time the stars were aligning.

One star was Sprint Chairman William T. Esrey, who had joined the project on the museum's side. For Esrey, head of the region's largest corporation, this was a way of getting involved in the community, something he felt guilty about not doing. Another star was Mercantile Bank Chairman Dick King, a low-key civic leader who was tapped to head the new Union Station Assistance Corp. King had the trust of Hallmark. He had once headed a Hallmark-controlled bank, and a Hallmark executive had suggested him to Cleaver for the Union Station post. One other star in Union Station's new constellation was Missouri's senior U.S. Senator, Jack Danforth. Up to now in his respected Sen-

ate career, he had not paid much attention to Kansas City. But in 1994 he was embarking on his final year in office and wanted to leave a legacy.

Together, these three men resolved to do what countless others couldn't for a quarter-century: raise millions of dollars for Union Station.

In the first months of the year, Esrey and King huddled in the nonprofit's new office, in a Trizec building. First they had to know how much money they needed. But no one could say for sure. Every time engineers and architects studied the building, its repair cost jumped. A 1980 study estimated rehabilitation costs at less than $15 million. In 1986 another study tagged those costs as probably exceeding $30 million. By decade's end, a station preservation group pegged the reconstruction bill at upwards of $88 million. That was five years before. The building's deterioration had worsened since its closing. Esrey and King figured they would need more than $100 million.

Of that, Esrey committed to raising half, which amounted to the then-largest private fund-raising campaign in Kansas City history. He set up meetings and made the rounds of fellow corporate chieftains. Drue Jennings at Kansas City Power & Light. Henry Bloch at H&R Block. Bill Nelson at Boatmen's bank. Richard Green Jr. at UtiliCorp United. And, of course, Hallmark. Esrey loathed asking people for money. But he realized that because of his standing, other corporate heads would give more readily if he asked. And he was right. Often all it took was his personal visit. Bloch, for instance, pledged $2 million while Esrey sat in his Plaza office — and Bloch later conceded he gave more because he heard the plea from Esrey himself. Soon, Esrey was on his way to more than $60 million.

The other half of Union Station's money was to come from taxes.

Federal money was a possibility. Kansas City's project thrilled Marc Solomon, Danforth's legislative assistant. Solomon had grown up in Kansas City and picked up a passion for Union Station from his architect father. Solomon convinced Danforth that the station was a project worth fighting for. So Danforth in the spring of 1994 made securing $50 million in federal fund-

ing his No. 1 public works priority for his last year in office. This was quintes-
sential pork politics, and Danforth at one point told Esrey, "I've railed my
whole life against this, but…."

Solomon ordered copies of the last three years' worth of Senate, House
and final appropriations bills. At 250-300 pages each, these created a stack
several feet high on his office floor. He pored over them at night and on week-
ends, looking for pots of funding where the station might fit. He found the obvious — economic development funds, urban redevelopment programs. He also unearthed some obscure fits, like the Fish and Wildlife Service construction
fund and the National Oceanic and Atmospheric Administration budget, because the science museum would include a weather exhibit.

The senator organized a lobbying alliance of Missouri and Kansas representatives from both parties, even Sen. Bob Dole of Kansas — which was surprising considering how the two states' congressional delegations had bickered
earlier in Union Station's history.

The response amounted to a going-away present for Danforth. He was able
to secure $12.7 million in federal commitments in his final year, and more
would come later, thanks to Sen. Kit Bond's follow-through. Still, it was a lot
less than $50 million. Station officials had to get more money from some-
where else. With private and federal sectors on board, that somewhere meant
local taxes.

And, in keeping with Union Station's newfound good fortune, a new kind of local tax was sprouting from the political landscape. It was something called the bistate cultural tax.

The bistate tax's genesis as a community issue can be traced to *The Kansas City Star*. In 1983 the newspaper published a series of articles titled "Blueprint for Progress" that scrutinized what other cities were doing right to stay vibrant and what Kansas City was doing wrong. The paper outlined ways Kansas City's private sector could improve the city. These included rallying the community around agreed-upon causes. Later that year, several civic groups launched an organization, Kansas City Consensus, which set out to research topics and report what it believed to be the community's consensus.

In 1985, Consensus came out for a metropolitan arts and cultural district funded by a regional sales tax. The idea wasn't entirely new, but it made perfect sense in an ever-expanding metropolis. The most popular museums, theaters and symphonies drew patrons from the entire region, so the entire region had a responsibility to keep them going, even if the primary attractions were in the city of Kansas City.

Consensus' stamp of approval led to tax bills being introduced in both Missouri and Kansas. These bills allowed a regionwide vote on a new regionwide sales tax. The bills languished for several years, then became a game of pingpong between the two states. Missouri passed it; Kansas altered it. The bills went back and forth three more times before the laws were identical in each state.

By the end of 1995 bistate had been more than a decade in the making. Its momentum was waning. At this point Steve Rose called together those Johnson County honchos to mull over bistate's chances.

"Should I do this?" Rose asked the group. The suburban leaders, seated in the conference room of Rose's newspaper building, didn't answer that directly. Instead, they debated bistate a bit.

Was it even a good idea? Yes, several immediately affirmed, it was good for Johnson County to participate in a regionwide endeavor. But no, Ed Eilert spoke up, bistate's proposed one-quarter-cent sales tax was too much. And no, others added, arts funding wasn't a good sell for a tax increase these days, not with federal arts subsidies under attack in Congress. And besides, Fred Logan chipped in, bistate's formula for distributing the potential tax revenue was too complicated.

Rose leaned back in his chair, listening, taking it all in. The discussion confirmed something he had thought about for months: Cut out the arts groups altogether and dedicate bistate proceeds to Union Station only. The simpler, the better. After all, when bistate organizers conducted their last public-opinion poll, 80 percent of respondents said they were more likely to vote for a bistate tax if it involved a science center at the station. Rose mentioned his idea to the group. Heads nodded up and down. It made sense. It crystallized everyone's thinking. It could be a winner.

The bistate tax, because it was an experiment, because it bridged the nettlesome state line, probably had only one shot. And that one shot couldn't be

The great clock was a rallying point for station supporters, although it required encouragement from repairmen to get it to work.

jeopardized by the political hot-potato of arts funding.

Now Rose posed his original question again: "Should I do this?" There was silence around the table. Who else would do it? Not those involved in Johnson County Community College's last bond election. It had lost. And certainly not the government heads and state officeholders sitting there. They knew Johnson County. They knew the antipathy many held toward Kansas City. They knew there were plenty of people like John Middleton of Leawood, who once wrote to *The Star*, "I would not give those yahoos in Kansas City one penny I found on the street."

That left Rose, who had only scant election campaign experience. Fred Logan piped up, breaking the silence: "You're the logical one to lead it, Steve."

Actually, it was logical. For a few years, Rose had been branching out, raising his personal profile, joining civic boards and going onto television. He could see himself becoming a Big Player. Bistate represented another step onto the metropolitan stage. It was a chance to do something momentous. He got back in touch with the Greater Kansas City chamber leaders who had taken him to breakfast. He was in. And Union Station's history took another turn.

THE TACTICIAN

In May, Jack Craft set up a meeting of the redevelopment and campaign sides to prepare for the big unveiling of Union Station's new re-use — the plan that would be sold to bistate voters that November, with $118 million from the one-eighth cent bistate tax.

Craft was Rose's counterpart on the Missouri side for the bistate election and he was the election's tactician. His parents had been Nebraska state legislators, and after coming to Kansas City in 1965, Craft had worked on and led statewide campaigns for Republicans Jack Danforth and Kit Bond. To Craft, winning elections took discipline. You stuck to tried-and-true strategies. One of those was offering proof of what you stood for. You didn't go to the public and say, "Trust me." With bistate, this boiled down to providing a detailed plan. So Craft told the project planners he wanted something on paper. He wanted drawings. He wanted cost estimates. He wanted a slick presentation.

Craft

> "You guys just don't get it You don't understand what we're trying to accomplish. We have one shot at this."

At this meeting he expected a dry run of that presentation. So the two sides met around the Union Station Assistance Corp.'s conference table, in a room dominated by a mural of Union Station along one entire wall. The project's lead consultants, from Hines Interests Limited Partnership of Houston, filled one side of the table. They had no drawings. They weren't prepared for a full-blown presentation. The campaign's need for a plan was six months ahead of the consultants' timetable. The locations of the science museum's theaters weren't exactly set.

After a half-hour, Craft had enough.

He and Steve Rose began a role-playing exercise. They asked the questions they knew bistate voters wanted answered. How much was the project going to cost? It depended on further study, the consultants replied. When was the project going to be completed? The consultants weren't sure yet.

Craft blew up. He called them "ninnies."

"You guys just don't get it," he bellowed at them. "You don't understand what we're trying to accomplish. We have one shot at this." He left in a huff, unsure whether he would be able to run the campaign he wanted. Already *The Star* was having doubts about bistate, with one editorial writer opining: "A bistate sales tax increase to renovate Union Station has a slim chance of passing."

After two weeks of late nights, the consultants pulled something together, guided by campaign manager Brad Scott and Kansas City Museum Vice President Bill Musgrave. The consultants presented posterboard-sized drawings and better cost estimates in early June. But Hines' lead man in Kansas City, Michael Fletcher, took little part in it. Soon afterward, Fletcher left the project altogether. This settled once and for all whether things were going to get done on the campaign's schedule or on the consultants' timetable.

THE POLITICS OF GOSSIP

It was mid-campaign, and Rose sat at the head table at an Olathe Rotary Club meeting. Olathe was one of Kansas City's farthest big suburbs, some 20 miles from downtown in Rose's Johnson County. Its thousands of new residents didn't have much attachment to Kansas City or Union Station. The town routinely opposed taxes. So Olathe had all the makings of a hostile audience for Rose.

In fact, as Rose ate his lunch, one Rotary leader sitting next to him predicted matter-of-factly that more Olatheans would vote against bistate than vote for

it. Why did Rose even bother coming here? It was another of Craft's grand strategies. He also wanted to bombard it with campaign speeches. Any group would do. Campaign speakers were hitting hundreds of them. Even gatherings in someone's living room. Craft called it "the politics of gossip." If voters heard a talk about some topic and went away impressed, they probably would chatter about it. The good will would spread.

Opposition flier

So here was Rose at the Olathe Holiday Inn, up on the dais, speaking to about 80 persons, mostly older men. His intent was simple. He was there to allay their fears. He was speaking as one of them.

"We have our mindset; we have our own culture in many ways. …We are autonomous. But I don't think it's unfair or unwise to ask the metropolitan area to pay one-eighth cent to renovate Union Station."

And: "Not one penny can be used for anything else — not stadiums, not schools, not anything. …I will stake my life and reputation that Kansas City will not get their hands on this money. That's a promise."

He had their attention. By their nodding heads, by their whispers, by the softening of their glares, he could feel he was getting to them. At the end, he asked for a show of hands among those intending to vote for bistate or leaning that way. Two-thirds of those in the room raised their hands.

> "I will stake my life and reputation that Kansas City will not get their hands on this money."

GETTING ON TV

In the summer, after bistate made it on all five county election ballots, Craft and Rose entered the downtown offices of KMBC-TV, Channel 9. They walked

Walter Cronkite, who once lived and worked in Kansas City, came back to encourage supporters and to film a commercial for the bistate tax,.

past some of the studio sets and control rooms and were ushered into General Manager Dino Dinovitz's office. They wanted to buy TV commercial time. Not just any time, but slots Channel 9 wouldn't sell them.

Craft and Rose were tailoring some election strategy to public-opinion polls, and those polls showed that the more people knew about the proposal, the more likely they would vote for it. Earlier that year a pollster used by presidential candidates, Neil Newhouse's Public Opinion Strategies, found 73 percent of metro respondents would probably "vote for" a sales tax just for Union Station. This same poll also pinpointed the issues that resulted in higher "vote for" percentages — that the tax would end and that it would be overseen by businessmen, not politicians.

So Craft and Rose decided to embark on a television blitz to highlight these issues. They already had ads shot inside the station with trusted journalist Walter Cronkite. The campaign committee could afford TV time, because Hallmark's Bill Hall was raising more money than any other issue-oriented campaign in the region's history, $1.5 million in all. A televi-

sion consultant told Craft and Rose that the most important spot for their ads was during the local news. Those programs had the heaviest concentration of voters. The networks' top-rated sitcoms had plenty of viewers but not informed voters. However, when the bistate campaign's media buyer tried to purchase time during the news, she was told no political advertising was allowed in those half-hours.

That's why Craft and Rose went to see Dinovitz. Channel 9 had the No. 1 ranked news program. They wanted that exposure. They wanted special treatment.

Dinovitz explained that there wasn't a written policy, but that he didn't want the news contaminated with political ads or his viewers wondering whether the station endorsed candidates being shown. Craft and Rose suggested Channel 9 should have a policy allowing political ads during news programs only to ballot issues affecting the Missouri-Kansas audience area.

Of course, there had never been such a ballot issue before — until now.

Dinovitz told them, "If I make an exception for this, I'll have to make exceptions for other things." To which Rose replied, "There'll never be another thing

like this." The bistate leaders also proposed paying the station's top ad rate, instead of the reduced price given to political campaigns. Dinovitz told them he'd think about it.

A few days later, Dinovitz called Rose and gave him the OK.

AN INSPIRATION

One Saturday in the fall, Steven and Annalee Sellars stood in line outside Union Station. They pushed their 9-month-old daughter in a stroller. The line inched forward. Over the cracked asphalt parking lot. Through the chain-link fence blockading the building. Past the west-side entrance marquee, which resembled a gap-toothed smile, what with some of its hanging glass pendants missing. And finally into one of the building's side doors. The couple came to pay respects.

Every Saturday during September and October, the bistate campaign unlocked the doors of the abandoned depot so voters could see its condition, remember the good old days and maybe dream of a better future. And the public came. Thousands each week. Even during drizzles. They brought parents. They brought children. They brought video cameras. The ruin was on display. The morning the Sellars family visited, in fact, a 3-foot clump of the Grand Hall ceiling fell 92 feet to the floor with a deafening splat, terrifying those setting up campaign materials. So the public inspection was confined to a covered walkway in the Grand Hall, along with the south balcony above.

The Sellarses climbed a staircase toward the balcony. The walls were a sea of curled-up paint chips. Steven touched a few, and they broke off to the floor. The couple stood above the Grand Hall floor and looked out. The clock didn't run. The stone walls were blackened. White, chalky streaks ran down the walls around the arched windows. The ceiling itself was a mess. There was no color to it, just a dirty brown, and big chunks were gone.

It was easy to see why the redevelopment cost was estimated at $234 million

— the most expensive single project ever put before the local electorate up to that point. "It's depressing. It's a heartbreak," Annalee remarked.

But the couple noticed something else on the balcony. Older folks whispered to each other, or pointed down to a particular spot, or scanned the hall with an open-mouthed look suggesting they were hearkening back to earlier times. It could have been seeing loved ones off to war, or leaving for college, or boarding a train for the first time. Steven Sellars had his own history there. He was a teen-ager in August 1966 when he boarded a train to Chicago. On the train he met and gabbed with some other teens going to see the Beatles in concert. It turned out to be the day John Lennon apologized at a packed press conference for uttering his infamous line, "We're more popular than Jesus now." The memory had stayed with Sellars all the intervening years.

The couple climbed back down the stairs and went back outside. Steven Sellars got out his video camera and started shooting the station facade. "It's a wonderful place to come back to," he narrated while panning the camera across the building. "It's history and it's beautiful. Even though it's messed up, there's a lot of hope for it."

For an election, Union Station was the perfect candidate. People stood in line to see it at every public appearance. It inspired awe. It reaped sympathy. It committed no blunders. It sold the couple on the bistate tax. They were going to vote for it.

CHASTAIN WEIGHS IN

A month before the election, three mothers picnicked on a blanket in Kansas City's Loose Park and tried to decipher what was going on. Just the day before, a judge had ordered a separate Union Station re-use proposal on the city's November ballot.

This proposal had some similarities

Clay Chastain

...as the station was finally progressing down a road of redemption, there was Chastain setting up bombs .

to bistate. It included a science center, and it sought funding from taxes. Unlike the bistate initiative, however, this proposal involved untried and untested ideas, such as for solar power, and had no support from the civic and political establishment. The picnicking moms munched some fruit on one of Kansas City's glorious Indian summer afternoons while their children scampered around the park playground. The women wanted to see Union Station renovated. But why were there different plans with different backers and different-sized taxes? One of the picnickers, Susan Finucane, shook her head. "We're more confused than we ever were," she declared.

The confusion could be traced to one man: Clay Chastain. Since 1991 this home remodeler had been stumping for assorted station re-uses. Typically they incorporated trains and transportation themes, even a downtown aerial gondola. Chastain attracted media attention like a public relations wizard, even running for mayor and City Council to publicize his dreams. The media dubbed him an activist, but he really was Wile E. Coyote to Union Station's Roadrunner; that is, as the station was finally progressing down a road of redevelopment, there was Chas-

tain setting up bombs.

First he demanded that city leaders do something with the station. After the Union Station Assistance Corp. was formed for that purpose, he felt slighted at not being included. He proceeded to fight a 1994 USAC plan that tore out part of the elegant waiting room. Then after the bistate plan promised to keep the station intact, he remained dissatisfied. In his autobiography, he explained his motivation as acting in the public interest. But he also referred to his efforts as a personal "obsession" guided by "my deep-seated insecurities to prove my self worth" as well as desires to make a name for himself — and even to get women "driven into my arms."

By the fall of 1996, he had sued the city for not putting one of his proposals on an election ballot. He pursued the case not because it was in the best interests of Union Station — his proposal was full of "harebrained" ideas, in the words of one city leader and not because voters had no voice in the station's future — they were getting their say through bistate. Based on interviews with reporters over several years, it was clear he simply wanted things done his way. A judge eventually sided with Chastain, because, as the ruling stated, cities could not discriminate against ballot issues — even those that might be "unsound policy."

So for several weeks before November, two saviors for Union Station vied for the public's attention. It was enough to make the picnickers' heads spin. "The thing about Union Station," Finucane said at one point, "is it just seems like it goes on forever. When you're inundated with it, you just go into overload. You just get tired of it."

LAST-MINUTE THREAT

The night before Halloween, Jack Craft, as usual, watched the 10 o'clock news for any mention of bistate. On KCTV, Channel 5, though, political commentator Steve Glorioso reported on rumors that

Hundreds of backers attended a campaign rally in September 1996.

long-awaited federal indictments were coming the next day. After the broadcast, Craft called Glorioso's cell phone.

Craft sounded nervous. His tone was somber, not upbeat, as it generally was. He was a man who could see all his work, his entire campaign, unravel right at the end. The indictments supposedly were aimed at some of Missouri's Democratic political establishment. "What have you heard? Who are the names?" Craft asked Glorioso, a longtime Democratic strategist. Glorioso repeated what was widely suspected — Missouri House Speaker Bob Griffin and probably labor leader Mike Fisher, a member of one of the bistate task forces that had asked the counties to put the issue on the ballot..

Of course, that's what Craft dreaded. Something linking bistate to corrupt Missouri-side politics. Six days before the election.

It could play right into the hands of bistate opponents. A one-time bistate official caught up in corruption. Bistate

would be branded guilty by association. This, after the campaign had prepared legal documents and run television ads touting that Union Station wouldn't be politics as usual, that Johnson Countians could feel at ease sending their tax dollars across the state line. Anxiety ran so high that some people with the campaign asked long-time Democratic operative Woody Overton to talk with his friend, U.S. Attorney Stephen Hill, about putting off the indictments until after the election. But Overton wouldn't do it.

Craft had reason to worry. The campaign's tracking polls were dipping. The probable "yes" vote in Johnson County had sunk below 60 percent for the first time. And the trend line extending out to Election Day put the outcome in the category of being too close to call. Now possible indictments. The whole election could "blow up in our face," Craft knew.

Opponents might exploit the news. The campaign wouldn't have time to respond. And that's what would stick in

people's minds when they stood in the voting booth and thought about which button to push, "yes" or "no." All Craft could do was wait for now.

And, indeed, the indictments came down the next day.

Charline Schmelzer remembered the day of the Union Station massacre in 1933 — because she was there, a teenager leaving the Fred Harvey lunch room. In 1995, she spoke to a luncheon crowd at the kickoff of a Science City Festival, aimed at drumming up support for the proposed science museum at the station.

Mission accomplished

On Nov. 5, 1996, Steve Rose awoke at his usual 5:30 a.m. for a treadmill workout. He hadn't slept much in anticipation of this day, Election Day.

The campaign had been one crisis after another. It never seemed to let up. The bistate election committee kept getting more and more money, but campaign coffers couldn't buy everything, like a smooth ride to election day. "Everyone felt one bad quote, one misstep, would doom the campaign," said Andy Scott of the Union Station Assistance Corp.

City and county officeholders weren't touching this issue. Even a couple of Johnson County commissioners, when they put bistate on the ballot, made it clear they weren't endorsing it. The conventional wisdom in suburban circles was that Steve Rose was in for a big fall. "Don't take this hard if it goes down," Rose had been told in the final days. He retorted, "Things look good."

In fact, Johnson County's tracking poll numbers had turned back up. Kansas City had gone to court to block activist Clay Chastain's plan for the station, and effectively knocked his competing idea off the ballot. And other bistate opponents had ignored unrelated indictments that snared Michael Fisher, a Missouri member of the bistate tax force.

As it was, the campaign had covered nearly all other circumstances and contingencies, from some 200 speeches to 20,000 yard signs, from paying election consultant Pat Gray $22,500 for handling Northeast Kansas City blocs to spending roughly $30,000 for political club Freedom Inc.'s get-out-the-vote effort in the central city.

Everything had come together by Election Day, as if it were synchronized, like a school of fish darting in different directions and then suddenly swimming in unison.

In midafternoon Rosemary Otte, a middle-age woman, walked into a voting booth at a Johnson County school. She hit the "yes" button for bistate. "It was a big decision for me," she acknowledged afterward. "I think Jackson County should take care of their own county. But I felt enough compassion about Union Station that I went ahead and voted for it."

That evening, campaign officials worked telephones bearing news of what they hoped would be an overwhelming number of votes like Otte's. The telephones kept them in contact with election boards of the five metro counties, and election returns were posted on a board facing the lobby of the Two Pershing Square building. There, hundreds of bistate boosters, some wearing white Union Station sweatshirts, some sipping free River Market Brewery beer, waited for history to unfold. Cheers and whistles from those closest to the board let those farther back know all was going well.

Indeed, it was a landslide, not even close. Jackson County approved the bistate tax by a two-thirds majority. Suburban Johnson, Clay and Platte counties each amassed "yes" votes of 60 percent or better. Only heavily taxed Wyandotte County rejected the tax. A breakdown of voting patterns revealed one clear trend: The wealthier you were, the more likely you were to vote for bistate. So Kansas City's Southwest Corridor south of the Country Club Plaza

At an election-night victory party Nov. 5, 1996, station backers Don and Dot Buell celebrated.

and Johnson County's Mission Hills section both topped 80 percent approval rates. Meanwhile, newer and more expensive subdivisions provided higher victory margins than older neighborhoods in the same suburb. This occurred in just about every big suburb with old and new sections — Overland Park, Olathe, Shawnee, Lee's Summit. Union Station's appeal, then, spanned geographic boundaries, and the pairing of preservation with science education boosted that appeal among younger parents not old enough to recall the building's heyday.

Around 9:30, Craft officially declared victory. There were balloons. There were hugs. There were speeches. The word "historic" filled the party like confetti in the air. Bistate was the nation's first cultural tax to cross a state line. It bridged Kansas City's psychological divide. Rose, working on television as a political commentator, blushed and beamed on the air when the news anchors congratulated him.

Everything had come together by Election Day, as if it were synchronized, like a school of fish darting in different directions and then suddenly swimming in unison.

As the victory party wound down, some campaign staffers didn't want to leave. They didn't want the night to end. So they agreed to meet in front of Union Station. They took the remaining beer keg with them.

Campaign volunteer Shirley Esher was there with her daughter, along with a few others. It was dark where they all stood, raising toasts. and recounting the ups and downs of what they had gone through that fall. Behind them, the arched windows glowed. The chandeliers were still on inside.

Soon, another car pulled into the parking lot. They didn't know who it was. The car circled by the group and then stopped. An older woman got out and walked toward them. "I just wanted to see what I voted for," the woman said.

After another half-hour, the after-party broke up. Esher, in her Union Station sweatshirt, was the last one to leave. She couldn't let go. She had grown up in the area, moved away to raise a family, and had just come back a few years before. Now she was involved in something historic. How cool was that?

She got in her van, pulled out onto Pershing Road, turned onto Main Street and looked over at the lighted-up station one last time for the night. It was finally going to become their science museum. And now it was up to them and their planners to turn it into the Next Big Thing.

CHAPTER 11

THE NEXT BIG THING

I ronically enough, David Ucko never wanted his science museum inside Union Station. It simply wasn't a good fit.

Exhibits couldn't go in the basements — the ceilings were too low and columns were in the way. Exhibits couldn't go in the Grand Hall or the waiting room, either — the ceilings were too high and the arched windows let in too much light. The station's architecture overwhelmed any accommodation. Ever since becoming president of the Kansas City Museum, in fact, Ucko had tried steering the museum anywhere but the station.

When Ucko interviewed for the job, Ron Manka, chairman of the Kansas City Museum board, drove him past a proposed university research park east of the Country Club Plaza, pointed and said, "That's where the science center will be." That project, though, never got going. Neither did several other deals Ucko pursued. Not a new development site closer to the Plaza. Or a site on Theis Mall pushed by J.C. Nichols head Miller Nichols.

Ucko and the Kansas City Museum board turned their attention to the west edge of downtown, where burgeoning DST Systems Inc. was reshaping the skyline. DST offered the museum free land.

Kansas City Mayor Emanuel Cleaver heard about the offer and asked leaders of the effort to update him. They gathered in May 1993 in the mayor's wood-paneled office on the 29th floor of City Hall. Cleaver sat on a couch while an architect moved the mayor's coffee table and spread the latest color renderings on the floor. The architect began going over the plan. The mayor followed along and then bowed his head. He slowly shook it from side to side. The room quieted.

"You guys," Cleaver announced, "are giving me a headache."

The Kansas City Museum leaders sat, stunned. Cleaver had something else in mind — Union Station. He urged Ucko and his board members to give the city government time to negotiate a settlement with Trizec Corp.

The mayor had made it his personal mission to reopen the station. But his pitch to Kansas City Museum leaders was purely financial: Major donors for

Facing page: **After years of vain hopes and discarded plans, Science City began to take form alongside Union Station.**

the science museum wanted it at Union Station, or at least wanted that alternative exhausted before the museum wound up anywhere else.

Ucko knew this. He knew leading businessmen on the Civic Council of Greater Kansas City had refused to endorse the science museum at one Plaza site. And he knew how one of the city's leading bankers, R. Crosby Kemper Jr., felt after visiting a railroad station-turned-science museum in Richmond, Va.: "I am very much in favor of doing the same thing here....I think the people would vote favorably on this, because their greatest priority is saving the station, and to combine the two would be an unbeatable idea." Though Ucko considered Union Station to be the Kansas City Museum's albatross, he had no choice.

This proposed science museum site achieved reality only in a scale model. It would have sat along Brush Creek between the Country Club Plaza and Theis Mall, now Theis Park.

So when the Trizec settlement was done, the Kansas City Museum went through a shotgun wedding. And it came, as promised, with presents — the two largest philanthropic gifts ever bestowed in Kansas City, a total of $45 million for exhibits and operations from the Hall Family, the Hallmark and the Kauffman foundations.

Now it was time to fit a 21st century museum into a building inspired by 19th century tastes. But first, everyone had to understand what it was Ucko wanted. And that would be an adventure all its own.

A vision develops

Just as the building of Union Station evolved from one man's vision, so too would the rebuilding. David Ucko was the latter-day Jarvis Hunt, the station's architect.

Although nearly a century separated them, the two had several things in common. Both attended the Massachusetts Institute of Technology. Both grew up on the East Coast and migrated from there. And both wanted to bring Kansas City something it desired — a major-league railroad station, in Hunt's case; a science museum for the largest U.S. city without one, in Ucko's case.

Yet in other ways the two couldn't have been more different. Hunt came from American aristocracy, Ucko from a recent immigrant family. Hunt was bombastic, Ucko soft-spoken. And Hunt was a man of the arts, Ucko a man of sciences.

That made Ucko a better fit for MIT. This New Yorker — whose parents had fled the Nazis — earned a Ph.D. in inorganic chemistry and became a chemist. He taught the science at small Antioch College in Ohio and wrote two textbooks. Nevertheless, when the college teetered on the verge of going broke, Ucko resolved to make a career change. But toward what? He liked teaching. And his expertise was science. "What about science museums?" his wife, Barbara, asked one day. That seemed a perfect fit.

So, in the late 1970s, Ucko became research coordinator for science exhibits at the famed Museum of Science and Industry in Chicago. He moved up

Facing page: David Ucko, president of the Kansas City Museum. He wanted "adventure" and he got it.

to vice president and later moved on to a deputy director's post at Los Angeles' science museum. While in this job, he had a life-changing experience. He envisioned the Next Big Thing in science museums.

Science-oriented museums evolved more than any other type of museum this century, following the accelerated pace of technological change. When the Chicago and the New York science centers opened in the 1930s, they broke from the standard of housing collections or artifacts in glass cases. At these science centers, visitors pushed buttons or turned knobs to get something to work. That's how science museums developed for three decades until 1969, when the Exploratorium opened in San Francisco.

As its name implied, the Exploratorium introduced an entirely new concept to museum visitors, the chance to explore exhibits themselves, to do more than merely push a button. One feature in the Exploratorium was the Bernoulli Blower. It was a geyser of air supporting a 10-inch rubber ball. Children pushed the ball, and it oscillated. Or they pulled the ball out of the airstream, and then threw the ball back in to see it captured in the current. These type of exhibits — learning by playing — became prototypes for an explosion of new science museums across the country in the 1970s and 1980s. By the late '80s, museum directors were again searching for a new formula.

It was then that Ucko visited Paris for the opening of that city's science museum. He wasn't impressed. It was more push-button, interactive stuff. But a separate building on the museum grounds housed a temporary exhibit. It was called Cites-Cines, or Cinema City. It immersed visitors in the look and the feel of a city, only on a film set. As you walked past a cityscape of building facades, scenes from classic movies were shown on TV monitors arranged throughout the set. Marilyn Monroe glanced at you. A taxi driven by Robert DeNiro cruised past. Peter Sellers searched for jewel thieves nearby. Whenever you entered one of the buildings, another montage of film clips added scenery. In a subway tunnel, for instance, you saw the train coming. "You felt like you were in a scene," Ucko told his colleagues.

This "immersion" experience became Ucko's inspiration. By the end of the decade, the Kansas City Museum was looking for someone who could develop a science center. A headhunting firm contacted Ucko. "David was thrilled by the opportunity to be No. 1 instead of No. 2," recalled his wife, Barbara. In the ensuing years, David Ucko retold the story of Cites-Cines dozens of times to describe what he had in mind for Kansas City. It became the guiding light for his own make-believe city, his own themed experience, his Science City.

As early as 1991, Ucko's vision appeared in an article he wrote for the newsletter of science and technology centers. It was headlined: "Science City:

Hands on: At the Exploratorium in San Francisco, the Tornado, a column of swirling mist, and the Bernoulli Blower.

Program for Cites-Cines.

A New Model for Science Centers." It began: "Imagine climbing inside a Kansas City fountain and discovering what makes it work, or playing golf on a special course where each hole demonstrates a principle of physics…. In contrast to the historical replicas of a 'living history' village, visitors to Science City will discover facades and mini-environments that form a 'living science' city of today."

The museum industry immediately took notice. This was cutting-edge. This was — well, what exactly was it? It had no artifacts to show off. No space capsule or prehistoric bones. It had no particular icon either, nothing like the mechanical dinosaur at the St. Louis Science Center. It had no glass cases and no storyboards for visitors to read. It sounded more like a theme park. It sounded like fun.

Funny this should come from a man like Ucko. He talked like a scientist, with little inflection or animation in his voice. And those who knew and worked with Ucko didn't leave a meeting with him thinking he was particularly fun-loving, a man capable of envisioning a playful experience for children and adults alike. Yet he had a playful side, hanging a poster of the "Periodic Table of Desserts" by his front door at home, or sitting on the floor and talking to his cat. To this outwardly cautious man, playfulness was a means to an end, a way for his vision to succeed.

His genius was finding a new way to combine science and playfulness: the theme-park setting. He, before others in the museum world, understood the evolving entertainment direction of the service industry.

Restaurants such as Rainforest Cafe and Hard Rock Cafe weren't just selling food; they also were selling the experience of being there. Stores such as Niketown or the Sharper Image, along with entire shopping centers such as the Mall of America, weren't just selling products; they were drawing consumers into fun environments with games and gadgets. It took years before the business press discerned the significance of what was happening. The *Harvard Business Review* published an article in 1998 titled "Welcome to the Experience Economy." The authors, from a consulting firm, said that "experiences have emerged as the next step in what we call the progression of economic value," beyond mere goods and services. Ucko grasped this trend early.

As William T. Esrey later related, "None of us knew what the hell he was doing." But, "if there wasn't a David Ucko, this wouldn't have gotten done."

Location, location, location — again

As Science City's vision danced around Ucko's head, the question for Union Station became: Where exactly will the museum go? Maybe in one of the majestic halls, or in one of the wings, or in one of the basements, or someplace else. Then there was the rest of the redevelopment, the eateries and the three theaters accompanying the museum. Where will they all fit?

Railroad stations throughout the country had been transformed into several things — hotels, shopping centers, convention halls, even traditional glass-case museums. But no railroad station quite approached all the attrac-

---

"None of us knew what the hell he was doing." But, "if there wasn't a David Ucko, this wouldn't have gotten done."

— *William T. Esrey*

Inside the Postal Museum in Washington, where exhibit space was created between wings of the U-shaped building.

tions Kansas City intended.

One project did resemble Union Station's retrofit, the conversion of Washington's beaux-arts Post Office building into government offices with a Postal Museum in the middle. The Post Office's decorative but decrepit lobby, with marble columns and a coffered ceiling, was fully restored. And exhibit space was attached outside, creating an atrium in the middle of the U-shaped building. Jim Bruns, the Postal Museum's director, raved about what was done: "I thought it was absolute brilliance." Those responsible included architects Coke Florance and David Greenbaum, along with construction planning consultant Glen Hopkins. All three were tapped for Science City at Union Station.

EARLY DESIGNS

A previous architecture team had tried fitting Science City into the station's main halls. The result was a fiasco.

That was in 1994, soon after the Union Station Assistance Corp. took over the building from Trizec. A team of volunteer local architects, led by Cary Goodman, a Kansas City Museum board member, recommended a plan to the museum and to the assistance corporation. The plan called for demolishing the waiting room's west wall and midway, along with much of the marble floor, and then placing an exhibit hall annex on the west side of the waiting room. This recommendation represented the first serious station plan in years and the first one for the new ownership. But it broke the federal government's historic-building rehabilitation rules.

This was no small failure.

These rules, known as the secretary of the interior's preservation standards, had to be followed to obtain federal money, which Union Station was counting on. No. 1 on the list of rules: "A property will be used as it was historically or be given a new use that requires minimal change to its distinctive materials, features, spaces and spatial relationships."

Goodman thought that the volunteer proposal amounted to "minimal change." Preservationists did not.

SCIENCE CITY AT UNION STATION

Volunteer architects' plan would have removed a waiting room wall and the floor.

In 1995 a historic-preservation consultant, Mary Oehrlein of Washington, was brought in. She took one look at the volunteer recommendation and flatly told project leaders, "You can't do this." Once when Oehrlein met with local preservation advocates, one of them, longtime Jackson County Historical Society leader Jane Fifield Flynn, sidled up to Oehrlein and asked innocently, "What do you think of this?"

Oehrlein replied, "I don't think it's right."

And Flynn looked back at her wide-eyed, "I'm so glad to hear you say that."

The Missouri preservation review board, which enforced the federal rules, took a dim view of it, too. By the time the project got around to officially hiring its architects, Goodman was passed over and the volunteer plan was scrapped. In terms of preservation, it became the prototype for what not to do.

It was their job to pick out space for the museum, its theaters and everything else, just as they had for new tenants in Washington's Post Office.

Maybe they could come up with the same solution with Union Station?

First, the architects cataloged the space required for the station's new tenants. They tallied some 225,000 square feet. The building, meanwhile, contained roughly 670,000 square feet from top to bottom, more than enough to accommodate everything planned. Yet there were other considerations. Like Ucko's own requirements. He wanted space that would conform to his vision, not the other way around. Ucko made sure this vision wouldn't be compromised. Over and over, he pleaded in meetings, "I gotta have..." or, "If I'm going to be in this project, I gotta have...." First and foremost, his museum had to have a 50-foot-high clearance, like a sky over his city. There were other things, too: continuous cityscape facades, real streets and curbs, natural light from above. All these couldn't be crammed just anywhere inside Union Station. The height and light demands by themselves ruled out anywhere in the T-shaped building except the two main halls.

Besides Ucko's requirements, the architects had to juggle federal preservation rules and public-relations considerations. Florance and Greenbaum produced "test-fits" for Science City. One placed exhibits inside the waiting room, with a planetarium bulging out the north end and the large-screen and stage theaters filling the basements under the Grand Hall. A second test-fit put exhibits in the back of the waiting room and under it, while all three theaters were in separate buildings outside.

Each of these plans had problems. The first required excavating under the station — and into the limestone bedrock — to make room for the large-screen theater. This was deemed more expensive than building a new structure. The second left only 20-foot ceiling heights for Science City under the waiting room. Back and forth the architects went, moving around the different exhibits like pieces on a chess board.

By March 1996, the one and only solution became obvious. If Ucko had to have his 50-foot ceilings, if federal preservation rules precluded altering the main halls, and if the budget imposed limitations, then Science City couldn't be done within the existing structure. The building simply would not do.

To save the beautiful beaux-arts station, adjoining structures would have to be added — for exhibits, the planetarium and the large-screen theater. With their last beaux-arts building, Florance and Greenbaum had placed the Postal Museum partly in the existing building and partly outside it. They would do the same with Science City. In the end, Union Station itself would contain only one small theater in the basement and a smattering of exhibit space in the west midway.

The building was getting restored, but for what? Not much of Science City was going in it. That was fine with Ucko. He was getting the free-standing structure he always wanted. Now Ucko could get on with developing exhibits.

'Adventure,' 'immersion' and 'experiences'

Ucko had this vision — a kind of science playland where the laws of physics, the hands of nature and the organisms of biology were all part of the museum visitor's experience. It would be the essence of his Next Big Thing. But how could this be done? Ucko wasn't an exhibit designer. For that, he turned to one of the nation's foremost museum design firms, Douglas/Gallagher, based in Washington, D.C.

Yet what Ucko wanted was not what Douglas/Gallagher was used to doing. First, the budget limited him to $300 per square foot of exhibit space, considerably less than the $500 per square foot that Douglas/Gallagher usually worked with. Second, he said there would be no glass cases, no artifacts, no graphics panels explaining how something worked.

So the designers spent their first months on the job basically learning a

In the idea stage, exhibit designers sketched, from the top: A space center ("Experience a simulated mission"), an aerodynamic feature called Go for a Glide ("Design a hang glider and test your design using a simulated ride") and a Secret City ("Explore the utility tunnels below the city").

...the designers spent their first months on the job basically learning a new language. Ucko held one meeting to define some terms. He didn't want the word "exhibit" used. He wanted his designers to think of "adventure" and "immersion."

new language. Ucko held one meeting to define some terms. He didn't want the word "exhibit" used. He wanted his designers to think of "adventure" and "immersion." To him, these brought to mind a theme park-like city with streets and curbs and even sewer grates, where each door off the streets opened into a different activity, and where character actors blended into the action and aided the visitor's discovery. Just like at Disneyland.

Fine, the designers thought. But how did this apply to dinosaurs and space and medicine? What kind of story lines did Ucko want with his adventures? And what, exactly, should a city of science look like? Ucko offered few suggestions. It was as if Ucko was imagining a symphony. The designers would have to read his mind to compose the music.

"I think David always had a vision, but he didn't know any more than we did how to get there," explained Cybelle Lewis, Douglas/Gallagher's exhibit design manager.

Once, Douglas/Gallagher prepared four renderings of a city facade, Science City's cityscape. Each one took weeks to produce, from the concepts to the artistry. One looked like downtown Kansas City. One looked like Disneyland. One looked like a movie set. And one looked cartoonish. Finally it came time to show Ucko.

"Which one is what you want?" he was asked.

"Well, none of these," he replied.

It was the same with early sketches for the science exhibits, the so-called experiences. The designers drew ideas. Ucko shot them down. The designers came back with what they thought hit the mark. Ucko retorted, "Where's the adventure?"

It was the same with character actors, who were to play along with museum visitors in the "experiences." All along, the designers deemed actors essential to the adventure. They were floored when Ucko asked them to plan ways to do without them.

To Ucko, all this kept the designers on their toes, always thinking, always striving to innovate. To the designers, they simply weren't getting any direction. They were just getting rejection. More than once, even Patrick Gallagher, the design principal of Douglas/Gallagher, ended a day looking in the mirror and muttering, "I don't think we can do this project." Often these disputes required mediation, and Glen Hopkins filled that role.

Slowly, the exhibit "experiences" evolved — 49 in all, with the help of market testing.

Ultimately there would be a space center, with a remote-control probe that could be driven on a red and mountainous surface of Mars. There would be a medical section, with a Cites-Cines-like walk-through of a pulsating and gurgling blood vessel. There would be a criminal laboratory, with investigative instruments to solve a crime. There would be a garage where a car was being repaired and a kitchen where bread was being baked. There would be a cave and a tree house to explore, a dinosaur site to dig into, a combine to harvest crops, a gravity-testing miniature golf course to play, even a hotel con-

taining optical illusions, called the Mr. E Hotel.

With this one, designers struggled. It lacked some pizazz. So Steve Snyder, Science City's science director, traveled with two designers to Las Vegas. They scheduled a meeting with magician Teller, of Penn and Teller, the duo that defied tradition by giving away their secrets to audiences. It was spring 1997. Snyder and the designers crammed into Teller's tiny office in an industrial park. Teller caught on to what Science City was after. He took a couple of books off the shelf and flipped them open to classic magic tricks. A head sitting on a tray. And a ghost image floating around a stage.

Snyder found a way to use some of the tricks. For one, a cafe was added in the hotel. On one table would be a head — of a museum character actor. There would be no body visible under the table. And the head would talk. It would mock the astonished look on a museum-goer's face. It would direct the person to come closer, check out the table, try to discover how a bodyless head could be talking. Would the visitor do it?

"This whole thing is a big risk," Ucko remarked about all the exhibits.

In 1998 a delegation from the American Association of Museums landed in Kansas City for the Kansas City Museum's accreditation. The delegation looked over Science City's plans. And its eventual report concluded, "The museum field is being given a new model."

Science City takes shape in miniature: Patrick Gallagher of the Douglas/Gallagher firm showed designers and others a scale model of the museum.

These exhibit designs made the cut. Concepts accepted for the final Science City plan included the astronaut training center, the treehouse as part of Natural Kansas City, and the walk through the human body.

Appearance counts

The decision to fit most of Science City into an annex had taken care of one problem but opened a Pandora's Box of other quandaries. Science City's annex was going on the west side of the waiting room. Museum parking was going west of this. It would be very convenient for visitors to park and walk directly into the annex. But what was the point of restoring Union Station then? And how would the station's other uses, like restaurants, generate crowds?

The architects proposed forcing museum visitors into the station at track level, bringing them up to the Grand Hall and making the museum entrance inside the old waiting room. So Science City's streetscape was devised to start at the waiting-room level, wind downward like a square corkscrew, and then wrap back underneath the station. Leaving Science City entailed going back up. Either way, coming or going, visitors would pass through Union Station's majestic halls.

That was fine for the Grand Hall. It kept the function it always had — lobby, mall, central hub all in one. As for the waiting room, that was something else. It wouldn't be a waiting room again — it was part of the museum now. It

couldn't be let alone for gawking — it wasn't as elaborately adorned as the Grand Hall. Something had to be done to make the room conform to Ueko's "city" theme. The architects dashed off dozens of drawings. One made the space a train station again, unloading at Science City. Another turned the room into one giant science exhibit, a walking tour of the human body. Mary Oehrlein, the preservation consultant, looked at some of these and curtly announced: No. "You're forcing the space to become something it's not," she said. The architects started over. The room was going to become part of a "city," so they studied photos of cities.

What did cities contain that could be in Science City, too? The answer leaped out of the photos: urban plazas.

Sometimes a city's most celebrated space was its plaza, like in Venice, Italy. The formula was simple: open space, people gathering, sculptures or fountains. The long, tall waiting room held that same potential — right down to the echo of shoes on its stone floor. All it needed was some furnishings. So the architects ringed the room with benches, tables, streetlights and banners, and then added a fountain and a carousel, although budget cuts eventually victimized the carousel. The new function wouldn't be out of character with how the room was used before — people pausing, lounging, watching. Once again, the new would mesh with the old.

And that was something David Greenbaum kept in mind with the architecture of Science City's new structure.

Passageway to Science City. Renovators settled on this plan for the waiting room containing a fountain and streetlight-like fixtures after scrapping ideas for a carousel and ornamental trees, right.

In Washington, a few blocks from the White House, Greenbaum sat at his drawing board. Pinned up around his desk were blueprints and photos of Union Station — building elevations, the old train sheds, an aerial view of the train complex.

Every now and then, Greenbaum paused and stared at his station spread. "I wanted to capture the spirit of the site," he said.

Science City's annex was going on track level. That's where the hard work of railroading occurred and where the train sheds exposed their steel supports. Greenbaum, then, gave the annex an industrial texture, a mixture of steel and glass. The more he stared at the station photos around this desk, the more he noticed various shapes — horizontal bands of train tracks, triangles in the sloping train sheds, X's in their roof trusses. These he incorporated too. A mesh screen covering the west facade would contain X-shaped bracketing. Glass skylights would take the form of right triangles. The roof's jagged shape would jut perpendicularly from the waiting room, just as the train tracks had. "We could keep the spirit of what Jarvis Hunt had without being slavish to the original design," Greenbaum said.

Actually, Greenbaum couldn't be slavish to the original architecture even if he wanted to. Federal preservation rules forbade any historic building addition from having the same materials and look as the historic building. The point was to differentiate old from new, no matter how strangely out of place the new looked. In his 1998 book, *The Architecture of Additions: Design and Regulation*, architecture professor Paul Spencer Byard decried new architecture that copied the old because it was "something that seeks the benefit of its success like a parasite." Byard, with Columbia University's graduate architecture school and a director of the New York Landmarks Conservancy, offered examples of universally admired but highly controversial additions — such as I.M. Pei's famous glass-sided entrance pyramid between the wings of Paris' Louvre.

Before the roof went on Science City, the foundation went in for the Iwerks three-dimensional theater.

In much the same sense, Kansas City government's preservation agency, the Landmarks Commission, had this to say about Greenbaum's design for Science City's annex: "Its materials are distinctive from the original station, yet reflect the industrial character of the property and are compatible with the character of the property."

As 1997 progressed, then, all the Union Station space dilemmas, all the architectural quandaries, all the science exhibit anxieties, had been resolved. Yet gremlins would continue to bedevil the project.

Science City would have mock stone walls created from a mixture of sand and cement and they would lie where limestone had been blasted away in the 1910s.

Constant blue skies would be guaranteed in parts of the new museum.

Like many of Science City's predecessors as Union Station's savior — a previous science center, the federal office complex and the Ambasz botanical garden, to name a few — planning or politics took a re-use idea only so far. At some point fate intervened and every idea was derailed. It had happened every time.

It looked as if it would happen with Science City, too.

In mid-August 1997, bond attorney David Queen sat, hands folded atop a table, in a conference room where a mural of Union Station covered an entire wall. A telephone call was in progress, a call he dreaded, a call that could unravel the station's complicated financing. This financing, which amounted to a construction loan, hinged on the participation of a foreign bank. The bank's top officials knew almost nothing about Kansas City or how much the station meant to its residents. The foreign bank, the Canadian Imperial Bank of Commerce, was supposed to have OK'd its participation at the end of July. But it asked for a week's extension. At the end of that week, it asked for another week's extension. That time had passed, too.

Now Queen and Union Station's budget gatekeeper, Clark Wallace, chatted with one of the bank's executives, Jeff Heckman. The speakerphone was on, and Heckman's voice on the other end told them: "We'll just step out of the way. I know that's not what you want to hear from me."

There it was, another bad break for a building that had been collecting them like puddles on its marble floor for years. The financing deal was off. It meant the project would not go forward and get done on time. It meant the people's trust in bistate could be broken. Who knows? Maybe fed-up suburbanites would start a petition to bolt from bistate altogether, killing the whole thing.

With the financing, the project faced sort of a Catch-22. Because the sales tax revenue would be spread out over six years, a loan was necessary to do the job in the three years promised to the voters. But the Bistate Commission, an agency

Banker Dick King of the Project Coordinating Committee.

overseeing the historic bistate sales tax, could not by law go into debt.

To get around these pitfalls, layers of bonds and guarantees to bondholders were set up. At the heart of these layers was something called a "credit enhancer," basically a bank that would guarantee the entire amount owed to buyers of Union Station bonds. At more than $100 million, this was too big and too complex for any local bank to handle, so the project solicited bids from some 20 banks. Only two responded, and only one — the Canadian bank — was serious enough to visit the site.

Yet, when Canadian bank officials investigated the project and came to town, they found it embroiled in a public relations mess.

Back in the bistate tax campaign, some of the campaign's television ads featured the faces of five businessmen who would essentially manage the project. Those businessmen formed a separate committee. William T. Esrey was the chairman. The four others were Louis Smith, Tom McDonnell, Dick King and Mike Brown.

The businessmen often made important decisions, such as the choice of the chief consultants, Hines Interests Limited

Partnership, and the entire layout of the redevelopment. The problem was that such decisions about spending public money were made in private, behind closed doors. That was against Missouri law when meetings dealt with tax money being spent by tax-supported agencies, such as the Kansas City Museum.

The Bistate Commission, composed mostly of politicians accustomed to holding open meetings, pushed for the businessmen to open theirs. And it had allies — the county prosecutor and *The Kansas City Star* editorial board.

Still, the businessmen were adamant, Esrey more so than the four others. He was used to making decisions in private.

With the two sides at an impasse, some forces behind the bistate election — Jack Craft, Steve Rose, attorney Terry Brady and Hallmark's Bill Hall — met with bistate Commissioner David Wysong. Wysong, who served in Johnson County's government, was not a typical politician. He was independently wealthy from advertising and investments. He knew King and Esrey from the Mission Hills Country Club, where he was then president. The bistate leaders knew that the situation was delicate, that Union Station needed the businessmen's stewardship, especially for the private fund raising. They also knew Union Station meetings had to be held in public. It was the law. They asked Wysong to intervene.

Every couple of days, Wysong bent Esrey's ear, sitting in Esrey's black, wrought-iron patio chairs, talking while Esrey was flying to see Microsoft's Bill Gates, touching base at Esrey's ranch in Colorado. Wysong told Esrey: "I come from private industry, too. I can see both sides. But there is a law, and that is the only way the project can go forward." Each time, Esrey replied: "We'll never have open meetings."

When Wysong reported this back to Craft, Rose and the others, one of them articulated what everyone was thinking: "We've got to get him to resign." The duty fell on Wysong's shoulders.

He met Esrey one last time on Esrey's patio. "Bill," he said, "I cannot conceive of one individual standing in the way of a project of this magnitude. Could you conceive of stepping aside?"

Esrey didn't answer then. But several days later, to the surprise of nearly everyone involved with Union Station, Esrey did suddenly announce his resignation from the project.

All during this, bond attorney Queen and budget-keeper Wallace were trying to put together the construction-financing deal, and the negative publicity was hurting the project's credibility to outsiders. The out-of-towners still needed convincing that Union Station could recover from Esrey's departure and that the partnership wounds were healed. So a luncheon was scheduled at a private room at the Kansas City Club downtown.

Three bistate commissioners and attorney Brady were there, along with a couple of the business leaders heading the project and project managers under them. On the Canadian bank's side, there was Heckman, head of U.S. public finance, and John Trahan, executive director of the bank's securities subsidiary. Trahan at one point asked how everyone was getting along. The bistate commissioners replied that there had been a disagreement, but

their primary concern was keeping the project going.

Meanwhile, Trahan studied the body language of the Kansas Citians. Did the representatives from the project side and the bistate side get along? Did they smile as if they meant it? They did.

After that, the financing deal sailed along. After months of attending meetings, exchanging telephone calls and faxes and soothing jittery nerves, Queen thought he had everything rock-solid. But he was dealing only with the bank's middle managers and wasn't certain the higher-level executives understood all the components.

Sure enough, when the deal got to that higher level, the international bank backed out, just five months before construction was scheduled to start.

What were the alternatives? Collect millions in private money immediately, which wasn't possible? Or resort to junk bonds as a form of financing, casting a black eye on Kansas City?

It turned out the Canadian bank's high-level executives were uneasy with the private fund-raising pledges. This money was merely pledged, not in hand. And while those pledges came from upstanding corporations like Hallmark and Sprint, those firms meant little in Canada. The bank wanted "complete comfort," Heckman said.

Queen had an idea. Before he fin-

ished that mid-August telephone call — the one in which Heckman dropped the bombshell — Queen asked him, "If I could solve that problem, will you stay?" Heckman stuttered a slow "yes," knowing it wasn't likely.

Immediately afterward, Queen called Dick King, chairman of Mercantile Bank in Kansas City. Queen explained the situation. The deal needed an infusion of money, fast.

"We need a letter of credit to cover the capital campaign," Queen told King.

"How much? Is it over $10 million?" King asked, knowing anything over that amount had to be approved by his bank's top officials in St. Louis.

"It's less," Queen replied.

"Then we can cover it," King proclaimed.

In a gesture reminiscent of the Kansas City Spirit of the city's bygone eras, when money was raised for civic projects and disaster relief, King acted decisively on his own. He prepared a letter of credit worth $9.1 million for the international bank. King authorized the transaction, then ran it by the bank's ad hoc loan committee, with himself being one of two members. "I didn't think it was a risk we shouldn't take," he said later.

King was in the right place at the right time for Union Station. Within a year, he would lose some of his titles and power in a bank reorganization. But by then Union Station was already under construction.

CHAPTER 12

BACK TO LIFE

A MAN WITH A BALANCING ACT

Jackhammers clanged and thumped under Union Station's old waiting room like a rock 'n' roll band gone amok. Donald McCormick ignored the racket as he hiked over mounds of mud, his charcoal-gray suit pants hanging over construction boots. Union Station was being sliced open like a patient in surgery, and McCormick was checking its vital signs.

It was early 1998. McCormick was an ex-military officer, and it still showed in his appearance. He was clean-shaven, and his black hair was neatly trimmed. He trudged under the room to its north end, where men wearing hard hats wielded the reverberating jackhammers and power saws. They were cracking open the concrete covering the steel columns holding up the waiting room.

McCormick stopped at one of the columns already uncovered. Years of rust had eaten away at the steel, leaving quarter-sized flakes. McCormick flicked off one of the flakes. Then he moved on to another column. Rust had gnawed a hole in this one. McCormick squatted and jabbed his fist into the hole.

"Look at this column," he exclaimed. "Look how bad it is. You're losing a lot of strength when you have a hole in it like this."

It was like this all over the building. Beams had rotted inside the concrete enclosures. Girders had broken loose from the structure. Some of the concrete had cracked and chipped off. There was one culprit — water. Water from cracked gutters, flowing down walls and oozing into columns. Water from restroom and kitchen mops, seeping through concrete in the floors. And, of

Watching the budget, watching the schedule: Project manager Donald McCormick, right, with J.E. Dunn's Scott Vath, left, and Hines' Glen Hopkins.

Facing page: Under the waiting room, beneath crumbling concrete, stood steel columns weakened by years of rust.

McCormick on watch: Balancing needs against the money available.

course, water from the roof, trickling down everywhere.

Rainwater leaks had been a constant problem since before the station even opened. Through the intervening decades, the slow-motion processes of seepage and corrosion, and freezing and thawing, acted the same way as the conditions creating potholes. Several repair estimates had been made in the last decade, but none of them could be taken seriously until the patient was cut open and examined.

The situation turned out worse than anyone had imagined. It was so bad that the reconstruction's main consultants, the Hines Interests Limited Partnership, began a weekly Monday morning meeting of architects, engineers and contractors to review a list of newly found structural problems. These were classified into 43 different jobs. Hines' McCormick was the man primarily responsible for balancing the repair needs with the budget ramifications.

The main contractor, J.E. Dunn Construction Co., had estimated that the repairs would cost $6 million — but only $1.5 million was allocated for this in Union Station's $38 million restoration budget. That budget was so tight, Mc-Cormick knew the project couldn't afford all the extra millions. So he released Dunn to do $4 million, figuring he would find ways to get the rest done.

He just didn't know how yet.

McCormick was a trained engineer, educated at West Point. His primary construction experience was on hotel and office skyscrapers. Those buildings were the specialty of his company. Hines' work could be found in the glass-sided skylines of Houston, Denver, Detroit and Minneapolis. Hines had earned a reputation for finishing projects on time and on or under budget.

Yet, historic building renovations, particularly railroad stations, were an entirely different breed. They were littered with examples of escalating costs. Washington's much-ballyhooed station redevelopment had ballooned from $130 million to $160 million, because consultants determined it needed more retail to support itself. And New York's Grand Central Terminal makeover started at $175 million and ended at $200 million.

For construction engineering expertise on Kansas City's station, though, Hines tapped McCormick, who hadn't worked on either of the company's high-profile restorations, Philadelphia's 30th Street Station or Washington's Post Office. McCormick had never handled an older building. He didn't have any experience dealing with decades of decay and neglect, so he didn't know how much damage to expect.

But this was what he lived for — building things. As a teen-ager he had built a 14-foot sailboat. And for his last house, in Boston, he had framed and wired and sided a 2,000-square-foot addition all by himself. To him Union Station wasn't much different from the office buildings he had engineered and managed in Boston. Sure, there were obvious contrasts, the same way today's Honda varies from yesterday's Studebaker. But it was still a building, framed with steel beams, poured with concrete, covered with a roof. And actually, Union Station seemed a pretty simple structure.

Work on the roof ran into unexpected problems, harbinger of later difficulties for the entire reconstruction.

Construction projects are nothing but constant troubleshooting, even if they are simple structures. Union Station provided a hint of what was to come with its first repair job: the roof. This job required Hines, as construction manager, to supervise the installation of concrete tiles so they duplicated the originals in every way but one — they couldn't leak. The tile manufacturer, however, couldn't fill the order. The roof repair contractor ended up sending its own men to the manufacturer's plant in Nebraska to finish the order. Later the troubleshooting involved the project budget. Bids for the main construction work came in nearly one-third higher than expected. Hines officials simply misread the tight construction market, resulting in fewer bidders. Those bidders sometimes crammed too much into the drawings, resulting in padded prices.

The $234 million project was threatened with a $29 million overrun. So parts of the plans were cut back, and the construction reserve fund was exhausted. Hines officials, including McCormick, received a tongue-lashing behind closed doors from business leaders managing the project. This budget problem would eventually be solved by paring the overrun and adding $20 million in private and federal funds. At this point, though, no one knew that, and the crisis only added pressure on McCormick to keep costs in check.

One day a construction worker noticed a crack in the concrete around a floor beam under the men's smoking room, just off the Grand Hall. This typically represented trouble, a sign that rusted steel had expanded inside the concrete. So the concrete was broken off. Sure enough, there was a hole in the steel. Replacing the beam would mean taking out the wall above it, and that wall contained decorative plastering. This one repair could cost upwards of $100,000, and the budget couldn't take that kind of hit. So McCormick improvised. He talked with other engineers and decided to add reinforcing beams on both sides of the deficient beam. It would cost one-third as much and still carry the needed floor weight.

Hopeful subcontractors collected rolls of documents in September 1997. When the bids came back, project managers faced some surprises.

"You're always balancing costs with what's the right thing to do for the building," he explained.

Structural issues like this got hashed out every Monday morning at Dunn's on-site headquarters inside the Express Building just west of the station. Sitting in folding chairs around folding tables, the men in white shirts and ties, with hard hats at their sides, went through a list of the latest structural revelations, usually a few dozen items. Another floor beam was found caked in rust. Two additional columns holding up the waiting room were unusable, raising the total to six columns. Girders holding up the carriage pavilion turnaround on the west end didn't look too good, either. On and on the lists went, week after week, each item coming with a price tag and requiring architectural revisions.

At the end of one meeting in November 1998, an engineer opened a book of blueprints and pointed out a new problem not on the list. McCormick put his head on the table and pounded his fists a couple of times. He expected these items to slack off as work progressed, but they hadn't. Over and over he asked himself, "When is it going to end?"

Julian Davis: British accent and rare skill.

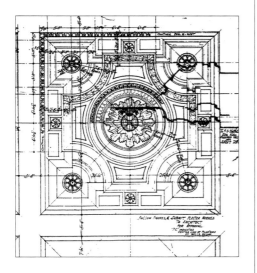

Ceiling design from Jarvis Hunt's original plans.

A PLASTERER'S NIGHTMARE

"Chewie" was nowhere to be found one November morning. Union Station's workday had started, as always, at 7:30 a.m., and now it was close to 9 a.m., and Julian Davis hadn't yet climbed the 110 steps to a scaffolding platform high above the Grand Hall floor. It was from this platform that the Englishman intended to magically resurrect Union Station's showpiece, its ornate Grand Hall ceiling.

This ceiling was the most decorative feature of the station's interior, with plastered swirls and ribbons and eggs and oak leaves and rosette medallions. Except no one could see its multicolored splendor anymore. In the 15 years since the building's heat was turned off and roof leaks were neglected, a quarter of the ceiling had broken apart and fallen to the floor. What remained were patches of brown and white, the colors of dirt and chalky moisture residue. The whole thing resembled a jigsaw puzzle with many pieces missing.

No other part of the interior renovation was as eagerly expected. Not the mundane job of running new heating and cooling ducts all over the building. Not the removal of several beams in the basement to accommodate a grand entrance staircase. Not even the repair of a less elaborate ceiling in the waiting

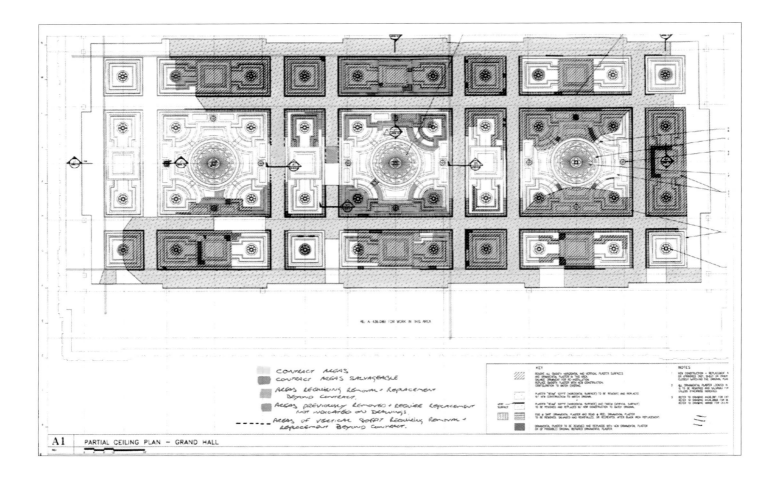

room. No, as Louis Smith, one of the businessmen managing the redevelopment, told project managers after the Grand Hall ceiling restoration began a few weeks earlier: "I think it defines the project."

Yet Chewie, the job's master plasterer and the brains behind putting the puzzle back together, still hadn't appeared for work this day. He had discovered an English-type pub serving English-style hard cider in Kansas City's Westport nightclub district. "We're not too happy with Chewie right now," said Gary Francis, the plastering superintendent.

So the morning's work went on without him. A dozen other men wearing coveralls and hard hats were up on the scaffolding platform. Some hammered out loose and damaged plaster. Others swept up plaster scraps in a haze of dust and dumped them down a yellow chute to a trash bin on the ground floor.

Finally, near midmorning, Chewie arrived up the scaffolding stairs. His head was pounding.

Here was the man, one of the few in all the world, who could accomplish Union Station's most eye-popping metamorphosis.

Julian Davis' path to the top of his profession couldn't have been scripted better by Hollywood. As a youth he was a wild child by his own account. Once, he was suspended from school for setting off a homemade firecracker in class. Another time he was suspended for sitting outside a classroom and drinking beer. Finally he was expelled for shooting someone with an air-pow-

The plasterer's task: Lobby ceiling areas colored in yellow, pink and blue all needed repair or replacement. White areas and the small spots marked in green were OK.

Smith

After ceiling repairs were complete on the west side of the Grand Hall, above, workers moved on to other sections. Deterioration was obvious before work began on the easternmost bay, right.

ered gun. He didn't return to school. He was 16 years old. His wavy hair flowed all the way down his back to his belt, so he was nicknamed after the hairy "Star Wars" character Chewbacca — Chewie.

He had scoured the newspaper want ads for a job. He didn't want to sit behind a desk. He saw something about a plastering apprenticeship and got the job in his native Bath. He thought plastering was all about putting up flat walls. It was — with new construction. Instead, he unknowingly landed in the renovation side of the industry. It was a side that was dying out as old theaters, mansions and government buildings fell by the wrecking ball, a side that literally depended on fires as a source of new work. "I didn't know what I was getting into," he said.

Chewie learned about plaster mixes, how the thick ones dried too quickly and the runny ones didn't stick. It was like understanding the nuances of cooking. In 1991, Chewie caught on with Hayles & Howe, then in the midst of winning the Plasterers' Trophy, the top industry award in Britain, three times in 10 years. His training advanced to surveying sites after fires and installing grids for hanging new plaster casts. He had a knack for visualizing things in three dimensions. His best marks in school had come in architectural drawing and geometry. "It's like hand-eye coordination for baseball," he explained. Increasingly his jobs became more complex — adding trim to new walls in English homes, installing curved plaster casts in France's EuroDisney, creating ornamental wall moldings from scratch for New York movie theaters.

Then Windsor Castle, a home of British monarchs for centuries and the largest inhabited castle in the world, burned. England's Heritage secretary called it "a national disaster." The country's three best ornamental plastering firms were called in to repair it. Chewie was part of Hayles & Howe's crew. In the Octagon Dining Room, with its arched windows, ribbed ceiling and Gothic motifs, the plasterers started with only photographs of what had been. From those they formed new casts and created molds of one-of-a-kind ornament shapes. Then Chewie pieced together everything on the floor to make sure it fit and installed it. The result pleased even persnickety architecture critic Prince Charles — and earned Hayles & Howe a Plasterers' Trophy.

In the United States, redevelopment managers of Kansas City's Union Station determined that only four businesses in the world were qualified to fix the Grand Hall ceiling. Only two of those bothered to bid on the $1.5 million job, and Hayles & Howe was selected. After a charred castle, what was Union Station other than a little run down?

Chewie soon found out. He was approaching 30 years old now. He had a round face with a matching round belly, which sometimes popped out of his T-shirts when he raised his arms over his head, which was often with a ceiling. His role as Union Station's plastering foreman encompassed two basic tasks early on: making an inventory of what needed replacing, and designing a new suspension system to hold the new plaster.

The Grand Hall ceiling, all 22,000 square feet of it, was divided into three bays. Each bay was exactly the same — several rectangular sections surrounding a central square. The sides of the rectangles and the square were framed with decorative molding in egg patterns. Inside each rectangle was a small rosette, while inside the square were rosettes in each corner plus concentric circles of various patterns — braids, ribbons and leafy swirls.

For an inventory, Chewie had to determine how much molding was needed to fill the various holes in the ceiling. Part of this task involved taking exact dimensions of all the moldings so duplicate casts could be created. Easy enough. Chewie took a measuring tape and held it across one of the football-sized eggs in the egg pattern. Then, to test the pattern's consistency along the same stretch of molding, he held the tape across another egg, and another.

Ninety-five feet above the floor, the plaster work went on.

"Ahhh, hell," he called out. The egg widths were slightly different. Not different enough to be noticed from the floor 95 feet below, but different nonetheless.

It seemed the original plasterers made the eggs smaller or larger as they proceeded along the side of a rectangle or square so that the final, corner egg was fully rounded and not cut off. Nearly a century later, Chewie's ceiling contract called for replicating everything. That meant mistakes and all. Chewie

Almost nine decades before Chewie and his crew, these men worked atop their own scaffolding in Union Station. They applied plaster to a grid similar to the modern renovators'.

didn't know how many egg casts he would have to make. "That's a huge problem," remarked Francis, the plastering superintendent.

Another huge one accompanied Chewie's other basic task, hanging the metal suspension rods. The original plaster had been applied by hand in three separate coats, while Hayles & Howe intended to replace much of it with pre-made plaster sheets and casts to save manpower and money. Nevertheless, both types of plastering were suspended the same way — from a grid. This grid had metal rods dropping vertically from the ceiling beams and joined horizontally. Chewie had to reconstruct this grid across the ceiling holes, to fill the voids. Again, easy enough, an ordinary level frame. Just determine the ceiling's base elevation level and extend the grid close to that point.

To do this, Chewie set up a laser almost level with the ceiling. He turned it on, and the red laser spun around like an ambulance's emergency light. The red beam circled in a perfectly level plane. Chewie stood on a platform that raised him almost to the ceiling, too. He took out a plastic measuring stick and hung it from one of the unadorned, flat areas of the remaining ceiling. The laser's red beam hit above the three-inch line on the measuring stick. He moved to another part of the flat area. The red beam hit below the three-inch line. The ceiling levels differed by roughly an inch in height — again, not much to the naked eye, but to a craftsman it was like walking over uneven floorboards. Again he had to replicate the original mistakes, by sloping some of the horizontal bars in his grid.

Why couldn't he just correct all the mistakes, make the eggs all one size and the ceiling one exact level? Because that would require ripping out the rest of the ceiling and building the whole thing new. No one had the money for that. "This is the nightmare part of the job," he muttered.

Dedicated by station planners as restaurant space, the former women's waiting room columns received finishing touches.

WOULD A RESTAURANT WORK?

Outside Union Station in the summer of 1998, excavators and dump trucks and cement trucks drowned out all conversation except for shouts. Inside Union Station, the Grand Hall sat empty and quiet, a lull between the high-pressure water cleaning just completed on the walls and the scaffolding being put together to rebuild the crumbling ceiling.

One afternoon, that silence was broken by hard-soled shoes echoing on the marble floor. Restaurateur Rod Anderson, who ran the Hereford House steakhouse a few blocks from the station, was touring the Grand Hall with his chef and the station's new leasing agents. Anderson was expanding his restaurant business and thinking about opening a new concept. Union Station, as Kansas City's next major attraction, offered an opportune location. He wanted a look. He had never been inside before.

Now, as his shoes clip-clapped across the floor, his mouth flung open and his head swiveled up and down, and then side to side. He had never seen anything like it in Kansas City. Such proportions. Such vastness. Such grandeur. "This is breathtaking," he thought.

Restaurateur Rod Anderson, right, visited the space for his future Pierpont's eatery in summer 1999. With him was architect Matthew Connolly.

He slipped into a daydream. He remembered being in New York's Grand Central Terminal and its jumble of heads, its frenzy of motion, its din of voices. It felt alive. He pictured that same scene here in this stately edifice. If the Grand Hall evoked such good vibes when it looked so bad — unlighted, unpainted and unrepaired — then in his mind it had the potential to be special. He wanted in.

The leasing agents walked Anderson and his chef to the northeast corner and into a dreary, high-ceilinged room with flaking green paint, broken plaster molding and dusty marble floors. This is where the station's one fancy restaurant will go, Anderson was told.

Redevelopment leaders had always promised to replace the Harvey House restaurant, that fixture of station lore with the prim waitresses and some of the best food in town. But the room directly east off the Grand Hall had been remodeled so many times, its original decor was gone. It would cost too much to rebuild the decor, so project managers moved the restaurant to a three-story section in the north end of the east wing. This encompassed the former women's waiting room and rest room on one level, a beauty salon one floor above and a women's and children's waiting room one floor below. Together they had comprised a women's oasis in the mostly masculine building.

This was where women went to powder their faces, or fall asleep on a couch between trains, or wash off soot in a small private bath, or take a crying baby for a feeding and a nap. And like so much of Union Station, these rooms left lasting impressions on some patrons. Just going to the rest room, seeing the long row of stalls, hearing the marble doors bang shut and stepping inside one was, for one young girl passing through during the station's heyday, "quite an experience for me, for the toilet I was used to was a building out behind our house." Now all the furnishings and equipment had been cleared out, leaving mere shells.

For Union Station's second life, these rooms were being transformed into something entirely different, something that attracted people after dark and produced income, something meant to prevent the building from becoming a white elephant again. And this transformation, more than anywhere else in the station, illustrated the challenge of marrying the new to the old, the modern to the obsolete.

Early on, the restaurant leasing firm proposed bringing in such high-profile national chains as Morton's steakhouse and Rainforest Cafe. These, though, preferred a plain box in which to plop their decor concept, not rooms with bulky columns and turn-of-the-century ornamentation. Besides, Union Station hadn't reopened yet. It had no track record as an attraction. So the national chains balked. The leasing agents then went to Plan B — local restaurateurs, such as Rod Anderson.

Anderson landed in Kansas City and got into the business purely by accident. He was a financial watchdog, an accountant by trade. But one day in 1987, while with Meridian Investment Co. in Boston, he was asked to analyze a property the company held as collateral on a loan. It was the Hereford House. The restaurant at 20th and Main streets was like most other downtown-area institutions at the time: in decline. It had a chummy core of long-time customers, but many were coming less frequently. Anderson felt the place skimped on portions and served commercial-grade meats instead of choice cuts. A year later a Meridian partner bought the restaurant and offered Anderson a stake in it — but only if Anderson would run it. Anderson agreed. He relished the challenge of rebuilding a business, any business. So what if he knew little about food? He knew plenty about general ledgers. By the end of that year, he restored hearty portions and choice cuts, and patronage doubled. The Hereford House was on its way to becoming among Kansas City's highest-volume restaurants.

At first he focused on food and service. His only edict on decor was that it not look shabby. He let an architect talk him into painting the walls gray. Only later, as theme restaurants took off, did he learn that gray was considered a dull and unpleasant color for eating. By 1997, Anderson was expanding the Hereford House to the suburbs, but when he heard Union Station was trolling for tenants so close to his Hereford House, he thought: "If someone is going to take away my business, let it be me."

So there he was on his first tour of the empty behemoth, absolutely overwhelmed. Anderson was a 6-foot-4-inch former small-college basketball player with flecks of gray beginning to show in his short, brown hair. He walked around the women's waiting room, and it occurred to him that this could be his theme restaurant. He turned to his chef: "Can you believe this decor?" and "Can you imagine what this will look like?" and "Can you see this room full of tables?"

Anderson walked out with what he called the "thrill factor." What better place than Union Station to make a personal statement as a restaurateur, that Rod Anderson was more than a steak-and-potatoes guy?

Soon, however, the thrill was gone.

In August, Anderson was back inside the station, this time accompanied by his architect, Matthew Connolly, and his concept designer, Paul Robinson, a former partner in the Gilbert/Robinson group, which had developed the Fedora Cafe and the Bristol and Plaza III restaurants on Kansas City's Country Club Plaza. Anderson explained his conception — an upscale eatery, something with seafood to fill a gap he perceived in Kansas City's market, basically another Bristol. As he talked, they walked. Anderson figured the station and the space would wow the two consultants as much as it did him. Finally, he asked what they thought.

"This is going to be a pain in the neck," Connolly told him. One of his last jobs had been the Cheesecake Factory on the Plaza. Connolly thought the Cheesecake Factory would never do a three-story restaurant again. The logistics of delivering hot food to different floors before it cooled were too much trouble. With Union Station, the rooms looked elegant, but would that matter if the food couldn't get there? "You don't need this," Connolly said.

Robinson, meanwhile, couldn't see the space fitting into a Bristol concept. "I don't feel it yet," he said.

After the tour, the three headed to the Hereford House for dinner. They stayed in a booth more than three hours, rehashing all that was wrong with the space. It was three floors. It had a dated decor that couldn't be replaced. It was chopped up by columns and walls. It had less usable square feet than either Hereford House. And it would cost a bundle to build out. For the next couple of months, Anderson crunched some numbers. He tried to figure out how he could turn a profit. How many tables did he need? How many tables actually fit? The answers didn't correlate.

The more he worked on it, the more dumbfounded he became. What did he get himself into?

"Everyday I looked at the plans," he said, "it looked more unmanageable."

Some of the renovation work took place outside Union Station. In St. Louis, workers at Antique Lighting Co., top, took apart light fixtures, sandblasted them and lacquered or painted them. *Above:* Stamped copper before and after restoration. *Left:* Back in Kansas City, electricians reinstalled fixtures high on the Union Station walls.

ON BALANCE, A SUCCESS

One balmy Indian summer day, Donald McCormick stood on the east wing's mezzanine level above the Grand Hall, glanced out a window and noticed two workers climbing on steel beams outside. They were installing framing for a new skylight over the old Harvey restaurant area, slated to become a fast-food court. McCormick was on one of his inspection tours with members of the regular Monday morning structural repairs meeting, and he had been wondering for weeks how this skylight was going. Usually it was covered with a tarp. Today the tarp was off.

As he looked out at the workers, he could plainly see that the perimeter framing — the horizontal strip that would eventually hold glass panels — was crooked. He stepped outside through a window opening, and a construction foreman introduced him to one of the skylight installers. "It doesn't look right," McCormick told him. McCormick, in his characteristic charcoal-gray suit, walked next to the knee-high base of the frame all around the skylight's four sides. The perimeter framing bowed outward, noticeably. To McCormick this just invited trouble from Union Station's old nemesis, rainwater. Water could seep into the gap and trickle down into the station.

He turned to Dunn senior project manager Bill Spillar: "I'm concerned whether everything will seal properly."

Spillar replied, "That was a good catch."

McCormick then asked for a string and instructed others to hold it across one base of the four-sided frame. The string acted as a carpenter's straightedge. The base meandered, compared with the string's straightness. "We're off three-fourths of an inch," McCormick declared. No detail was too small to get past his attention. That's how he had to be to keep structural costs from spiraling out of control.

While McCormick was agonizing over inches and dollars, the rest of the station was undergoing so much change that old-time train travelers would scarcely have recognized it. All the stairways leading from the waiting-room midways to the track platforms were gone, except for two. The ground directly under the waiting room was topped with concrete. The area where passengers once boarded trains on the waiting room's west side was sprouting columns and walls for Science City's museum box. Out in front of the building, a special backhoe equipped with shears as large as a man chomped away at the steel frame under the driveway deck, which was close to collapsing. The shears, nicknamed "Jaws," bit into the metal, twisted it and ripped it away like an animal feeding on a carcass. Once the deck was gone, the station resembled a castle surrounded by a moat.

Meanwhile, the structural repairs were coming along. The vertical beams supporting the waiting room — the ones so decayed that McCormick could flick off steel flakes or put his fist through a hole — those had been taken out. A truck-sized jack had propped up the room's

New light fixtures went up in the entrance to Science City's theater district, inside the old station at the foot of the entrance staircase to the Grand Hall.

To make way for new parking space, the old driveway deck was removed along with more rock and dirt.

north end while an ironworker with a torch had severed each of the six worst columns at its top and bottom. Then a crane had hoisted a new I-beam in its place. On the southwest corner of the building, construction engineers had originally expected to save about half the steel frame holding up the old carriage pavilion connected to the west wing. But everywhere that jackhammers cut open the concrete to examine more steel beams, there was rust. Finally project managers decided to demolish the entire frame and rebuild it from scratch.

Then there was the skylight. After McCormick's inspection, Dunn's Spillar had quickly dispatched a letter to the skylight installation company, ordering work stopped until the perimeter framing was fixed. A week later, after the next Monday morning structural meeting, McCormick and his structural watchdogs went back up to check the progress. No one else was around the skylight as they peered at the horizontal base frame through the east-wing mezzanine windows. "The line's a lot better," observed architect Michael Fountain.

McCormick remained silent until he had scrutinized it. Then the skylight installers appeared, carrying out a piece of glass. McCormick told them, "The glass is going in, looks nice."

In mid-December, McCormick arrived at the Monday morning meeting,

Pressure-washing the outside of the station.

sat on a metal folding chair and grabbed an agenda. "OK, I love that list," he announced. The usual three-page slate of problems was down to one. By January 1999 it was down to a couple of items, and the meeting was abandoned.

In the final tally, all the structural repairs had come to $3.3 million, less than the $4 million allowed and barely more than half the original $6 million estimate, thanks in part to McCormick's vigilance and Dunn's cooperation. So at the end of that month, McCormick rounded up the Monday morning regulars — Spillar, Fountain, other Dunn managers and engineering consultants — and treated them and their wives to a "thank you" dinner.

He arranged for a special room at JJ's bistro on the Country Club Plaza. Seventeen were there in all. In the midst of the $1,500 feast, with the wine flowing at a pace of a nearly bottle per person, McCormick stood up and addressed the wives with a toast. "The reason why we're here," he said, "is your husbands have done a tremendous job. They have saved the project a tremendous amount of money. You should all be proud."

And with that, they clinked glasses and drank some more.

A British plasterer had to climb through the ornamentation to attach anchors for the ceiling.

A PLASTERER'S MASTERPIECE

With the new year, too, Chewie's work on the Grand Hall ceiling progressed from planning to installing. He was more than ready.

He had spent much of the fall consumed with eggs and rods. One week he measured hundreds of ornamental molding eggs, unsure of how many different sizes he would find, unsure of how many different replacement casts he would have to make. He settled on three sizes, one cast for each size. Other weeks he held his arms overhead for hours, screwing vertical metal rods to the roof beams and screwing horizontal rods across vertical rods, filling the ceiling holes with his suspension grid. But the work — like putting up picket fences around a yard, only upside down — was repetitive and boring. It wasn't plastering. Finally he was getting into ornamental installation, the finish work instead of the prep work.

Installation followed a logical progression: flat surfaces such as backgrounds and beams first, and then the ornaments.

One morning in February, beam cases and egg casts sat in a line on the scaffolding platform. They had come from Hayles & Howe's warehouse in Baltimore. For casts of the side-by-side eggs, craftsmen there had started with intact pieces from a salvaged section of the ceiling. They poured rubber over the eggs to prepare a reverse mold and later filled that mold with plaster to produce a cast. Then the old eggs and the new eggs were joined and the process repeated, eventually forming an 8-foot-long egg section.

Several of these beam cases and egg-cast sections were shipped weekly to Kansas City. On this morning, Chewie and a partner picked one off the floor. The beam cases were lifted into place and mounted on the ceiling grid. Then the eggs — with the three dif-

ferent sizes alternating — were held up, fastened to angle brackets on the beams and tied with wire to the grid above the beams. It all entailed the same principles as hanging kitchen cabinets.

With that done, Chewie got to do a little actual plastering. Holes from the drilling and joints between the casts had to be filled. And in every rectangle and square with egg molding, an oak leaf had to embellish each corner.

In one, Chewie gobbed plaster matting and a milkshake-thick plaster mix over the corner eggs. He lighted a cigarette and pressed a plaster oak leaf against the wet plaster. The rounded cast stuck in place like a suction cup. Then he laid out a pouch resembling a mechanic's wrench set. These were his plastering tools, which weren't much different from those used by the ceiling's original crews. Chewie chose one resembling a butter knife. He began smoothing out the gobs around the oak leaf, as if he were spreading butter on bread. Back and forth, up and down, he shaped the edges with short, quick strokes, his cigarette burning almost to the butt. He selected another tool, this one with a narrower end, like a scalpel. He scraped away the excess plaster. The edges looked seamless, as if the oak leaf and the eggs were one cast.

Chewie didn't have to make them that way. The oak leaf sat almost 100 feet above the floor. No one would be able to discern how smooth his plaster edges were from that far away. But Chewie was a craftsman. He took pride in making the reproduction look better than the original.

"They're much cleaner edges," he remarked while he peered at the corner.

Over his shoulder, one-third of the platform was empty now. The first

With the so-called egg sections — non-matching plaster work that bedeviled restorers — finally installed behind him, a painter touches up a floral detail, a rosette.

bay of the ceiling was finished, restored in all its former glory. Or so everyone presumed. They would know for sure tomorrow. That was inspection day.

The next morning, Mary Oehrlein climbed the 110 steps to the top of the scaffolding. She was the preservation consultant, with some architecture award to her credit in almost every year since the mid-1980s. She had been the one who made the painters redo part of the waiting room ceiling after the scaffolding came down. And she had been the one who was lifted to the Grand Hall ceiling in a bucket truck a few years back and flaked off layers of dirt to uncover the original blue, red, silver and chestnut hues. Her word was gospel. Now she had to sign off on the first third of that Grand Hall ceiling.

It was mid-February. Floodlights on the scaffolding illuminated the completed bay. Oehrlein — tall, sandy-haired and soft-spoken — strolled around the platform, under the new beams and rosettes and ribbons and eggs. She had been there a couple of times before, to review 15 newly applied paint colors that had been brushed on, sprayed on and even patted on with rags to achieve a layered look, like an impressionist painting. But they hadn't been consistent enough for her. This time, as she strolled around the scaffolding, she thought, "This is it." She finally saw what she wanted — chestnut glazing with short brush strokes on much of the molding, plus silvery clouds obscuring bright reds and blues in rectangular side sections. To the modern eye, the ornate Victorian-era ceiling looked odd, even slightly garish. But that didn't matter to Oehrlein. "This is as close as we're going to get," she said, "to the original ceiling."

Chewie saw her from the opposite end of the scaffolding platform, where he was installing the third bay. He couldn't tell what she was saying. Still, he felt a bit triumphant. The once-wild child had gotten the job done. He fit the puzzle back together. "Chewie cracked it," said Stephan Meyers, Hayles & Howe's project manager.

The last day for the ceiling work came in April. Late that afternoon the plasterers, the painters and a host of project officials gathered for a sort of topping-out ceremony on the Grand Hall floor. The last rosette was being signed — just as the original workers had signed one of the original ornaments. After the plasterers and painters all signed, everyone applauded and the TV cameras left, the plasterers left, too — to go to Chewie's favorite bar, Finnegan's in Westport.

The whole crew, 17 of them, sat around several tables, downing beers and ciders, pumping quarters in the jukebox, waiting for their moment in the spotlight — the 5 o'clock news. When it came, Chewie yelled to the bar: "We're on TV. Turn it up. Jukebox off."

The room hushed. The big-screen TV blared. On Channel 9, there was Julian Davis' signature on the rosette. Then the channel was switched. On Channel 41, there was Chewie helping hoist the rosette. The plasterers whooped and clapped. In a few minutes it was over. The TV was turned down, the jukebox turned up, another round was ordered, and Chewie went back to his favorite diversion, his English-style hard cider.

The old, the new: Workmen left their names in pencil on the center rosette of the Grand Hall ceiling early in the century. Similarly, Julian Davis signed his work 85 years later.

MAKING A RESTAURANT FIT

Some 1,860 miles from Kansas City, Rod Anderson again sat at a restaurant table with his architect, Matthew Connolly, his concept designer, Paul Robinson, and two Hereford House executives. They were in Seattle, home to dozens of eateries with turn-of-the-century decor, many of them specializing in seafood — a combination Anderson kept pursuing for his three-story Union Station grill.

It was November 1998, and the group had been there nearly a week, eating too much, drinking too much and critiquing too much. They had seen plush private dining sections with wine themes and custom-made fixtures. They had seen long, wide bars that were treated as destinations instead of holding cells for diners. They had seen "display kitchens," where patrons sat at countertops adjacent to the grills and stoves and ovens. So as they sat that evening waiting for their steaks to arrive, Anderson's Union Station venture started coming together. "Everybody was pumped," Anderson said.

He took out a pen, reached for a napkin and began sketching where to move his bar in Union Station — along one wall of the women's waiting room, instead of around the central columns. Except he couldn't draw. Connolly grabbed the pen out of his hands, picked out some more napkins and finished the drawing. Then he took other napkins and put a display kitchen in the back of the former women's restroom, taking up more space than the previous enclosed kitchen. He added stools along the bar and tables everywhere else on that floor. For the downstairs, the former women's and children's room, he drew another display kitchen in one half and walls in the other half. This created private dining rooms, taking the place of the previous lounge-like arrangement of leather chairs and ottomans. Only the upstairs, the former beauty shop, stayed the same — banquet rooms.

"Things just seemed to fall into place," Connolly said later. Even Robinson, who had been most skeptical of a restaurant fitting into the station space, could visualize it now.

Once back in Kansas City, Anderson again crunched some numbers. He had hoped to get 150 seats on the main level; the latest blueprints incorporating the Seattle designs provided for 110. He nixed the display kitchens and ordered more tables. Connolly squeezed them in, boosting the total to 142. That was good enough. Along with banquet and private rooms, it all worked. Finally.

"When I left for Seattle, I was looking at all the challenges," Anderson said. "When I got back, I was looking at all the opportunities."

Six months later, Anderson led his consultants on another tour of the station's restaurant space, this time to discuss some of the smaller details. At one point they started down the stairs from the former women's waiting room to the women's and children's room. The stairs were marble and U-shaped and included a marble ledge in the middle.

Connolly inquired about the ledge on the way down: "We need something to dress it up."

Union Station's famed clock was removed in March 1998, top, and shipped to a Massachusetts company for restoration. The work entailed refinishing its brass numbers, trim rings and wooden hands, sandblasting its steel enclosure and removing dirt. A Kansas City company helped with the $50,000 job on the 1,100-pound clock, which is 6 1/2 feet in diameter. By November it was back in town, left.

In 1999 the clock was displayed at various shopping malls before being returned to the station, above.

"I think so, too," piped up Ron Barkley, who headed operations for Anderson's growing restaurant family, "but you can't do anything with these marble walls."

He was right. It was a lesson they all had been learning, reluctantly. Like almost everywhere in the building, there were preservation considerations. And because this restaurant space had much of its original architecture intact, those considerations were magnified. They boiled down to this: Nothing could be altered unless the alterations could be easily undone.

With some things, this merely posed an inconvenience. Anderson and his group would, for instance, put the carpet runners down with two-sided tape instead of glue, so that the marble would remain intact. They would not anchor the bar or eating booths to the walls in the women's waiting room, so that the floral and pilaster trim would remain intact. And they would run electrical and soda lines under the floor and behind the walls in that room, so that the ornamental scroll ceiling would remain intact.

Yet, there were other things the restaurant creators could not live with. Like the wood benches around the columns in the downstairs room: They stuck out, and food carts wouldn't be able to get by. And the former waiting room's gray-colored walls: Anderson knew from experience that was "a very bad restaurant color."

To change any of that, Anderson's contract required him to get approval from a group of nine local preservation buffs formed by the station's owner. He won their OK to remove the benches after Connolly, with archival photographs, convinced the preservationists that wicker benches had been in the women's and children's room originally and that the wood ones were latecomers. In mid-June, Connolly met with the preservationists again. This time it involved the gray color. Connolly brought along a palette of yellowy tan colors. At the meeting, no votes were taken and no consensus stated. No dissent represented approval, and Connolly left the meeting relieved.

"We were sweating this," he said outside the door. "If they told us no, I was going to be committing suicide right here."

Still, with all these changes and accommodations — not to mention reconfiguring booths and adding more fire escapes, based on building code inspections — Anderson's development cost tripled from what he initially thought, to about $2.4 million.

Yes, this restaurant was turning out to be some personal statement on his part. A statement about the hardships of marrying the new to the old at Union Station.

> **"We were sweating this. If they told us no, I was going to be committing suicide right here."**
>
> — *Martin Connolly, architect*

One day in summer 1999, men in shirts and ties and women in business suits strolled onto the reconstruction job site, all wearing hard hats. There were about 20 of them, civic leaders from the Greater Kansas City Chamber of Commerce's executive committee, along with chamber administrators. They were getting a pre-opening, VIP tour of the station, from its innards and its additions to the Grand Hall and Rod Anderson's restaurant.

It was a little past noon, lunchtime. The building was quiet. Almost everywhere the tour went, the chamber executives could see the finished product but not the toil that characterized the project in progress. Consider, for instance, concreting, the seemingly simple tasks of making forms and making pours. Or as field superintendent Harold Jansen put it: "There's no new technology. There's no rocket science. There's nothing new." There was just a lot of concreting done. Just about everywhere the chamber executives looked. The holes in the midway floors where train passengers used to climb to and from the trains. The 60-foot-high

Detail from the ceiling, restored.

walls of the big-screen theater. The ramp serving as Science City's winding main street. The new deck in front of the station and the two-story garage under it. Not to mention all the floors and columns that were replaced. The chamber executives could only marvel at the grandness of the place, the sheer scope of the job spread over a site the size of six city blocks. But concreting was not what they had come to see.

Up the stairs they went, the new grand stairs, the tunnel from the basement toward the light — the Grand Hall. There, in that sun-drenched expanse, the chamber executives paused and craned their necks upward.

"Isn't that gorgeous?" asked one.

"Wow," declared another.

"Oh, it's breathtaking," uttered a third.

With that, the ceiling had one of its first public reviews.

From there the tour crossed the Grand Hall, veered to the northeast corner and entered Rod Anderson's space. All the plaster trim had been repaired. All the walls were painted tan. And it was in here where one tour participant, Doug Luciani, really grasped the magnificence of Union Station.

This had been a simple ladies' lounge, he thought, and yet it was so fancy, so formal, so representative of a city brimming with self-confidence around the turn of the century. Luciani was a senior vice president with the chamber. He had no long affinity for Union Station. In fact, he had preferred it be demolished.

Early in the 1990s the chamber had put out a report highlighting an often overlooked crisis: "deferred maintenance," the billion-dollar-plus backlog of bridge, street and sewer repairs in the metro area. Luciani headed the chamber's transportation group then, and he couldn't believe some civic leaders were clamoring to save Union Station. The decrepit depot was going to cost a couple of hundred million dollars — money he thought should be spent on something more important. Then bistate came along, Luciani got swept up in the two-state partnership, and he voted for it — in suburban Johnson County.

So he understood the restoration's historic context, and he knew it was viewed as the most visible embodiment of Kansas City's end-of-the-century comeback, in which the heart of the city was regaining population, adding jobs, cutting crime, building attractions and becoming a hot place to live. This, of course, made Union Station a symbol of its city and its times — yet again.

And now Luciani had finally seen what the fuss was all about. As the tour left the station, he turned to a companion and expressed one of the universal feelings about Union Station: "I was for tearing this down years ago. It was going to take too much money to save it. I wondered if it might not be better to have it torn down. But I'm glad it wasn't."

APPENDIX

Chronology of main events in the background and history of Union Station.

1850: The Town of Kansas is incorporated by Jackson County.

1878: Union Depot is built in the West Bottoms.

1888: Pointing to crowded conditions at Union Depot, *The Kansas City Star* issues the first of many calls for a new railroad station.

1898: Union Depot is expanded.

1906: Six railroads, eventually joined by six more, decide to build a new station along O.K. Creek.

1909: Kansas City voters approve altering streets for Kansas City Terminal Railway tracks.

1910: Work begins on excavation for Union Station.

1914: On Oct. 30, Union Station is opened and shortly after midnight Nov. 1 the first regularly scheduled train arrives.

1917: Number of trains through Union Station hits its non-war peak.

1921: The hill opposite Union Station is dedicated as the site for a war memorial.

1926: The Liberty Memorial is formally dedicated.

1933: Five people die in a gangland-style shootout, the Union Station Massacre.

1934: First regularly scheduled streamliner, the Pioneer Zephyr, goes into service at Union Station.

1957: Glass-walled shops are built into the Grand Hall.

1967: Wooden benches are removed from the waiting room, replaced by colorful plastic seats.

1968: The Fred Harvey restaurant is closed.

1969: Proposal to turn Union Station into a museum is defeated by voters.

1971: Amtrak takes over most U.S. railroad passenger service.

■ A consultant for the Kansas City Terminal Railway proposes to redevelop the area around Union Station and demolish the building.

1974: A redevelopment partnership, including a subsidiary of Trizec Corp. of Canada, proposes to renovate Union Station instead of demolishing it.

1977: Voters reject plan to turn Union Station into a science museum.

1984: To save money on heating, Amtrak moves its operations into a polyester dome called the "bubble" in the Grand Hall.

1985: Amtrak moves into a new, small space next to Two Pershing Square, an office building constructed ajacent to the East side of Union Station.

1988: Kansas City sues to recover damages from Trizec for failure to redevelop the station.

1990: The Kansas City Terminal Railway sells Union Station to an affiliate of Trizec.

1993: Kansas City wins several million dollars in its court case, but can collect little of it and does not win ownership of the station.

1994: City settles court case with Trizec to pass Union Station to a new non-profit corporation. Union Station Assistance Corp. is formed to redevelop the station.

1996: Voters in Jackson, Clay and Platte counties in Missouri and Johnson County in Kansas approve a one-eighth cent sales tax to redevelop Union Station as a science museum.

1999: Union Station reopens as Science City/Union Station.

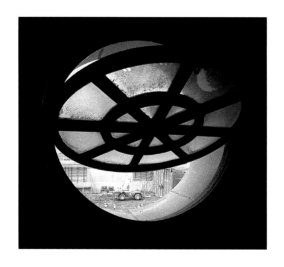

ONCE AGAIN, A SYMBOL OF PROGRESS

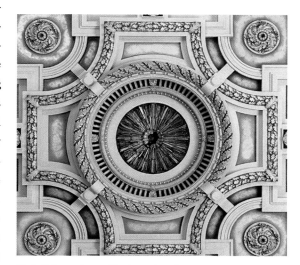

APPENDIX

Union Station primary ownership and development groups 1994-1999

Union Station Assistance Corp.:
Richard C. King, chairman
Mary Birch
John C. Brown
Sharon Hoffman
Patricia Shaughnessy
Louis W. Smith
Andy Scott, executive director

Kansas City Museum:
Michael J. Brown, chairman
Mary S. Bloch, vice-chairman
Nancy J. Dillingham, secretary
Peter K. Yelorda, treasurer
Gary F. Ballard
Arthur D. Brookfield II
Angela M. Browne
Polly P. Brunkhardt
Barton J. Cohen
Andrew W. Dahl
Marjorie D. Grant
Michael R. Haverty
Steven C. Hawn
Shirley B. Helzberg
John L. Hoffman
Ronald T. LeMay
Georgia Q. Lynch
Carl D. Peterson
Richardson K. Powell
Carl A. Ricketts
James L. Spigarelli
Sally Von Werlhof-Uhlmann
Dale Wittenborn
David A. Ucko, president

Union Station Project Consultants Inc. (formerly Project Coordinating Committee):
Thomas A. McDonnell, chairman
William T. Esrey, past chairman
Mary S. Bloch

Michael J. Brown
Richard C. King
Louis W. Smith

Metropolitan Cultural District (Bistate Commission):
Lisa A. Adkins, Kansas
Thomas M. Brandom, Clay County
John Patrick Burnett, Dennis Waits, Jackson County
Michael Copeland, Olathe
Ed Eilert, Overland Park
Karen K. Holland, Missouri
Michael L. Short, Platte County
E. Mark Swope, Al Van Iten, Independence
Mary Williams-Neal, Kansas City
David Wysong, Annabeth T. Surbaugh, Johnson County
Sandi Hackman, Molly McGovern, administrator

Campaign for Science City at Union Station (private fund-raising committee):
William T. Esrey, founding chairman
William A. Hall, co-chairman
A. Drue Jennings, co-chairman
Mary S. Bloch
Arthur D. Brookfield II
Polly P. Brunkhardt
William H. Dunn Sr.
Debbie Sosland-Edelman

Friends of Union Station (volunteer station advocacy group):
Phelps Murdock, president
Gary Brahl
Pat Caruthers
Jody Craig

Tim Freund
Allan Gray
Sharon Hoffman
Martha Immenschuh
Diana Johnson
Janet Kelley
Sean Kelley
Vince Latona
Sara Morgan
Joy Snyder
Daniel Windham

Hines Interests Limited Partnership (on-site reconstruction managers):
Donald McCormick, project manager
Glen Hopkins, project manager
Tom Marko, M.A. Mortenson Co.
Chuck McNabney
Rob Reynolds
Clark Wallace

J.E. Dunn Construction Co. (main contractor), project and site management:
Scott Vath, vice president
Willis Bowers
Eric Floyd
Gordon Hocker
Harold Jansen
Sharon King
Chris Liermann
Bill Spillar

This book, a history of Union Station as a public place, could not have been done without the cooperation and assistance of the public. In 1994 and 1999, *The Kansas City Star* asked readers to send in their memories and mementos. Several hundred people responded each time, recounting the station's heyday, its operations and its special events. The richness of these letters led to a crucial early decision to populate the book with people's stories, to make it as much of a social history as a structural history. Many of these letter writers were contacted and interviewed later, and their remembrances appear throughout these pages. Many others provided descriptions of sights and sounds that helped us communicate what the station was like. These latter people do not appear in the book, but among those who were especially helpful were Allen Welch, Annabel Shannon Jones, Richard Salts, Marion Lyon Henry, Doris Yake White, Hazel Hooper, Steve Stewart, Lloyd Elliott and Charlotte Davis. To everyone who wrote letters, we would like to extend our heartfelt thanks.

Much of the research for this book, whether for the writing or the pictures, was done at local and regional archives. The Kansas City Terminal Railway years ago donated its old records to the Kansas Collection at the University of Kansas. These records included a treasure chest of correspondence and memos going back to the station's original planning and construction period. The staff there graciously handled our requests for most of the Terminal Railway's 400-plus boxes and photo envelopes. We also would like to recognize several other archivists: David Boutros and Jennifer Parker at the Western Historical Manuscript Collection, Charlie Pitcher at Kansas City Southern Lines, Connie Menninger at the Kansas Historical Society and Fred Bauman at the Library of Congress. Stuart Hinds of the Special Collections department, Kansas City Public Library, helped immensely in our search for photographs and other information. There were several out-of-town repositories that lent time to our project, too. Among them were the Massachusetts Institute of Technology archives, the Weathersfield, Vt. Historical Society, the Brattleboro, Vt., Historical Society, the Wheaton, Ill., History Center, the Chicago Public Library Special Collections department, the Audrain County, Mo., Historical Society and the University of Arizona main library Special Collections department. And special thanks go to Sue Collins at Ohio State University's main library for digging out an obscure article on Edward Harriman and to Mary Woolever at the Art Institute of Chicago for retrieving Jarvis Hunt's correspondence with Daniel Burnham.

In the two years it took to gather the material for this book, there were countless people who graciously gave their expertise or some materials they had saved about Union Station. These people included Vicki Chenier, Jim Schaid, Nell Peniston, Bob Wade, Joe Maciel Jr., Diana Hunt Edgerton, Edith Hunter, Kimberly Shilland, Wayne Carhart, Rebecca Ofiesh, Terry Brady and David Wharton.

Union Station's current owner and redevelopment partners also contributed to this undertaking in myriad ways. The Union Station Assistance Corp.'s Andy Scott, Patty Markley and Bonnie Murry went out of their way to provide information and graphic material. The Kansas City Museum's David Ucko, Maria Meyers, Steve Snyder and Bill Musgrave offered insights into the creation of a museum. Hines Interests Limited Partnership's Glen Hopkins and Donald McCormick spent many hours explaining the intricacies and complexities of the construction process. Hopkins, especially, was one of the project's unsung heroes. And J.E. Dunn Construction Co.'s Scott Vath, Bill Spillar, Ron Welhoff and Harold Jansen provided almost unlimited access and information about the project, which was unusual for any private contractor.

At *The Star*, this book would not have turned out as it did without the outstanding service of the library, especially Derek Donovan and Janelle Hopkins. A former columnist, Jennifer Howe, solicited letters about the station in 1994. Tom Jackman and Elaine Adams provided valuable documents from their days of reporting about Union Station for *The Star*. Greg Reeves both taught and provided the computer database expertise that proved to be a crucial research tool. The staffs of the photography and imaging departments also took time to handle our requests.

We also want to thank the management of *The Star* for the opportunity to do this project and their support during it.

Finally, we owe our greatest debt to our families, who provided inspiration, encouragement, solitude, understanding and more than a little patience.

Jeffrey Spivak
Monroe Dodd

SELECTED BIBLIOGRAPHY

BOOKS

Abramson, Rudy. *Spanning the Century: The Life of W. Averell Harriman, 1891-1986.* New York: William Morrow and Company Inc., 1992.

Allen, Geoffrey Freeman. *Luxury Trains of the World.* New York: Everest House, 1979.

Appelbaum, Stanley. *The Chicago World's Fair of 1893: A Photographic Record.* New York: Dover Publications Inc., 1980.

Atlas Portland Cement Co. *Concrete in Railroad Construction.* New York: The Atlas Portland Cement Co., 1909.

Baker, Paul R. *Richard Morris Hunt.* Cambridge, Mass.: The MIT Press, 1980.

Ball, Don Jr., and Whitaker, Rogers E.M. *The Decade of the Trains: The 1940s.* Boston: Bulfinch Press, 1977.

Bosworth, F.H. Jr., and Jones, Roy Childs. *A Study of Architectural Schools.* New York: Charles Scribner's Sons, 1932.

Boyne, Eleanor L. *Brick Row: A Brief History and Comments on the Officers' Quarters at the U.S. Naval Training Center, Great Lakes, Illinois.* Crawfordsville, Ill.: R.R. Donnelley & Sons Co., 1984.

Bruccoli, Matthew J. (ed). *Ernest Hemingway, Cub Reporter: Kansas City Star Stories.* Pittsburgh: University of Pittsburgh Press, 1970.

Bruce, Alfred W. *The Steam Locomotive in America: Its Development in the Twentieth Century.* New York: Bonanza Books, 1952.

Bryant, Keith L. Jr. *History of the Atchison, Topeka and Santa Fe Railway.* New York: Macmillan Publishing Co. Inc., 1974.

Bush, Donald J. *The Streamlined Decade.* New York: George Braziller Inc., 1975.

Byard, Paul Spencer. *The Architecture of Additions: Design and Regulation.* New York: W.W. Norton & Co., 1998.

Casdorph, Paul D. *Let the Good Times Roll: Life at Home in America during World War II.* New York: Paragon House, 1989.

Clifford, Clark. *Counsel to the President.* New York: Random House Inc., 1991.

Condit, Carl W. *American Building Art: The Twentieth Century.* New York: Oxford University Press, 1961.

————. *The Railroad and the City.* Columbus, Ohio: Ohio State University Press, 1977.

————. *The Chicago School of Architecture: A History of Commercial and Public Building in the Chicago Area, 1875-1925.* Chicago: The University of Chicago Press, 1964.

Couper, William. *History of the Engineering, Construction and Equipment of the Pennsylvania Railroad Company's New York Terminal and Approaches.* New York: Isaac H. Blanchard Co., 1912.

Crittenden, H.H. *The Crittenden Memoirs.* New York: G.P. Putnam's Sons, 1936.

Cronkite, Walter. *A Reporter's Life.* New York: Alfred A. Knopf, 1996.

Cutts, Mary Pepperell Sparhawk. *The Life and Times of Hon. William Jarvis, of Weathersfield, Vermont.* Weathersfield, Vt.: The Weathersfield Historical Society, 1991.

Diehl, Lorraine B. *The Late, Great Pennsylvania Station.* Boston: Houghton Mifflin Co., 1985.

Douglas, George H. *All Aboard! The Railroad in American Life.* New York: Paragon House, 1992.

Droege, John. *Passenger Terminals and Trains.* New York: McGraw-Hill Book Co. Inc., 1916.

Drury, George H. *The Historical Guide to North American Railroads.* Milwaukee: Kalmbach Publishing Co., 1985.

Ehrlich, George. *Kansas City, Missouri: An Architectural History, 1826-1976.* Kansas City: Historic Kansas City Foundation, 1979.

Floyd, Margaret Henderson. *Architectural Education and Boston.* Boston: Boston Architectural Center, 1989.

Fink, Gary M. (ed). *Labor Unions.* The Greenwood Encyclopedia of American Institutions. Westport, Conn.: Greenwood Press Inc., 1977.

Foner, Philip S. *History of the Labor Movement in the United States,* Volume IV: "The Industrial Workers of the World, 1905-1917." New York: International Publishers Co. Inc., 1965.

————. *History of the Labor Movement in the United States,* Volume V: "The AFL in the Progressive Era, 1910-1915." New York: International Publishers Co. Inc., 1980.

Frailey, Fred W. *Twilight of the Great Trains.* Waukesha, Wis.: Kalmbach Publishing Co., 1998.

Friedman, Donald. *Historical Building Construction: Design, Materials and Technology.* New York: W.W. Norton & Co., 1995.

Garvin, Alexander. *The American City: What Works, What Doesn't.* New York: McGraw-Hill Cos. Inc., 1996.

Glaab, Charles N. *Kansas City and the Railroads.* Lawrence, Kan.: University Press of Kansas, 1993.

Goddard, Stephen B. *Getting There: The Epic Struggle Between Road and Rail in the American Century.* New York: BasicBooks, 1994.

Gordon, Sarah H. *Passage to Union: How the Railroads Transformed American Life, 1829-1929.* Chicago: Ivan R. Dee Inc., 1997.

Gowans, Alan. *Styles and Types of North American Architecture.* New York: HarperCollins Publishers Inc., 1992.

Grant, H. Roger (ed). *We Took the Train.* DeKalb, Ill.: Northern Illinois University Press, 1990.

Halberstadt, Hans H. and April. *The American Train Depot & Roundhouse.* Osceola, Wis.: Motorbooks International Publishers & Wholesalers, 1995.

Haskell, Henry C. Jr., and Fowler, Richard B. *City of the Future: A Narrative History of Kansas City, 1850-1950.* Kansas City: Kansas City Star Co. and Frank Glenn Publishing Co. Inc., 1950.

Hechler, Ken. *Working With Truman: A Personal Memoir of the White House Years.* New York: G.P. Putnam's Sons, 1982.

Henderson, James David. *Meals by Fred Harvey: A Phenomenon of the American West.* Fort Worth, Texas: Texas Christian University Press, 1969.

Highsmith, Carol M., and Landphair, Ted. *Union Station: A Decorative History of Washington's Grand Terminal.* Washington, D.C.: Chelsea Publishing Inc., 1988.

Hines, Thomas S. *Burnham of Chicago: Architect and Planner.* Chicago: The University of Chicago Press Inc., 1979.

Holbrook, Stewart H. *The Story of American Railroads.* New York: Crown Publishers, 1947.

Hungerford, Edward. *Daniel Willard*

Rides the Line: The Story of a Great Railroad Man. New York: G.P. Putnam's Sons, 1938.

Itzkoff, Donald M. *Off the Track: The Decline of the Intercity Passenger Train in the United States.* Westport, Conn.: Greenwood Press, 1985.

Kay, N.W. (ed). *The Modern Building Encyclopaedia.* London: Odhams Press Ltd., 1955.

Kidder, Tracy. *House.* Boston: Houghton Mifflin Co., 1985.

Kirkeby, Ed. *Ain't Misbehavin': The Story of Fats Waller.* New York: Dodd, Mead & Co., 1966.

Kisor, Henry. *Zephyr: Tracking A Dream Across America.* New York: Times Books, 1994.

Klein, Maury. *Union Pacific: The Rebirth, 1894-1969.* New York: Doubleday, 1989.

Larsen, Lawrence H., and Hulston, Nancy J. *Pendergast!* Columbia, Mo.: University of Missouri Press, 1997.

Long, Bryant A., and Dennis, William Jefferson. *Mail by Rail: The Story of the Postal Transportation Service.* New York: Simmons-Boardman Publishing Corp., 1951.

Loughlin, Caroline, and Anderson, Catherine. *Forest Park.* St. Louis: The Junior League of St. Louis, 1986.

Lyon, Peter. *To Hell in a Day Coach: An Exasperated Look at American Railroads.* Philadelphia: J.B. Lippincott Co., 1968.

Lynch, Terry. *Railroads of Kansas City.* Boulder, Colo.: Pruett Publishing Company, 1984.

McCullough, David. *Truman.* New York: Simon & Schuster, 1992.

————————. *The Great Bridge.* New York: Avon, 1972.

Meeks, Carroll L.V. *The Railroad Station.* New Haven, Conn.: Yale University Press, 1956.

Members of The Kansas City Star staff. *William Rockhill Nelson: The Story of a Man, a Newspaper and a City.* Cambridge, Mass.: The Riverside Press, 1915.

Mercer, Lloyd J. *E.H. Harriman: Master Railroader.* Boston: Twayne Publishers, 1985.

Mitchell, Giles Carroll. *There Is No Limit: Architecture and Sculpture in Kansas City.* Kansas City: Brown-White Co., 1934.

Morse, Charles Fessenden. *A Sketch of My Life, Written for My Children.* Cambridge, Mass.: Riverside Press, 1927.

Museum of Science and Industry, Chicago. "Pioneer Zephyr," 1998.

Noffsinger, James Philip. *The Influence of the Ecole des Beaux-Arts on the Architects of the United States.* Washington, D.C.: The Catholic University of America Press, 1955.

Orrock, J.W. *Railroad Structures and Estimates.* New York: John Wiley & Sons, 1909.

Overton, Richard C. *Burlington Route: A History of the Burlington Lines.* New York: Alfred A. Knopf Inc., 1965.

Parissien, Steven. *Station to Station.* London: Phaidon Press Ltd., 1997.

Pindell, Terry. *Making Tracks: An American Rail Odyssey.* New York: Grove Weidenfeld, 1990.

Poling-Kempes, Lesley. *The Harvey Girls: Women Who Opened the West.* New York: Paragon House, 1989.

Potter, Janet Greenstein. *Great American Railroad Stations.* New York: John Wiley & Sons Inc., 1996.

Reddig, William M. *Tom's Town: Kansas City and the Pendergast Legend.* Philadelphia: J.B. Lippincott Co., 1947.

Richards, Jeffrey, and MacKenzie, John M. *The Railway Station: A Social History.* Oxford, England: Oxford University Press, 1986.

Roth, Leland H. *Understanding Architecture: Its Elements, History and Meaning.* New York: HarperCollins Publishers Inc., 1993.

Sabbagh, Karl. *Skyscraper: The Making of a Building.* New York: Penguin Books, 1989.

Salvadori, Mario. *Building: The Fight Against Gravity.* Canada: McCelland and Stewart Ltd., 1979.

————————. *Why Buildings Stand Up: The Strength of Architecture.* New York: W.W. Norton & Company Inc., 1980.

Stout, Greg. *Route of the Eagles: Missouri Pacific in the Streamlined Era.* Kansas City: White River Productions, 1995.

Stover, John F. *The Life and Decline of the American Railroad.* New York: Oxford University Press, 1970.

Sullivan, Louis H. *The Autobiography of an Idea.* New York: Dover Publications Inc., 1956.

Sullivan, Mark, and Rather, Dan. *Our Times: America at the Birth of the 20th Century.* New York: Scribner, 1996.

Szwajkart, John. *Train Watchers Guide to Kansas City.* Brookfield, Ill.: self-published, 1991.

Tauranac, John. *The Empire State Building: The Making of a Landmark.* New York: St. Martin's Press, 1995.

Truman, Margaret. *Harry S. Truman.* New York: William Morrow & Co. Inc., 1973.

Twombly, Robert. *Louis Sullivan: His Life and Work.* New York: Viking Penguin Inc., 1986.

Unger, Robert. *The Union Station Massacre: The Original Sin of J. Edgar Hoover's FBI.* Kansas City: Andrews McMeel Publishing, 1997.

Werner Co.. *Photographs of the World's Fair.* Chicago: The Werner Co., 1894.

Whiffen, Marcus. *American Architecture Since 1870: A Guide to Styles.* Cambridge, Mass.: The MIT Press, 1992.

White, John H. Jr. *The American Railroad Passenger Car.* Baltimore: The Johns Hopkins University Press, 1978.

Wilson, William H. *The City Beautiful Movement.* Baltimore: The Johns Hopkins University Press, 1989.

————————. *The City Beautiful Movement in Kansas City.* Kansas City: Lowell Press Inc., 1990.

Withers, Bob. *The President Travels by Train: Politics and Pullmans.* Lynchburg, Va.: TLC Publishing Inc., 1996.

Withey, Henry F., and Withey, Elsie Rathburn. *Biographical Dictionary of American Architects (Deceased).* Los Angeles: New Age Publishing Co., 1956.

Wright, Gwendolyn, and Parks, Janet. *The History of History in American Schools of Architecture, 1865-1975.* New York: The Temple Hoyne Buell Center for the Study of American Architecture and Princeton Architectural Press, 1990.

Yenne, Bill (ed). *All Aboard! The Golden Age of American Rail Travel.* Greenwich, Conn.: Brompton Books Corp., 1989.

HISTORICAL ARTICLES

Baldwin, A.S. "Factors Governing the Design of Passenger Terminals." *Railway Age*

Gazette, Vol. 73, Sept. 2, 1922.

Bell, Larry. "Scientist for a Day: Elbow Grease and Discovery in the New Science Museum." *MIT's Technology Review,* February/March 1997.

Bohasseck, Charles. "Loramoor, Estate of Jas. Hobart Moore, Esq., Lake Geneva, Wisconsin." *The Architectural Record,* Vol. 15, March 1904.

————————. "Gordon Hall, The House of Dan R. Hanna, Cleveland, Ohio." *The Architectural Record,* Vol. 15, January 1904.

Burks, Walter. "Still a Bloody Puzzle after 60 Years." *The Squire,* June 10, 1993.

Busfield, T.L. "The Design of Large Passenger Terminals." *Railway Age Gazette,* Vol. 60, May 5, 1916.

————————. "Alderman Jim Pendergast." *The Bulletin of the Missouri Historical Society,* Vol. 21, October 1964.

Eberlein, Harold D. "Recent Railway Stations in American Cities." *The Architectural Record,* Vol. 36, August 1914.

Felton, Samuel M. "The Genius of Edward H. Harriman." *The American Magazine,* April 1925.

Gallagher, Patrick. "Captivate & Educate: Museums are busy redefining themselves as lively, interactive learning environments." *Urban Land,* February 1998.

Garrity, John. "Deathwatch at Union Station." *Corporate Report Kansas City,* November 1984.

Grasty, Charles H. "The Best Newspaper in America: The Kansas City Star and What It Stands For — Mr. W.R. Nelson, the Man Behind It." *World's Work,* Vol. 18, June 1909.

Gregerson, John. "Postal Square: Daniel Burnham's monument to mail undergoes a postcard-perfect restoration for its new role as a government office center." *Building Design & Construction,* October 1993.

Hands, W.O. "The Kansas City Flood." *Street Railway Journal,* July 4, 1903.

Howe, Frank Maynard. "The Development of Architecture in Kansas City, Missouri." *The Architectural Record,* Vol. 15, February 1904.

"The Kansas City Terminal Railway." *Engineering News,* Vol. 70, No. 6, Aug. 7, 1913.

Kohr, Harry F. "Huge Railroad Station that Can Expand." *Technical World*

Magazine, Vol. 20, September 1913.

"K.C.S.-L. & A. Streamliner 'Southern Belle.'" *Railway Age,* Oct. 5, 1940.

Kuchinsky, Wayne. "Kansas City! Her trains, her railroads, her stations." *Passenger Train Journal.* Vol. 19, No. 10, October 1988.

McDonald, Lawrence L. "60th Anniversary: The Kansas City, Mo., Union Station, 1914-1974." Kansas City Chapter Historical Bulletin, National Railway Historical Society Inc.

McIntyre, H.H. "Vermont at the World's Fair." *The New England Magazine,* Vol. X, March 1894.

Mumford, Lewis. "Mother Jacobs' Home Remedies." *New Yorker,* Vol. 38, Dec. 1, 1962.

"New Kansas City, Mo., Passenger Terminal." *Railway Age Gazette,* Vol. 54, May 23, 1913.

"The New Kansas City, Mo., Union Passenger Station." *Railway Age Gazette,* Vol. 57, Oct. 14, 1914.

O'Neill, Hugh, and Steele, John M. "Kansas City — A City that is Finding Itself." World To-Day, Vol. 11, November 1906.

O'Sheel, Shaemus. "Kansas City, The Crossroads of the Continent." *The New Republic,* May 16, 1928.

"Party Walls in Chicago." *The Architectural Record,* Vol. 17, February 1905.

Pine, B. Joseph II, and Gilmore, James H. "Welcome to the Experience Economy." *Harvard Business Review,* July-August 1998.

Risher, Howard W. Jr. *The Negro in the Railroad Industry.* Report No. 16 on the Racial Policies of American Industry for the Industrial Research Unit at the Wharton School of Finance and Commerce. Philadelphia: University of Pennsylvania, 1971.

Schmidt, Leone. "A Vermonter . . . Looking for Something to Do." *DuPage History,* Vol. II, DuPage County Historical Society, 1994.

Semper, Robert J. "Science Museums as Environments for Learning." *Physics Today,* November 1990.

Sturgis, Russell. "The Warehouse and Factory in Architecture — II." *The Architectural Record,* Vol. 15, part 2, February 1904.

"Trainshed of the Kansas City Union Station." *Engineering News,* Vol. 72, Oct. 8, 1914.

Ucko, David A. "Science City: A New Model for Science Center." ASTC Newsletter, September/October 1991.

————————. "Science Literacy and Science Museum Exhibits." *Curator,* Vol. 28, No. 4, 1985.

"The Ultramodern Super Chief Marches Forward." *The Santa Fe Magazine,* Vol. XXXI, No. 7, June 1937.

"Union Passenger Station, Kansas City, Mo." *Architecture and Building,* Vol. 47, June 1915.

"Union Passenger Station Situation at Kansas City." *Railway Age Gazette,* Vol. 45, Oct. 23, 1908.

GOVERNMENT DOCUMENTS

Board of Public Welfare, Kansas City, Mo. "Report on Housing Conditions in Kansas City, Missouri." June 1912.

————————. Factory Inspection Department. "Report of Investigation of 100 Industrial Accidents in Kansas City During the Year of 1912." 1912.

————————. The Research Bureau. "Social Prospectus of Kansas City, Missouri." August 1913.

Ciruli Associates. "Kansas City Metropolitan Area Cultural Needs Assessment." Executive Summary, February 1993.

City Council, Kansas City, Mo. "Union Station Ordinance, No. 2336." Approved July 7, 1909.

————————. "Ordinance No. 9701, Modifying and Amending Union Station Ordinance No. 2336." Approved August 19, 1911.

City Planning and Development Department, Kansas City, Mo. "Kansas City in Context: A Data Analysis Workbook, Population and Demographics." January 30, 1993.

Clarus Corp. "Assessment of Community Opinion for the Bistate Cultural District Initiative: Summary of Results." April 1994.

Commission on Chicago Historical and Architectural Landmarks. "900 North Michigan Avenue." Preliminary Summary of Information. Jan. 4, 1982.

Ehrenkrantz & Eckstut/Keyes Condon Florance. "Science City at Union Station Kansas City, Mo.: Programming Phase Report." March 28, 1996.

Emilio Ambasz & Associates Inc., and Black & Veatch Engineers-Architects. "Preliminary Estimate of Construction Cost for Conceptual Design for Partial Renovation of Union Station, Kansas City, Missouri." Jan. 5, 1988.

Environmental Research Center. "Cultural Resource Investigations, Phase 1 Survey, Kansas City Union Station Project, Jackson County, Missouri." Kansas City: Union Station Assistance Corp., March 1998.

Harrison Price Co. "Attendance and Financial Analysis for Science City at Union Station Kansas City, Missouri." June 1995, Revised May 1996.

HNTB Architects Engineers Planners, Smith & Boucher Inc. and Boyd, Brown, Stude and Cambern. "Kansas City Union Station: Cost Update and Budget Projections of the 1986 Condition and Rehabilitation Report." April 1990.

Howard Needles Tammen & Bergendoff. "Condition Analysis and Rehabilitation: Union Station, Kansas City, Missouri." July 25, 1986.

Interstate Commerce Commission, Division of Valuation. ICC Classification for Kansas City Terminal Railway Company, Station and Office Buildings. Approved August 12, 1916.

Kansas and Missouri Task Forces for the Bistate Initiative. "Science City at Union Station Bistate Redevelopment Project." July 8, 1996.

Kansas City Terminal Railway Co. "Kansas City Union Station Development." 1972.

Kansas City Union Station Inc. "Kansas City Union Station: Framework for Redevelopment." August 1990.

Market Directions. "Science City Concept Test." May 1995.

——————. "Student Evaluation of Neighborhood Activities." October 1996.

Mid-America Regional Council. "Metropolitan Kansas City's Urban Core: What's Occurring, Why It's Important and What We Can Do." A report of the Urban Core Growth Strategies Committee, 1993.

Oehrlein & Associates Architects, and Robinson & Associates Inc. "Historic Structures Report/Treatment Plan: Kansas City Union Station." July 1, 1996.

Robinson & Associates Inc., in association with Oehrlein & Associates Architects. "Kansas City Terminal Railway Company, Union Station Rail Yard, Kansas City, Missouri: Historic Resources Survey." January 1998.

Union Station Task Force. "Union Station Redevelopment." March 1986.

United States Bureau of the Census. *The Statistical History of the United States.* New York: BasicBooks, 1976.

United States Department of the Interior. National Register of Historic Places Inventory — Nomination Form. "Kansas City Union Station." Prepared by the Kansas City: Landmarks Commission, 1971.

ARCHIVES AND MANUSCRIPT COLLECTIONS

Fred Harvey Collection, Special Collections, University of Arizona, Tucson.

Kansas Collection, University of Kansas, Lawrence.

Kansas State Historical Society, Topeka.

Special Collections department, Kansas City Public Library, Kansas City.

Western Historical Manuscripts Collection-Kansas City, University of Missouri-Kansas City.

THESES AND DISSERTATIONS

Dorsett, Lyle Wesley. "Alderman Jim Pendergast." Unpublished master's thesis, the University of Kansas City, Kansas City, 1962.

PAMPHLETS, BROCHURES AND LECTURES

Commercial Club, Convention and Publicity Division. "Between Trains in Kansas City." 1915.

Oppenheimer, Frank, and the staff of the Exploratorium. "Working Prototypes: Exhibit Design at the Exploratorium." San Francisco: The Exploratorium, 1986.

Serda, Daniel. "Boston Investors and the Early Development of Kansas City, Missouri." Lecture for Midwest Research Institute's Midcontinent Perspectives, Jan. 23, 1992.

INTERNET

Rose, Julie K. *World's Columbian Exposition.* University of Virginia internet site: http://xroads.virginia.edu/~MA96 CE, 1996.

These are the main sources of information for each chapter. A complete description of the materials cited is in the bibliography. Newspaper articles used as resources for this chapter and throughout the book are too numerous to list.

Chapter 1

The primary material for this chapter came from minutes of Union Depot and Kansas City Terminal Railway board meetings. The minutes were found in the Terminal Railway's local office and at the Kansas Historical Society.

The author also combed *The Kansas City Star* and *The Kansas City Times* day by day for the late 1890s-early 1900s period. William Wilson's book provided a solid foundation for some of the twists and turns to expect.

As for the interrelationships among Edward Harriman's railroad empire, the Burlington's obstinateness and Kansas City's station situation, Richard Overton's and Maury Klein's books, as well as Samuel Felton's article, were most helpful.

Chapter 2

Oehrlein and Robinson's "Historic Structures Report" was invaluable as the basis for research on the topics in this chapter. Kansas City Terminal Railway board minutes, correspondence at the Kansas Collection and newspaper accounts provided much of the material for Jarvis Hunt's initial station plans and how they changed.

Hunt's background was obtained from many sources, including archives in Chicago and Vermont, magazine critiques of his work and his granddaughter, Diana Hunt Edgerton. Hunt's relation with Daniel Burnham came to light in letters uncovered at the Burnham Library at the Art Institute of Chicago, plus descriptions of Burnham's life in Thomas Hines' biography. It was gratifying that one architectural historian, Cydney Millstein, noted a "striking similarity" between Hunt's first building in Kansas City, for Commerce Bank, and a Burnham bank building, as reported in Millstein's nomination form for the Commerce building to be placed on the National Register of Historic Places.

For the analysis of railroad station architecture, T.L. Busfield's article and Carroll Meeks' book were noteworthy.

Chapter 3

Much of the information detailing Union Station's construction, including types of work,

deaths and strikes, was found in the Kansas City Terminal Railway archives at the Kansas Collection. A day-by-day construction log was kept from August 1911 through the November 1914 opening. This information was buttressed with newspaper reports in *The Star* and *The Times* as well as from *The Labor Herald*, available at the Jackson County Historical Society in Independence. In addition, some descriptions of the construction work were drawn from photographs included in Terminal Railway archives and from the Fuller collection donated to the Union Station Assistance Corp.

Oehrlein and Robinson's "Historic Structures Report" again provided technical assistance in describing the station's architectural features.

Details of Union Station's opening-day ceremonies came from various newspaper accounts, along with a few interviews with and letters from participants. Woodrow Wilson's papers at the Library of Congress provided his schedule and activities on Oct. 30, 1914, which showed he did not open the station's doors.

Chapter 4

The anecdotal scenes in this chapter were drawn primarily from newspaper accounts, supported if possible by interviews with surviving participants. The section on presidential visits was helped also by Bob Withers' book.

Descriptions of the station were drawn from remembrances sent in by *Star* readers, along with Oehrlein and Robinson's "Historic Structures Report" and the author's observations on visits to the building from 1994 to 1999.

The Kansas City Terminal Railway's archives at the Kansas Collection provided the material for the building's early foul-ups. Information on Fats Waller came from the musician's biography and a recounting in *The Star* by Joe Popper.

Chapter 5

For the Fred Harvey section, descriptions of Harvey's Union Station operations and practices came from interviews with former Harvey Girls, newspaper accounts and books about the company. Information about the wedding of the Harvey Girl came from the couple's children.

For the New Year's Eve section, the events were reconstructed from newspaper clippings, interviews with participants and letters from *Star* readers when they were asked to contribute Union Station memories. By far the most popular subject for Union Station memory letters was

the New Year's Eves under the clock.

For the Massacre section, Robert Unger's book provided the basis for much of the fact-finding. Unger was the only author to acquire the FBI's full file on the case. With the bullet holes, the author observed the tests conducted by the Kansas City Police Department's crime lab analysts, except for John Cayton's shooting.

Chapter 6

The importance of the Burlington Zephyr and the Union Pacific M10000 trains was derived from the archives of the two railroads, many railroad books and articles and, in the Zephyr's case, a history compiled for an exhibit at Chicago's Museum of Science and Industry. Donald Bush's book was particularly helpful in understanding the significance of streamlining.

Information about Union Station's railroad operations came from the Kansas City Terminal Railway's archives at the Kansas Collection, coupled with letters from *Star* readers and interviews with local members of Railway Express and post office historical societies. Readers' letters and railroad books also supplied insight about what it was like to ride a train decades ago.

The anecdote about Thomas Pendergast is something that William Reddig and a few articles recounted before the boss died.

Chapter 7

The story of Pearl Harbor day at Union Station was reconstructed from local folklore and a few interviews. The station's appearance was derived from historic photographs along with newspaper clippings kept at the Jackson County Historical Society. Information about train travel and the station's operations during World War II came from the Kansas City Terminal Railway's archives, especially its annual reports.

Subjects for the six oral histories were chosen from the several hundred *Star* readers who sent in their station memories in 1994 and 1999. These letters served as the basis for interviews, which were tape-recorded and edited for brevity.

Chapter 8

The decline of railroad passenger service has been the subject of many books, articles and federal reports this century. Those that were most helpful to this chapter were the books by Peter Lyon and John Stover. Changes in railroad operations at Union Station were drawn from the Kansas City Terminal Railway's archives and a log of year-by-year changes kept by a longtime station employee, Bob Blowers. Changes in the station's appearance were drawn from the railway's archives, which included memorandums about the Harvey operations, and Oehrlein and Robinson's "Historic Structures Report."

Analysis of Kansas City's postwar decline came from the author's own research on Kansas City history, especially its sprawl effects, plus local reports such as the Mid-America Regional Council's urban core report.

Material for station events in the 1960s and '70s was taken primarily from letters sent in by *Star* readers, interviews with participants and newspaper clippings. Early preservation efforts were documented by George Ehrlich in the Western Historical Manuscript Collection and were also found in the Kansas City Terminal Railway's archives. The scene of the station's auction was reconstructed with help from the auctioneer, Jerry Hertzog, station employees and participants.

Chapter 9

Loyd Dillinger was the source for much of what was written about him, buttressed by the memories of other station workers, documents about water leaks in the Kansas City Terminal Railway's archives, plus details about general deterioration from station re-use studies. For information and insights about the various station re-use ideas, newspaper articles and court records that were part of the later Kansas City-Trizec lawsuit formed the basis for some of the scenes. Also, most every participant named was interviewed. Former Terminal Railway President Vernon Coe and former Pershing Square Redevelopment head Garold Osborne were particularly helpful confirming what happened.

For the Trizec/Edward Smith section, many participants and lawyers involved were interviewed. Those especially helpful included Emanuel Cleaver, Phelps Murdock, Phil Bledsoe, William Levi, Irvine O. Hockaday Jr. and Judge David Shinn. Information also came from court documents and the attorneys' own files.

Chapter 10

Most of the election-period scenes described in this chapter were reconstructed from interviews with participants. The memories and notes of Steve Rose, Jack Craft, Brad Scott and Andy Scott were most helpful. In the cases of the Olathe Rotary luncheon, the Loose Park picnic and Union Station's open house, the author was there. In the case of Clay Chastain's saga, the author drew from Chastain's autobiography and from the author's own notes and observations in covering Chastain's activities from 1994 to 1998.

Information on federal funding, the Trizec settlement and bistate's background was supplemented by interviews but started with documents, including Jack Danforth's congressional correspondence, records kept on pre-settlement offers and the author's notes from covering these issues.

Chapter 11

The bulk of material in this chapter was obtained from interviews with the participants, notably David Ucko, Glen Hopkins, Patrick Gallagher, Cybelle Lewis, Denis Kuhn and David Greenbaum. The author also sat in on some Science City planning meetings and exhibit presentations and had access to various planning documents, from programming and market-testing reports to incremental sketches of exhibits.

For the construction financing section, all the main participants were interviewed, including David Queen, Clark Wallace, Dick King, Jeff Heckman, William Esrey and David Wysong. The scenes described in this section were verified by more than one participant.

Chapter 12

For the Donald McCormick section, the author sat in on meetings and tours involving McCormick on the station construction site. For scenes such as the skylight, the author was there. Interviews with others on the job site and documents pertaining to the station's budget provided supporting information.

For the Julian Davis section, the author observed the plastering progress on many occasions and visited Hayles & Howe's cast-making warehouse in Baltimore. Information on Windsor Castle and plastering practices was culled from newspaper articles, a television documentary, books on the subject and interviews with other plastering experts. The celebration at Finnigan's was reconstructed from interviews and tapes of that night's television news.

For Rod Anderson's section, most of the station tours were reconstructed from interviews with the participants, although the author witnessed one incident and was present for one preservation meeting. History of the restaurant space was provided by Glen Hopkins and the Oehrlein and Robinson's "Historic Structures Report."

For the chamber tour, the author accompanied the entourage and interviewed Doug Luciani afterward.

Invaluable assistance in illustrating this book came from readers of *The Kansas City Star* who answered our plea for photographs and other memorabilia of Union Station.

To the archivists, librarians, collectors and photographers contacted for illustrations in this book, we extend our gratitude. We'd particularly like to thank Stuart Hinds of the Special Collections Department, Kansas City Public Library; David Boutros and his staff at the Western Historical Manuscript Collection; Kristin Eshelman, Becky Schulte and Sheryl Williams of the Kansas Collection at the University of Kansas, and Andy Scott and David Ucko and their colleagues at the Union Station Assistance Corp. and the Kansas City Museum.

On The *Star's* photography staff, Fred Blocher contributed new pictures and also retrieved from the newspaper's electronic archive photos related to station renovation. *Star* staff photographer Julie Jacobson photographed the people whose memories of the station and World War II appear in Chapter 7. Also taking new pictures was Peggy Bair. Other *Star* photographers whose work appears in this volume include Kevin Anderson, Talis Bergmanis, Beverly Bynum, Joe Ledford, David Pulliam and Wendy Yang.

Photographs and other illustrations not credited here are from the files of *The Kansas City Star* library.

These sources have been abbreviated:
SC/KCPL: Special Collections Department, formerly the Missouri Valley Room, Kansas City Public Library.
WHMC: Western Historical Manuscript Collection, University of Missouri-Kansas City.

Dustjacket: Collection of Art Evans
Endsheets: Kansas Collection, University of Kansas Libraries.
ii-iii: SC/KCPL
vii: Collection of Art Evans.
4. Chicago Public Library, Special Collections.
5. Map Collections, Library of Congress.
6-7. Right: Kansas City Terminal Railway Collection, Kansas Collection, University of Kansas Libraries.
8. Lower left: SC/KCPL. Lower right: Fred Harvey Collection photographs, Box 6, Special Collections, The University of Arizona Library.

10-11. Top: SC/KCPL. Bottom: Collection of Don Harmon.
12-13. Bottom: WHMC.
14. Top: Chicago Public Library, Special Collections.
15. Kansas City Southern Lines.
16. SC/KCPL.
17. Diana Hunt Edgerton.
20. Audrain County Historical Society.
21. Diana Hunt Edgerton.
22-23. Chicago Public Library, Special Collections.
24. Courtesy of the Illinois State Historical Library.
26. Chicago Public Library, Special Collections.
33, 34-35. Kansas City Terminal Railway Collection, Kansas Collection, University of Kansas Libraries.
38-39. WHMC.
40. Kansas City Terminal Railway Collection, Kansas Collection, University of Kansas Libraries.
41. Top, right center and bottom: Kansas City Terminal Railway Collection, Kansas Collection, University of Kansas Libraries. Left center: WHMC.
42-43, 44. Kansas City Terminal Railway Collection, Kansas Collection, University of Kansas Libraries.
46. Union Station Assistance Corp.
47. Left four pictures: WHMC. Right: Kansas City Terminal Railway Collection, Kansas Collection, University of Kansas Libraries.
48. WHMC.
49. Top: WHMC. Lower left: SC/KCPL. Lower right: Kansas City Terminal Railway Collection, Kansas Collection, University of Kansas Libraries.
50. WHMC.
51. Kansas Collection, University of Kansas Libraries.
53. Kansas City Terminal Railway Collection, Kansas Collection, University of Kansas Libraries.
54-55. Top: Union Station Assistance Corp.
55. Bottom: Collection of Robert and Luella Smith.
57. Top right: SC/KCPL.
58-59: Collection of Don Harmon.
63: Collection of Art Evans.
64-65: Wilborn & Associates.
66: Right: Collection of Sandra Barnes.
67: Collection of Don Harmon.

68. Collection of Don Harmon.
70. Fred Harvey Collection photographs, Box 6, Special Collections, The University of Arizona Library.
72. Top: Fred Harvey Collection photographs, Box 6, Special Collections, The University of Arizona Library. Bottom: Collection of Betty Neely Flood.
74-75. SC/KCPL.
76. Fred Harvey Collection photographs, Box 6, Special Collections, The University of Arizona Library.
77. Fred Harvey Collection photographs, Box 6, Special Collections, The University of Arizona Library.
78. Collection of Art Evans.
80. Collection of Glen V. Duston.
81. Top left: Collection of Don Harmon. Top right: Fred Harvey Collection photographs, Box 6, Special Collections, The University of Arizona Library.
82. WHMC.
83. Collection of Don Harmon.
84. Bottom: SC/KCPL.
92-93. Right: Fred Harvey Collection photographs, Box 6, Special Collections, The University of Arizona Library.
94. Top: Kansas State Historical Society.
95. Collection of Ruth and Don Coppage.
96. Fred Harvey Collection photographs, Box 6, Special Collections, The University of Arizona Library.
98: Bottom: Collection of Pauline McKenzie.
109: Jack Wally for the *Kansas City Journal-Post.*
114-115. Collection of Jennie V. Holcomb, donated in memory of her father, Phil C. Rogers.
116. WHMC.
117. WHMC.
118. Bottom: Kansas State Historical Society.
119. Detroit Publishing Co. Collection, Library of Congress.
120. Kansas State Historical Society.
121. Kansas City Terminal Railway Collection, Kansas Collection, University of Kansas Libraries.
122. Collection of Dave Eames.
123. Wilborn & Associates.
124. Top: Kansas City Terminal Railway Collection, Kansas Collection, University of Kansas Libraries.
125. Top and bottom: SC/KCPL. Middle: Collection of Pauline Johnson.
127. Fred Harvey Collection photographs,

Box 6, Special Collections, The University of Arizona Library.

128. Top and second from top: SC/KCPL. Second from bottom: *Kansas City Journal-Post*. Bottom: Jack Wally.

129. All except bottom: Jack Wally. Bottom: SC/KCPL.

130. WHMC.

132. WHMC.

133. Collection of Mary Eleanor Edwards.

134. Collection of Dave Eames.

135. Kansas State Historical Society.

136. Collection of Harold K. Vollrath, from Kansas City Southern Archives.

137. Collection of Dave Eames.

139. Collection of Midge Proctor Chinn.

140, 141. Collection of Marjorie Siegrist Ebling.

142, 143. Wilborn & Associates.

144. Collection of Bill Lawrence.

146. Top: Collection of Sally Martin Rice.

147. Bottom: Collection of David Pence.

148. Collection of Mr. and Mrs. R. L. Bauer.

149. Wilborn & Associates.

152. Collection of Walter Lewis.

153. Bottom: Collection of Edna Sutton.

154. Collection of Izak Federman.

155. Left: Collection of Izak Federman.

158. Left: Collection of Sandra Barnes.

158-159: Right: Collection of Don Harmon.

160. Bottom: Collection of Harold K. Vollrath.

161. Top: WHMC. Bottom: SC/KCPL.

164. Collection of Dave Eames.

166, 167. SC/KCPL.

168. Collection of Hazel Odessa Surratt.

174. Collection of George Ehrlich.

175. Collection of Jerry Hertzog

178-179. Tom Taylor.

186. Tom Taylor

189. Bottom: Tom Taylor

205. Union Station Assistance Corp.

216. Bottom: Collection of David Ucko.

218. Knight Ridder Tribune.

223. Kansas City Museum.

224-225. Top: Union Station Assistance Corp.

235. WHMC.

236. Hayles & Howe

240. SC/KCPL.

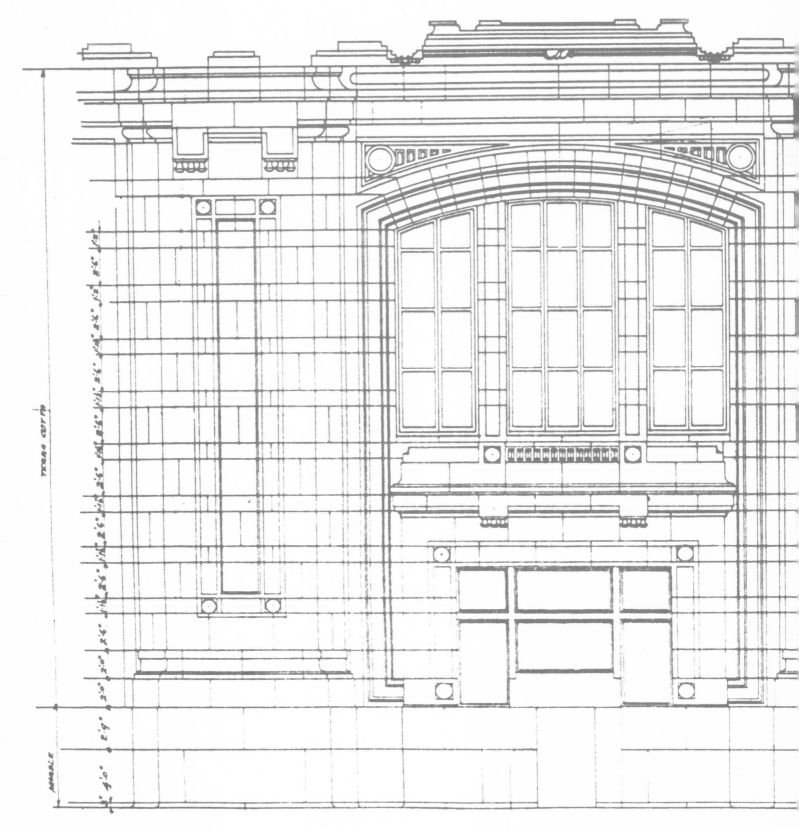

ELEVATION

1/4" SCALE DETAIL OF TERRA CO
UNION STATION, KANSAS CITY,

JARVIS HUNT, ARCHITECT, CHICAGO, ILL.